COLOR:
THE PROFESSIONAL'S GUIDE

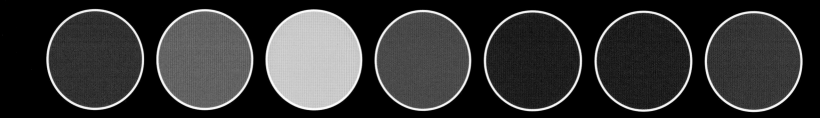

COLOR:
THE PROFESSIONAL'S GUIDE

KAREN TRIEDMAN

Understanding, appreciating and
mastering color in art and design

NORTH LIGHT BOOKS
CINCINNATI, OHIO
www.artistsnetwork.com

COLOR: THE PROFESSIONAL'S GUIDE

Copyright © 2015 by Ilex Press

Manufactured in China. All rights reserved.

No other part of this book may be reproduced in any form or by any electronic or mechanical means including information storage and retrieval systems without permission in writing from the publisher, except by a reviewer, who may quote brief passages in a review.

Published in the United States by
North Light Books, an imprint of F+W Media, Inc.,
10151 Carver Road, Suite 200, Blue Ash,
Ohio 45242. (800) 289-0963.

First edition.

Other fine North Light products are available from your local bookstore, art supply store or online retailer.
Visit our website at fwmedia.com.

19 18 17 16 15   5 4 3 2 1

ISBN-13: 978-1-4403-3898-4

This book was conceived, designed, and produced by
Ilex Press, a division of Octopus Publishing Group Ltd
Octopus Publishing Group
Carmelite House
50 Victoria Embankment
London, EC4Y 0DZ
www.octopusbooks.co.uk

Publisher: Roly Allen
Commissioning Editor: Zara Larcombe
Senior Project Editor: Natalia Price-Cabrera
Editor: Rachel Silverlight
Managing Specialist Editor: Frank Gallaugher
Art Director: Julie Weir
Picture Researcher: Katie Greenwood
Designer: JC Lanaway
Production Controller: Meskerem Berhane

Cover image © Itana/Shutterstock

a content + ecommerce company

CONTENTS

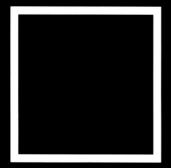

INTRODUCTION

COLOR: THE PROFESSIONAL'S GUIDE

Color is a dynamic force that influences our everyday experiences in many ways. Whether appreciating a piece of art or buying a new kitchen appliance, our response to color plays a significant role in daily life and is the result of a combination of theoretical, cultural, and personal experiences that we have accumulated over a lifetime. Color is such a complex and exciting subject that it is important to be studied from a multidisciplinary perspective. Not only can color be seen from both an art and design perspective, but it must be viewed from a scientific perspective that includes physics, chemistry, and biology. In addition, psychological, sociological, political, and cultural perspectives must also be taken into account. While it is impossible to talk in great detail in each specific area, I have taken a holistic approach by providing a strong foundation for exploration, presenting solid information in such a way as to suggest relationships between different color topics with the hope that it might prompt further study on the part of the reader. I have therefore placed an interview with an expert in the field at the beginning of each chapter to talk about his or her work. These experts help me in describing the enormous possibilities

for expansion and development with respect to where the field of color has come from and where it can take us in the future. Many factors influence our choices and they must be explored in order to understand and gain positive control when making color decisions. To create a successful color palette it is important for the designer to be well versed in theoretical principles—harmonies and contrasts, theoretical color schemes, and color and light. In addition to mastering the theoretical and scientific aspects of color, it is critical to understand the biological, psychological, and cultural responses of individuals and population groups. The greater the understanding of art, culture, and trends, the greater the ability to deduce and create symbolic meaning. Knowledge of theory, human behavior, and observation must be interpreted and utilized to create successful design. These skills must be applied within the parameters of world sentiment. In a world where the need for sustainability is apparent, the designer must be able to determine what goes into colored materials, and must make material choices based on aesthetics and an awareness of things that are harmful to the environment.

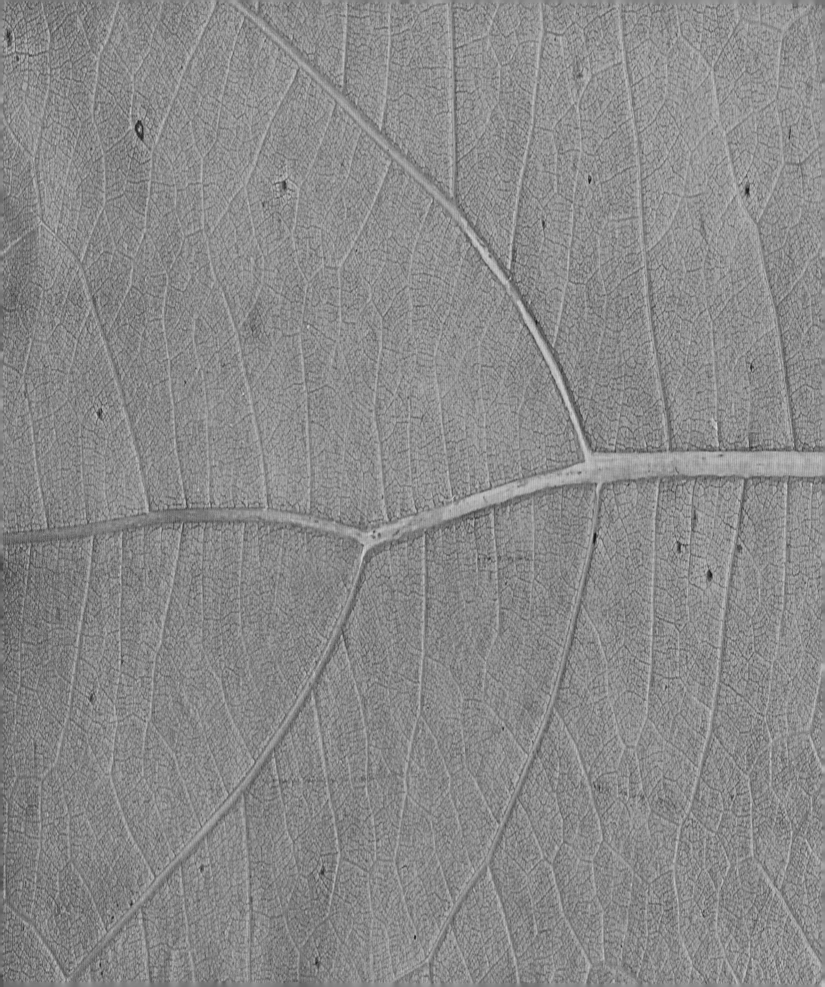

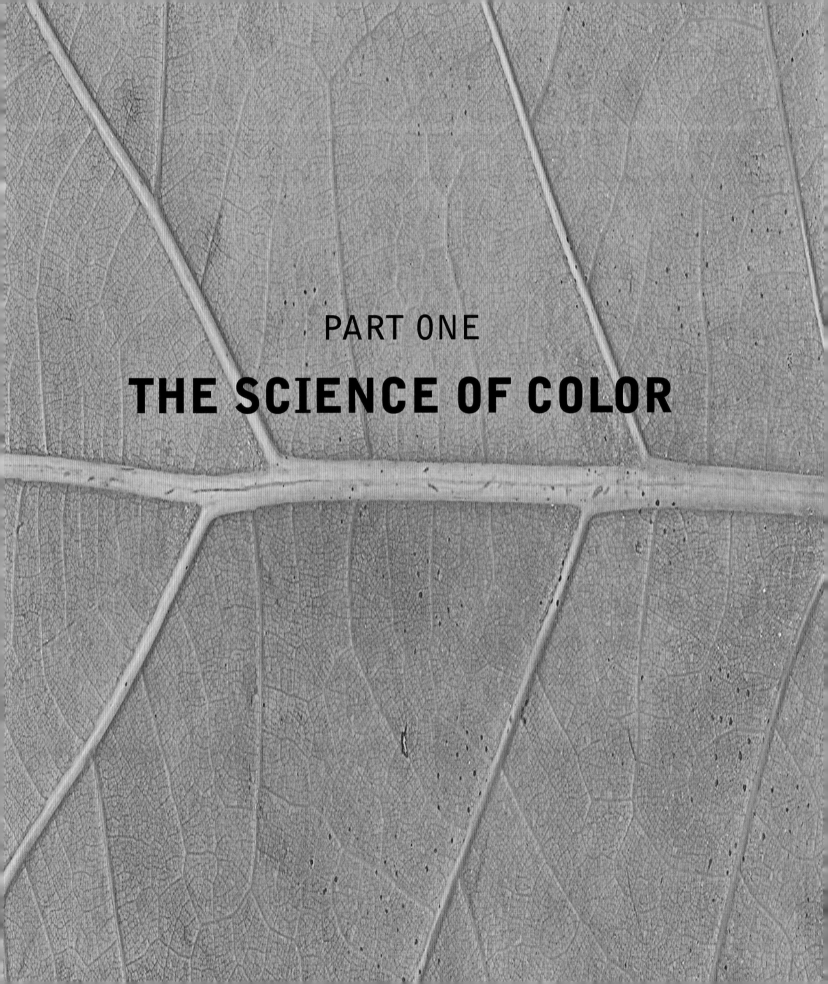

PART ONE

THE SCIENCE OF COLOR

CHAPTER ONE

COLOR IN NATURE

EXPERT: **DR JULIA HARTLING**
Evolutionary Biologist Ph.D., Yale University, and also an accomplished artist-illustrator.

Could you tell me a little bit about your background?
I studied art for years as a child but in college it seemed more responsible to study something more practical like biology. I stuck with this idea for years and received a Ph.D. in Evolutionary Biology from Yale University where I studied the evolution of protein structures. After that I had a child and a realization that I did not want to pursue a career in biology, but art so I became an artist-illustrator.

Why are plants green?
It's interesting to think about why plants appear green to the human eye. Green color is a part of the visible spectrum of sunlight containing red, orange, yellow, green, blue, indigo, and violet. One way to think of light is as a wave, with different colors having a different average wavelength. Another way is as photons, which are particles of light. Photons of different colors have different energies—redder photons have lower energy than bluer ones. Plants harvest energy by capturing photons of light, and using the process of photosynthesis to produce other molecules, most importantly cellulose, for growth. The central molecule in photosynthesis is chlorophyll, a pigment that initially captures the photon and converts its light energy into chemical energy. Interestingly, it does not use photons from all colors of the spectrum. It predominantly uses photons from the red and blue parts of the spectrum. Because photons of the green part of the spectrum get absorbed much less during photosynthesis they get reflected and can be detected by the eye, therefore making plants appear green to us.

From the perspective of evolutionary biology, why don't plants use green photons?
One possible theory is that early oceans contained two types of single-celled life—Archaebacteria and Cyanobacteria. Both are able to convert the light energy of photons into chemical energy. But Archaebacteria uses the green part of the spectrum and reflects back blue and red, therefore appearing purple, while chlorophyll-containing Cyanobacteria absorb blue and red, and reflect green. Some evidence indicates that bacteria that utilized green photons appeared first and there was a niche for an organism to evolve that used blue and red photons. The availability of resources allowed organisms that utilize the blue and red part of the spectrum to flourish. In turn these Cyanobacteria were incorporated into other cells and became the chloroplasts of modern plant cells. All chlorophyll is found inside the chloroplasts of plants, and as a result of this absorption and reflection of colors, plants appear green.

BIOMETRIC COLOR Acknowledging and engaging in the rich cultural and environmental diversity of biometric life is critical to how we think, experience, and gather information from our environment. It enables us to applaud "natural color" and take an holistic approach to studying it within the context of the biome—a geographical region that can be defined by its climate, land formations, and flora and fauna. Here we can discover nature's complex color combinations and define biometric color in terms of the ecosystems in which it exists. We can see how these elements distinguish themselves to form distinct color palettes, creating color identities that will enrich us culturally.

Let us explore the color of several exemplary biomes, including desert, tundra, tropical rainforest, temperate forest, temperate grasslands, as well as the aquatic biomes. Our initial impressions when we think about the desert biome, is of a place of little coloration. The landscape, plants, and animals of this biome, characterized by a dry harsh environment, might seemingly have less color, but this is really not the case. Georgia O'Keeffe, an artist who called the desert of New Mexico her home, had an extremely heightened sense of color that she used to communicate feelings about the desert landscape. If one experiences the desert, you can understand how well she captures the colors of northern New Mexico, with earthy reds, mauves, and ochers. She uses these subdued, warm, rich earth tones on the hills in contrast to the intensity of the oversized red flowers, giving them great clarity and purpose against the desert vastness.

Also characterized by sparse vegetation, the color palette of the tundra biome is very different from the warm palette of the desert. A treeless biome that occurs in the northern hemisphere (just under the Arctic Circle), the grays and whites of the vast mountain landscape and permafrost dominate the colors of the tundra. This is contrasted only by greens from mosses and dwarf shrubs, a variety of floral pinks and violets in the spring, and autumnal oranges and reds. The whiteness and fur of the arctic fox and the polar bear seem to be an important color adaptation of the animal to life in the tundra.

While color is seasonal in the tundra, it is in abundance all year round in the rainforest biome. Of all the forest biomes, the rainforest is teeming with the most vibrantly colored plants and wildlife. There is a plethora of brightly colored flowers and a rich greenery in the canopy of giant trees and woody vines. Like the polar bears of the tundra, rainforest wildlife has also adapted to its environs. Bright yellow tree frogs, bright orange toucans, and intensely colored and highly patterned butterflies live within the trees that flower and produce fruit year round. The main distinction between the rainforest and temperate forest is based not only on the

Below left: In winter, animals such as this Arctic fox, blend into the achromatic background of the Arctic tundra.

Below: The landscape appears to have a blue cast because of the light bounced back from the reflective surfaces.

Right: This desert landscape with capped sandstone towers at sunset, in Bisti Badlands Wilderness Area, New Mexico, USA is a beautiful sight to behold. The bold light of the south enhances the intensity of rich reds, oranges, and yellows, which are complemented by the vast blue sky.

Below left & right: The gray barren snow-covered mountains are in deep contrast with the low-lying shrubland of late summer, which exudes a plethora of color enveloping the rolling plains. Such extremes are common to tundra regions.

dominate, the temperate forest sees far more seasonal color changes. In the spring and summer, flowering trees give way to varying green vegetation dependent upon the species. Both the Japanese cherry tree and the flowering plum tree produce an abundance of pink flowers that stay for about 10 days in the spring, before giving way to dark green and dark red leaves. The green leaves of oak and maple trees turn a beautiful deep red, bright yellow, and orange in the fall. Flowers and plants are also subject to seasonal color change in the temperate forest, and different flowering species can come in a multitude of colors, such as hydrangeas in blues, pinks, violets, and yellows.

While rainforest animals are brightly colored, the animals of the temperate forest—squirrels, rabbits, skunks, and foxes, for example—have gray, black, and brown colorations that allow them to blend into the forest habitat, especially in the winter when color is sparse. Although animal coloration is far more subdued in the temperate forest, anyone who has experienced fall or spring in New England, USA, will understand that color is both as varied and beautiful as the rainforest, but far more ephemeral.

The forest holds a great variety of color, but grass greens are the dominant color of the grassland biome. While an occasional cottonwood or oak tree might be seen, the land is colored by a variety of grasses. Purple needlegrass, blue grama grass, buffalograss, and galleta grass are interspersed with wildflowers such as goldenrods, sunflowers, clover, and wild indigo. In the

Below left: The brightly colored bill of the toucan not only makes it identifiable to people the world over, but also helps to attract the opposite sex. Both males and females possess this colorful beak, which they employ during their mating ritual.

Below: In New England during the first week of May, the Japanese cherry tree blossoms are in full bloom with pink soft-edged flowers. While they are rich and full blossoms, within five days there is a blanket of pink fallen flowers on the ground giving way to greenery. Many spring rituals have developed in different countries around the world with the advent of the blossoming.

fall, the big sky and wide-open rolling plains imbue our vision with colors of gold, ocher, and rust. While little more than prairie dogs, ferrets, and coyotes live among the grasses (contributing only browns and grays to the biome's coloration), man contributes by using the rich and fertile soil to plant crops that provide color dependent upon choice. While land-based biomes are influenced by the vastness of the blue sky, the color blue dominates the water biomes. The color of both freshwater and saltwater shifts according to what's on the surface and the quality or clarity of the water, its depth, and the salt content. At the bottom of the ocean, where little light is present, fish rely on other senses and color is sparse. However, there are areas with an abundance of color. Comprised of colorful coral and

beautiful fish, coral reefs are filled with great diversity and color intensity. The colors range from bright yellows and cobalt blues through to vivid greens and intense reds. Some freshwater biomes are also teaming with color and life, such as salamanders, marshlands filled with blue irises, and plankton and algae floating on the surface of the water.[1]

Below: Research suggests that sea anemones have a symbiotic relationship with two forms of algae, one of which, the unicellular zooxanthellae dinoflagullate, serves as a source for photosynthesis and may be responsible for the bright colors as they use their fluorescent pigments to provide some protective function against light in the tropical shallow water.

STRUCTURAL COLOR: COLOR THAT SUPPORTS LIFE

In nature, color is intrinsically important to plant and animal life. This life-supporting color is of purpose to the environment, as a source of energy, for regeneration of species, to encourage behaviors, and to provide personal safety. For some animals, colors are intrinsic to their genetics, as is the case with the melanin in hair and fur, or the bioluminescence that emits light in the firefly. Others have to eat their color, as with the flamingo, which gets it coloration from the carotenoids in the shrimp and algae it consumes. Some animals (peacocks, for example) alter their color with structural shifts in their surface texture—due to the movement of layered surfaces (in the peacock's case, feathers) light is reflected in different ways, apparently changing the creature's color.

While biological pigments in living organisms absorb and reflect light in the same way as inanimate objects, they are colored not by personal choice but by genetics. These genetic colorations have evolved for very specific purposes. In the plant kingdom, the color green is vital to the metabolic process of photosynthesis: "chlorophyll green" converts water and carbon dioxide into glucose. Many of us are curious as to the reason why chlorophyll is green and there are many theoretical possibilities proposed, some of which consider the absorption of red and blue light versus green and suggest that as green light is absorbed less in the process of photosynthesis, more of it bounces back to the eye than red and blue light. Lots more research has to be done, however, to answer this seemingly simple color question.

Color is widely responsible for the regeneration of many species of plant life. A symbiotic relationship exists in which brightly colored flowers entice insects of all varieties to come to them, enabling the spread of pollen. Some floral colors are actually specific to species of pollinators—for example, flowers that need bees to pollinate them are mostly yellow, as bees cannot detect reds, while other flowers are red to attract species such as butterflies, which can see the color. A yellow flower's outer petals reflect both visible spectrum color yellow and ultraviolet light, while the inside reflects only the yellow thus directing the bees to the nectar. Many flowers also use stripes or dots.[2]

Animals also use color to entice members of their own species to mate. An article on the color preferences of zebra finches found that the male birds' bills became redder with age. It was also deduced that females of this species preferred to associate with males with the brightest red bills.[3] Lizards are a great species to talk about when it comes to color and mating. Barry Sinervoa, Donald B. Milesc, W. Anthony Frankinob, Matthew Klukowskib, and Dale F. DeNardo, studied the throat color of the side-blotched lizard. These lizards' throats are colored orange, blue, or yellow, and the study suggests that the colors "advertise hierarchical statue and male reproductively within the side blotched community."[4] It found that orange males have control over the greatest amount of territory and have the greatest harems (most female lizards). The lizards with blue and yellow throats have less territory and smaller harems. Another type of lizard, the chameleon, uses its ability to change color to protect itself, in addition to using its color to attract a mate. In this way, color is used in the animal kingdom as both a communication tool and a form of protection through camouflage, mimicry, or as a warning deterrent.

Fish in the coral reef are brightly colored to help them stay hidden from view of predators. In the article, "Communication and Camouflage," Professor Justin Marshall, of the University of Queensland in Australia, and Professor George Losey, of the University of Hawaii, study protection with respect to "bright" colors in reef fish. Using "non-subjective spectrophotometric measurements" they studied the colors of fishes and their habitat. By determining the average reef color by refraction, they were able to determine blue and yellow were the dominant colors. Interestingly enough, many of the colors of coral fish fall within this spectrum of average reef color. While humans can easily see the contrasting colors, the fish cannot distinguish colors as clearly because they lack long wavelength reflectors, with the result that the fish are camouflaged against the reef.[5]

Opposite top: If you have ever wondered why flamingos are pink, it is due to the food they eat. They commonly ingest aqueous bacteria and foods that are high in alpha and beta carotenoid pigments. These birds are a variety of pinks dependent upon species and how much pigment they ingest.

Opposite center left: The chameleon has the ability to change its color, which it uses to protect itself from predators, as well as to attract a mate.

Opposite center right: The colors of a peacock's tail are produced by intricate crystal-like structures that allow for some light rays to filter through while other are reflected back creating a beautiful array of colors.

Opposite bottom left: Made up of vibrant coral and beautiful fish, coral reefs are filled with great diversity and intense color. The colors range from bright yellows, cobalt blues, bright greens, and intense reds. Sea horses adapt very well to the environment using color to protect themselves from life-threatening predators.

Opposite bottom right: Clown fish have a symbiotic relationship with sea anemones. They get food in exchange for protecting the host by driving predators away.

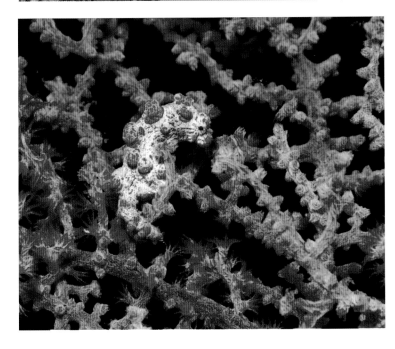

OUT-OF-SIGHT COLOR: MICROSCOPIC AND TELESCOPIC With technological innovation and growth, our knowledge of physics and particulate matter has enabled us to answer color questions that were not easily answered in the past. Not only are we able to see and understand more about "universal" color, but color has allowed us to define what we cannot see with the naked eye: with telescopes we have the opportunity to look at galaxies beyond our own, while microscopes enable us to experience color at a cellular level.

Scientific discovery has also given us an explanation as to why the sky is blue. Within the atmosphere there are gases and other particulate matter that collide with light waves. When light waves collide with particulate matter, the light waves bounce off in different directions, but the light remains "white" because all of the wavelengths that combine to make "white light" are still present. However, when the light waves hit gases, some of the wavelengths are absorbed and then later released as the same color. This is known as Rayleigh scattering,

after Lord Rayleigh, the English physicist who first described it in the 1870s. Blue wavelengths are more readily absorbed and released, which gives us the reason as to why the sky is blue.

Another atmospheric interaction with particulate matter results in beautiful colors. This occurs when highly charged electrons from solar wind interact with the atmosphere creating the Aurora Borealis (the northern lights) and the Aurora Australis (the southern lights).[6]

Left: The colors of the Aurora Borealis depend on which highly-charged electrons from solar winds—oxygen or nitrogen—hit them and at what altitude they hit. Colors can vary between green, red, blue, and purple.

Opposite: The advent of sophisticated telescopes and digital camera technology allow a wide range of colors to be detected with greater clarity. Colors are made possible by the combination of hydrogen (reds), doubly ionized oxygen (greens), and nitrogen-based compounds (blues), in the nebula's environment.

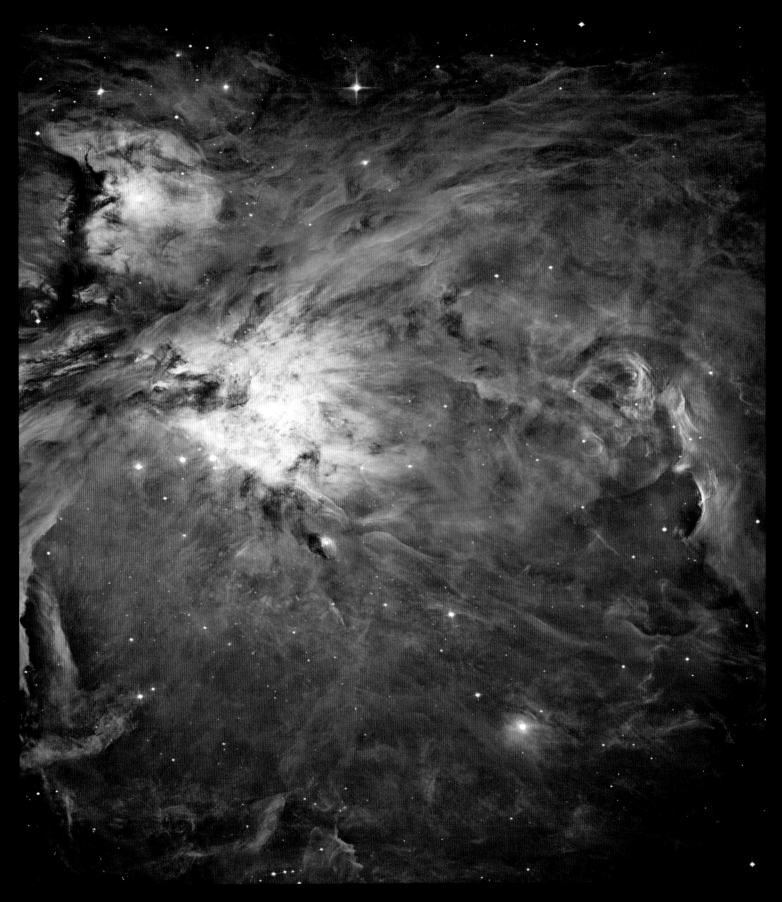

The development of new color-aided visualization, combined with advanced exploration technology has allowed us to use pigments and colored filters to enhance our scientific visualization in space. Colorization techniques are being used to make photographs of planets more readable, and as we discover planets and solar systems we can use color to create contrast and definition.

Scientists also use colored filters to enhance their "astronomical seeing." Filters act by letting the color of the filter through, while blocking the other hues. Jeff Beish, former A.L.P.O Senior Mars Recorder, wrote an article on filtering and Mars entitled "Observing the Planets with Color Filters," in which he listed filtering suggestions that would make images of the "Red Planet" clearer.

JEFF BEISH COLOR SUGGESTIONS

Yellow (W12, W15) to brighten desert regions; darkens bluish and brownish features.

Orange (W21, W23A) further increases contrast between light and dark features, penetrates hazes and most clouds, and limited detection of dust clouds.

Red (W25, W29) gives maximum contrast of surface features, enhances fine surface details, dust clouds boundaries, and polar cap boundaries.

Green (W57) darkens red and blue features, enhances frost patches, surface fogs, and polar projections.

Blue-Green (W64) helps detect ice fogs and polar hazes.

Blue (W80A, W38, W38A) and deep blue (W46, W47) show atmospheric clouds, discrete white clouds, and limb hazes, equatorial cloud bands, polar cloud hoods, and darkens reddish features.

Magenta (W30, W32) will enhance red and blue features and darken green ones. Improves polar region features and some Martian clouds.[7]

Color has not only been an asset in space, it has also aided microscopic imaging research. One such technique involves medical testing. When taking an MRI, a medical diagnostic test, dye injected into patients allows for greater contrast sensitivity and clarity of the scanned area. A technique called fluorescence microscopy—a process by which a microscope with an intense light source excites fluorescent dyes and proteins to enhance microscopic images—is a key diagnostic technique for immunology and microbiology. In addition, fluorescence is also useful in the areas of environmental science and geology.

Advances in technology have also allowed us to look at color under the sea. New underwater vehicles allow us to stay underwater longer and utilize photographic equipment such as high-resolution video and digital cameras and lighting at greater depths. We know that light is selectively filtered out as you descend—for example, red disappears at a depth of 10 ft (3m), and only violet can be viewed at 100 ft (30m). However, with the aid of special filters, lenses, and strobes we can counter the blue-green affect of the water and capture truer color. Low-light monochrome cameras can also be used to photograph organisms that are sensitive to light.

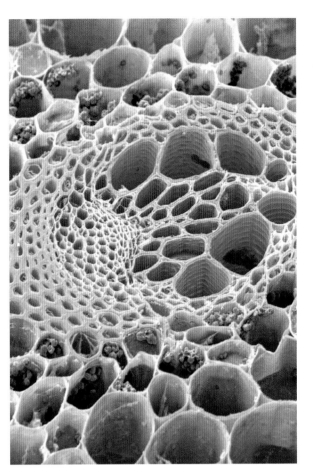

Opposite: As early as the 1950s precise spectrographs revealed that the color of Mars was really a dark yellowish brown. At the summer solstice, the Syrtis Blue Cloud with its aerosols and ice crystals allows for scattering and, in turn, makes the color blue become visible.

Left: This color-scanned micrograph of a cross section of a buttercup was made possible by the use of a focused electron beam that reads electrons of the object and produces a three-dimensional image. The color used to add definition and clarification is the result of natural or artificial color specific staining.

Below: Fluorescent light micrograph of two fibroblast cells, showing their nuclei (green) and cytoskeleton.

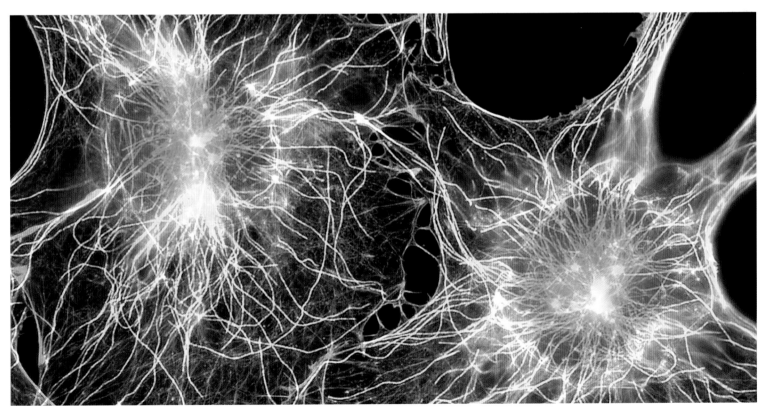

CHAPTER TWO

COLOR AND LIGHT PERCEPTION

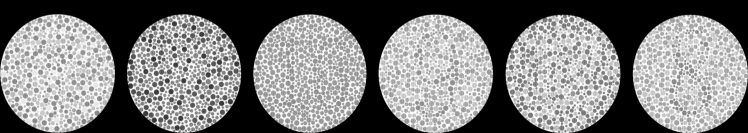

EXPERT: **DR JOSEPH MARKOFF PhD, MD**
Joseph Markoff is the CEO of Gabrieli Biotech Consulting, LLC. Prior to that he was Global Director of Scientific Affairs for Ophthalmology at Merck & Co., Inc. Prior to joining Merck, Dr Markoff founded Philadelphia Eye Associates in 1978 after completing his Residency at the Wills Eye Hospital. Dr Markoff received his undergraduate degree from Oberlin College where currently he serves as an honorary trustee. He received a Ph.D. in the neurosciences from Syracuse University and was a Senior Principal Research Scientist at the Honeywell Corporation prior to receiving his MD from the University of Minnesota in Minneapolis. Dr Markoff holds the rank of Attending Surgeon at Wills Eye Hospital and is a Clinical Professor of Ophthalmology at Thomas Jefferson University School of Medicine. He lectures nationally and internationally on cataract surgery, glaucoma, retinal disease, and basic physiology of the eye. He has published and presented more than one hundred fifty scientific papers. He served as an associate examiner for the American Board of Ophthalmology. He has been chief of ophthalmology at the Albert Einstein and St. Agnes Medical Centers in Philadelphia. He served as an advisor to Pfizer, Johnson and Johnson, Bausch and Lomb, Chiron and Alcon. He has been the principal investigator on more than 50 clinical trials and served as the grants officer for the International Retinal Research Foundation. He was named in Consumer Research Council's guide to "America's Top Ophthalmologists." Dr Markoff is also a professional trumpet player having performed with the orchestras of Syracuse, Minnesota, St. Paul and Philadelphia. He has also done research into the acoustics of musical instruments. A *New York Times* article about this work appeared in its Science Section on November 2, 1999.

Tell me about the function of vision.
The function of vision is to locate objects in space, determine if they are moving or static, and make an interpretive decision.

What are the components of the visual system?
There are three components. The first one is optical, in which an image must fall clearly on the retina. The second is retino-cortical, in which neural signals travel from the retina to the cortex without interruption. The third component is integrative, in which signals are encoded.

Please define the tasks of the rods and cone.
The rods outnumber cones 20:1. There are 120 million rods and six million cones. Cones are responsible for fine spatial vision like reading and driving. Rhodopsin is the primary pigment in the rods. There are three types of photo-pigments (short, medium, and long wavelength). While the rods have no color mediation, they are responsible for mediating vision at low light levels. They also mediate motion, but have poor spatial resolution.

What causes color blindness?
Deficiencies in the red, green, and blue cones will result in loss of color sensitivity. When one of the three cones—blue, green, or red—is absent or abnormal, color deficiencies develop.

Please define different types of color blindness.
Protanopia color deficiency is a red deficiency (long wavelength cone) and therefore people who suffer from this are less sensitive to red light. Deuteranopia color deficiency is a green defect (medium wavelength cone). Tritanopia occurs when there is an abnormality in blue cones (short wavelength cones).

What are the causes of color blindness?
Color blindness or deficiency can be congenital or acquired. Congenital defects primarily affect males. They are usually symmetric and most commonly red-green. Acquired defects affect both males and females equally, are asymmetric and progressive. Certain drugs such as digitalis and ethambutol can produce acquired defects.

LIGHT THEORY AND SOURCES In order to understand how we see color it is necessary to examine the relationship between a light source, our perception, and the object being perceived. It is the interaction between these three that allows us to see and experience the world around us. The interaction is so consequential that the alteration of any of them will change what is being seen. Understanding what light is and how it works is of primary importance, because without light we cannot see color. Light can be defined as a series of electromagnetic wavelengths that emanate from an energy source. It is a form of energy released by atoms made up of particles called light photons. Most come in the form of white light from the sun, the moon, and the stars (referred to as natural light), while artificial light uses electricity to convert energy into electromagnetic radiation (as in a lamp). Other natural sources include animal bioluminescence and fire.

In the late 1800s a scientist named James Maxwell developed an electromagnetic scale that included everything from radio waves, through gamma waves, including microwaves, infrared rays, ultraviolet rays, and x-rays, all of which vary in length, frequency, and energy. The entire electromagnetic spectrum is not perceivable to humans—what we see we call the "visible spectrum," which exists on the scale between ultraviolet and infrared. The scale is measured in nanometers (nm), with the visible spectrum ranging from approximately 400–700nm.

We use two variables to describe a wavelength: size and frequency. The size of a light wave is measured from the "peak to peak" or "trough to trough" of the wave, while the frequency is the number of waves that pass a point in a specified time frame. When we refer to a wavelength's frequency as being fast we call it high frequency, and when we refer to it as being slow we call it low frequency. As the low frequency wavelengths move slower, they have less energy than higher frequency wavelengths. Oddly enough, the two variables: size and frequency are inversely proportional. This means, for example, that red has the longest wavelength and the lowest frequency reading on the visible electromagnetic spectrum (around 700nm), while violet has the shortest wavelength and the highest frequency (around 400nm). Greens and yellows read at about 500–600nm on the scale. Yellow-green is regarded as the most easily visible color on the spectrum.[1]

Unless there are no other light sources present, the light we experience is a combination of natural and artificial light. While artificial light can emanate from energy sources such as oil, wood, and gas, electric lamps are most commonly used today. However, different

VISIBLE SPECTRUM

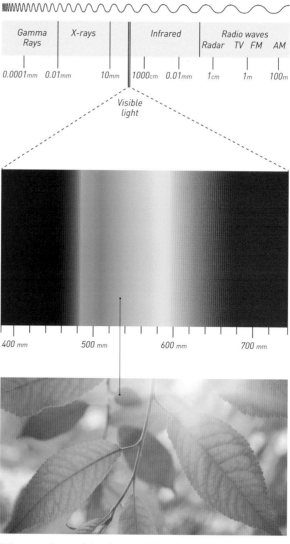

Yellow-green is regarded as the most visible on the color spectrum

Left: The electromagnetic spectrum is used to describe the range of light from radio waves to gamma waves. The part of the spectrum that is visible to the human eye is a very small part of the spectrum and is referred to as the visible spectrum. The colors in this spectrum are known as spectral colors. While there are millions of colors that are detected by the human eye they are all made from a dominant spectral color. Yellow-green is the most visible color to the human eye.

Opposite top: Light comes from both natural and artificial sources. It originates from the sun in the form of ultraviolet, infrared and visible light. The intensity of moonlight is not as great as the sun and it varies due to its position with respect to the earth. Light can also be generated from within a plant or animal. This is referred to as biofluorescence and bioluminescence.

Opposite bottom: A rainbow is caused by the reflection, refraction, and dispersion of light after it rains causing a spectrum to be revealed. Each droplet acts as a prism and disperses light reflecting it back at the viewer.

NATURAL SOURCES OF LIGHT

Sunlight

Moonlight

Animal bioluminescence

Fire

LIGHT THEORY AND SOURCES

types of artificial light release energy in different ways, and consequently give off different qualities and colors of light. For example, incandescent lights, which are commonly used in interiors, create light by heating a metal filament until it glows, while fluorescent lamps use discharged energy from argon gas and mercury and a phosphorous powder coating on the inside of the glass, which are then stimulated by electrodes and converted into light. LED, or Light Emitting Diode lamps, which are gaining popularity because of their light quality and energy efficiency, create light by the movement of electrodes through a semi conductive material.

Because of the work of Isaac Newton, we understand that the sum total of the visible spectrum of light is white. This means that when all the colors of the visible light spectrum are mixed together they create white light. This theoretical concept applies to both natural and artificial light—while natural light seems to have greater purity, this is more to do with the inability of artificial light to replicate natural light than the color of the light itself.

Electric bulbs vary in terms of their brightness or wattage. For example, an incandescent bulb may come in 40, 60, or 80 watts. They can also vary in the

COLOR TEMPERATURE

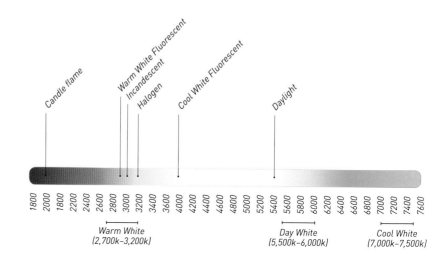

Above: **Color temperature is expressed in degrees Kelvin and refers to how warm or cool the light quality is. Candlelight has a low color temperature whereas daylight is about 5500K at noon so is very cool.**

Below left: **Modern bulbs can offer different color temperatures. A warm yellow light has a low color temperature, creating a cozy atmosphere.**

Below: **Cool white fluorescent lighting is often used in offices to enhance levels of concentration. Cooler, higher color temperature light is also traditionally found in hospitals and gives off a bluish cast.**

ARTIFICIAL SOURCES OF LIGHT

Incandescent

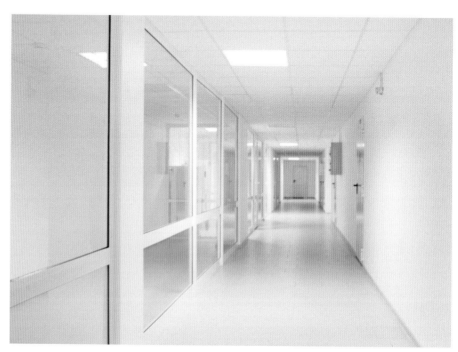

Flourescent

COLOR RENDERING INDEX (CRI) VALUES OF COMMON LIGHT SOURCES

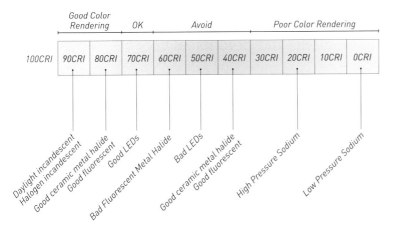

	Good Color Rendering		OK	Avoid			Poor Color Rendering			
100CRI	90CRI	80CRI	70CRI	60CRI	50CRI	40CRI	30CRI	20CRI	10CRI	0CRI

Daylight incandescent
Halogen incandescent
Good ceramic metal halide
Good fluorescent
Good LEDs
Bad Fluorescent Metal Halide
Bad LEDs
Good ceramic metal halide
Good fluorescent
High Pressure Sodium
Low Pressure Sodium

Above: **The Color Rendering index refers to a numerical system that rates the color-rendering ability of a light as compared to natural daylight out of 100.**

Below: **Inspired by Dante's epic poem, *The Divine Comedy*, the piece *The Walk*, created by light artist Titia Ex for the 2012 international light art festival in Eindhoven, the Netherlands, creates an intensity of color and movement that portrays a journey to enlightenment. Titia Ex uses 35000 LED lightbulbs using the additive color system to create the vivid colors and engage her audience.**

color of light that they give off. Florescent lights can come in cool, warm, or full spectrum variants, with cool lights emitting more low frequency light, while warm lights emit a higher frequency light. Full spectrum fluorescent lights balance all frequencies and are closest to the white of natural light.

To compare the accuracy of light bulbs to natural light, the Color Temperature Index and the Color Rendering Index were created. The Color Temperature Index describes whether the color of a light is warm, neutral, or cool: the higher the temperature (measured on the Kelvin scale), the cooler of the light; the lower the temperature, the warmer the color of the light. Sunlight varies in temperature: at noon on a clear day it measures 5500 Kelvin (K), whereas on a cloudy day it measures 6500–7500K. Incandescent lamps measure around 2700K, while halogen lamps measure around 3200K. Fluorescent have a wide range dependent on cool or warm extending from 27000–6500K Kelvin. The Color Rendering Index measures light's ability to show color "realistically or naturally" as compared to a natural light source: the closer it is, the higher the CRI, and the more "accurate" the light source is.[2]

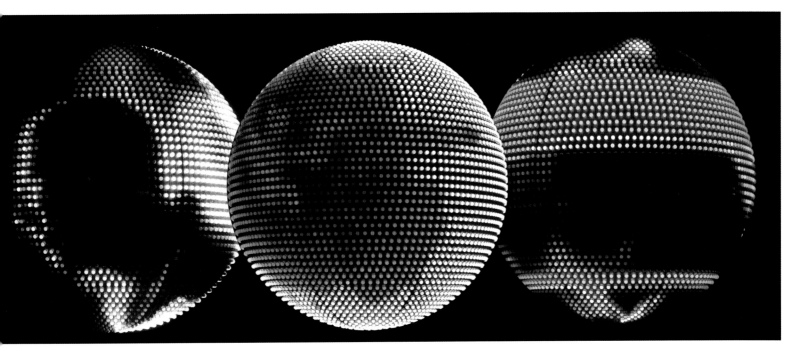

LED

COLOR VISION We are aware from our previous discussion that there are many variables regarding light that come into play when perceiving the color of an object. While we now understand the process by which light transmits energy to the eye, what needs to be explored is how the eye senses, perceives, and interprets that light. Although scientists can describe the physics of light and the anatomy of the eye and brain, perceptions and interpretations are grounded more in cognitive studies and psychology. Vision capability stems from a combination of sensory elements and perceptual interpretations within the mind.

The eye is responsible for receiving the light waves and transmitting signals to the brain. It is a chain reaction of sorts, where each part of the eye acts as a link in the process of visual perception. A study of the anatomy of the eye begins at the point of light entry into the cornea, the clear covering of the eye. It is a structural element responsible for bending and refracting the light, and focusing it for sharpness and acuity. The cornea protects the iris, which contains the pupil, whose job is to regulate the flow of light that enters the eye by expanding and contracting as the light intensities change. Situated behind the iris, the lens further refracts the light and sends impulses through the vitreous cavity to the retina, which is located on the inside surface of the back of the eye. The retina is a layer of nerves lining the back of the eye, which senses the light and transmits information through electrical impulses to the optic nerve. In turn, the optic nerve relays information to the visual cortical areas in the brain, which are responsible for our vision acuity and color perception.

Specific areas of the human retina contain two types of photoreceptors: the rods and the cones. These are crucial to vision. The rods are responsible for our ability to see more clearly in dim light. They also assist in our peripheral vision. The cones (which are located in the central fovea) are specifically responsible for our color vision and for high spatial acuity. There are three types of cone-shaped cells, each of which is sensitive to either long, medium, or short wavelengths of light.

While various theories of color vision have evolved, scientists have come to believe the answer to how the brain "sees" lies in two important theories:

Right: Light enters the eye through the pupil and is focused by the lens onto the retina, where it stimulates the rods and cones. Information about what we are seeing is transmitted to the brain via the optic nerve.

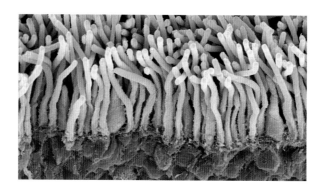

Left: This is an electron micrographic image of the rods, which are yellow and the cones, which are purple within the retina of the eye.

STRUCTURE OF THE HUMAN EYE

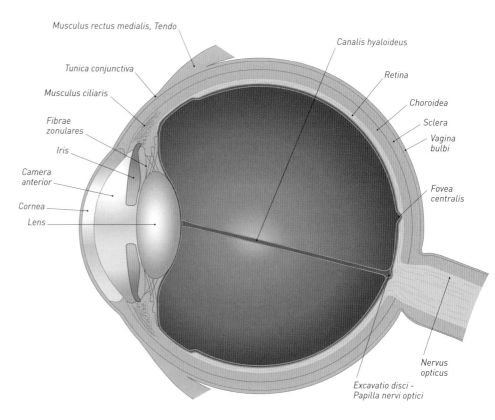

Musculus rectus medialis, Tendo

Canalis hyaloideus

Tunica conjunctiva

Retina

Musculus ciliaris

Choroidea

Fibrae zonulares

Sclera

Vagina bulbi

Iris

Camera anterior

Fovea centralis

Cornea

Lens

Nervus opticus

Excavatio disci - Papilla nervi optici

Above left & right: **According to the trichromatic theory and the opponent-process theory of color vision, receptors in our eyes receive the colored light and send a message to the brain. If we didn't have these color vision receptors we would see in black and white.**

the trichromatic theory and the opponent-process theory of color vision.

The trichromatic theory originated in the work of Thomas Young and was confirmed and expanded upon by Hermann Von Helmholtz. In 1802, Young considered the idea of three types of photoreceptors, each sensitive to a specific part of the visual spectrum. In 1850, Von Helmholtz proposed that each color viewed by the eye was a combination of three basic colors: red, green, and blue. When an individual sees color, a certain number of each type of receptor registers the light, which is interpreted as color by the brain.[3]

In his *Theory of Colors*, Goethe acknowledged a relationship between diametrically opposed colors, but it was Ewald Hering who proposed the opponent-process theory in 1892. Based upon the subjective appearances of color, Hering suggests that the visual system might be capable of generating two opposing signals at the same time. The opponent-process theory suggested that there were four, not three, elementary color sensations: red and green, and yellow and blue, which oppose each other. A third achromatic pair, black and white, was added to the primaries to account for luminance. These pairs do not create white light when mixed together as the mixture of red, green, and blue in the trichromatic theory proposes, but rather let it occur through the negation of each color in a pair. It is now believed that these systems work in conjunction:

the trichromatic system relates to the way in which the retina creates color using three types of cones, while the opponent-process theory relates to the retrieval and processing of color information on a more complex level.[4]

However, the question arises as to whether physiological differences in the eye can cause individuals to see differently. Assuming the anatomy is correct, perception of color should theoretically be consistent, but if the individual has dysfunctional cones due to genetics or ill health, he or she may be colorblind. Many scientists have wondered whether colors appear differently to different individuals, even if their relative physiology is healthy. Martha Livingston, in her book, *The Biology of Seeing*, poses the question: "Do you see red like I see red?"[5] She talks about a basic physiological similarity and response to the color red, but suggests that perhaps a higher level of consciousness mixed with experience might enhance or change that color. She suggests that just as a musician may hear musical notes with a greater clarity of sound, so an individual who has been trained visually might see color with greater clarity. This is a reasonable premise, which undoubtedly warrants further research and investigation.[6]

OBJECT COLOR: LIGHT, SURFACE, AND ENVIRONMENT Now that we have covered the physics of light and physiology of perception, we must explore how light interacts with the object's color and material attributes. We understand that the light (natural or artificial), its placement, and its intensity will influence the color of an object, but the color will also be affected by an object's surface reflectance, its degree of transparency/opacity, and its surface texture. Material attributes can affect the way in which light interacts with the surface. When a light wave hits a surface it reacts in each of three possible ways: reflectance, transmission, and refraction. When talking about color, reflectance can be described as the light waves that are not absorbed by the object and instead bounce off the object to be perceived by the eye as its color. A highly reflective surface would be a mirror or glass-like pond in which the image and the color are mostly reflected and not absorbed.

Transmission refers to the light waves that pass through the object. The amount of light that is transmitted is directly related to the degree of transparency of the material quality: if the object is transparent, like a window, for example, light will travel through it without a great deal of scattering and the color of the objects behind can be seen. However, if an object is opaque, it will not transmit any light and its color will be the result of its reflectance and refraction.

Refraction occurs when the light waves hit materials that change the velocity of the wavelength, causing the wave to bend. If one looks at the paintings of Janet Fish one can see her great attentiveness as to the way light hits an object. Her elegant still lifes are all about transparency, translucency, and reflectivity. You can study the intertwined layers of translucent cloth, transparent colored glass, and mirrored reflections. Not only is the transparency of the surface material a relevant color concern, but so too is the surface reflectance. Let's use a painted wall as an example. When you paint a wall your paint finish options are matte/flat, eggshell/satin/semi-gloss, and high gloss. Matte paint reflects less light/absorbs more light, as a result of which cracks and uneven areas are smoothed out and appear less obvious. However, gloss paint reflects more light, creating a more active surface that can cause glare and highlight bumps and textures: the color of the paint may remain constant, but the surface quality changes due to the texture of the wall and the reflected light.

With the exception of pure outdoor daylight, the way we see objects typically depends on a combination of natural and artificial light, and their variables. For natural light, variables include weather conditions, the time of day, the geographic location, and even the season. For artificial light we must consider the color and wattage of a bulb, the number of lights in a space, the time of day, and whether there are any windows allowing natural light into the space. With so many variables, it is understandable that our perceptual brains might play tricks on us.

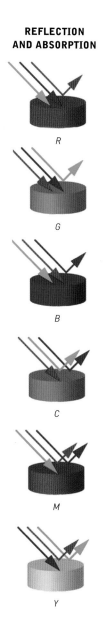

REFLECTION AND ABSORPTION

R

G

B

C

M

Y

Opposite left: **Color viewed through clear glass should be completely accurate, but due to both natural and artificial light there can be distortion. Translucent surfaces allow light to pass through, but diffuse it so that images and color are not as clear or intense.**

Opposite: **Reflective color is what we see when we look at the color of an object. The color that we see is that which is reflected, while the colors that we cannot see are those that are absorbed.**

Left: **Janet Fish's paintings, like** *Pears*, **1972, seen here involve the woven intermingling of intense color and form and light. She employs reflectance when she paints areas of the plastic wrap white, transmission in clear areas exhibiting the fruit below, and refraction when all colors are absorbed except the beautiful greens of the fruit and box.**

In some instances, the brain makes up for changes in light, which we describe as color constancy. In other instances, it perceives the difference, which we define as metameric failure. Color constancy occurs when our brain assumes that colors are the same, even when they are not. The color of a white house is perceived as white at all times of day, when in reality the color shifts dramatically, as we see when we view Monet's *Haystack* or *Rouen Cathedral* series. In this way, the brain understands a familiar color and maintains that perception, even when environmental factors have changed its appearance.

On the other hand, metameric failure occurs when two swatches of the same color appear to be the same under one light source and different under another light source. The reason for this difference stems from the fact that the eye creates the same color in different ways, with varying combinations of red, green, and blue receptors depending on which light rays enter the eye. In other words: 2 + 2 = 4 and 1 + 3 = 4. As different light sources emit slightly different wavelengths, the perceived colors of an object can sometimes shift when the sources change. The goal for commercially reproduced color in the print, product, and digital worlds is to achieve a metameric color match regardless of lighting conditions, so an object appears to exhibit the same colors, regardless of the light source used to illuminate it.[7]

Below & opposite: **Monet** was interested in perceiving the color shifts with the change in times of day. If you are observant and view what you think of as a white house in the early morning, high noon, and early evening light it will become apparent that it never really is white. Morning light tends to have a warm pink and orange cast, while evening light has a purplish-bluish cast. The most accurate color that appears yellowish occurs at noon.

MONET'S ROUEN CATHEDRAL SERIES

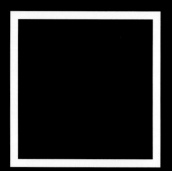

CHAPTER THREE

THEORETICAL COLOR

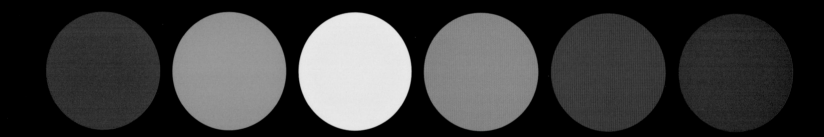

EXPERT: **MARGARET S. LIVINGSTONE, Ph.D**
A visual neurophysiologist, Margaret S. Livingstone is a professor of Neurobiology at Harvard
Medical School. She is a graduate of MIT and Harvard with a post doctoral from Princeton
University. In addition to her main body of research, Dr Livingstone uses her sophisticated
knowledge of visual neurobiology to understand some of the visual insights that artists have
expressed in their work. In her book *Vision and Art, The Biology of Seeing* she explains the
science of vision and studies art works from the perspective of "underlying visual phenomena."

**In a lecture "What Art Can Tell Us About The Brain"
at the University of Michigan School of Art and Design,
you suggested that many works of art are great because
they reveal important things about how we see. One such
topic was color and luminance (value). Could you talk
about it with respect to science and art?**

Picasso said "colors are only symbols. Reality is to be found
in luminance alone." We have three cones in the retina:
blue, green, and red that allow us to see color. Luminance
is not just the sum but the envelop of the three cones.
Usually color contrasts have a luminance contrast but
sometimes you can have a color contrast that has no
luminance contrast. An example is *Impression, Sunrise*
by Monet (see page 123). I received a small grant to
measure the luminance of the sun in this painting. The
sun, despite how brilliant it appears, is the same luminance
as the background. The basis of this phenomena is that
your visual system, which starts in the retina goes onto
the mid brain and then onto the primary visual cortex
then splits into two major processing streams—the
Ventral stream, the "what" pathway, and the Dorsal
stream, the "where" pathway. The Dorsal stream
navigates the environment coarsely and is colorblind.
If you showed a red spot on a green background to your
Dorsal system, it would see it as a gray spot on a gray
background and you can imagine changing the relative
brightness of the red spot in such a way that it would be
invisible to your "where" system. That's called equal
luminance. At equal luminance depth and motion go
away. If your ability to see depth from shading is carried
by a colorblind part of your visual system then it doesn't
matter what color the shadows are as long as the
luminance is right in order to give you a sense of
three-dimensionality.

**In your book you talk about how science underlies
different illusions used by artists to create a feeling of
depth and movement. What other cues are you taking
from artists?**

I am interested now in film editing. I think it tells us a lot
about how the world remains stable despite our moving
our eyes constantly.

What current research are you working on?

We study the normal development and functional
organizational principles of inferotemporal cortex by
performing functional magnetic resonance imaging
(fMRI) on alert infant monkeys over their first two years.
We have developed non-invasive techniques for scanning
that are not harmful to the monkeys. We monitor the
earliest functional organization in the inferotemporal
cortex, the emergent properties of the system, and how
category selectivity emerges during development. In
humans and other primates the ability to see, to process
visual information, is not mature at birth. The normal
maturation of primary sensory cortical areas requires
early experience and can be dramatically disrupted
by abnormal early experience. For example, visual
acuity in humans increases 50 fold over the first three
to five years of life, but misalignment of the two eyes
can result in permanent poor visual acuity in one eye.
It is unknown what aspects of this organization are innate
and what aspects emerge as a consequence of visual
experience, and we do not know what the significance
is of having specialized domains for processing certain
object categories.

COLOR MIXING: THREE APPROACHES: RGB, RYB, CMYK

What would color be without mixing? If colors could not be mixed, our entire palette would consist only of the primary colors. This would limit our creative expression and it would make it difficult to differentiate between products, environments, signage, and so on. An extensive color palette is therefore not only important to personal expression, but it is a critical element in our reasoning powers and experience.

There are several ways in which color can be mixed. When mixing colored light, we use the additive process, which involves mixing two or more light sources together. Conversely, the subtractive process involves the subtraction or absorption of light by mixing pigments or dyes and applying them to objects. Both processes use all the colors of the visible spectrum.

The additive mixing process is based on the three light primaries, red, green, and blue, and colored light is the mixing material. Colored wavelengths directly from the source mix together in the eye to create color: the process that occurs is called emission and there is no refracted object involved.

When two additive colors are mixed together they become lighter, so the additive secondary colors (yellow, magenta, and cyan) are brighter and lighter than the primaries. When all wavelengths of light are mixed together, the light becomes white. Additive color mixing takes place with all virtual technologies, such as computer monitors, cell phone screens, and televisions. If you look through a magnifying glass at a computer screen, you will see light primaries placed adjacently to create color. It is also used in stage lighting, which employs both additive (stage lights of varying colors) and subtractive processes.

Subtractive color is based on absorption, rather than emission. It is object dependent and revolves around the principle of subtracting rather than adding color. It requires that colored materials absorb all light except for the color of the object itself, which bounces off into the eye. It involves the use of a mixture of surface pigments and dyes that are applied to the object or that are intrinsic in its material. Rather than having multiple light sources, color is perceived by the retina under a single light source, with secondary colors darker than the primaries.

The subtractive system has several color models. The RYB model, which will be familiar to painters, uses three primary colors—red, yellow, and blue—with secondary colors of orange, violet, and green. When mixed together they form a deep neutral gray.

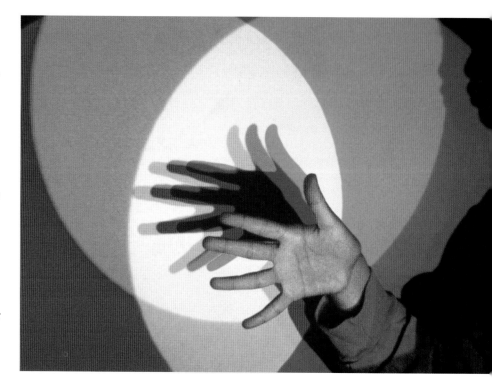

ADDITIVE AND SUBTRACTIVE COLOR SYNTHESIS

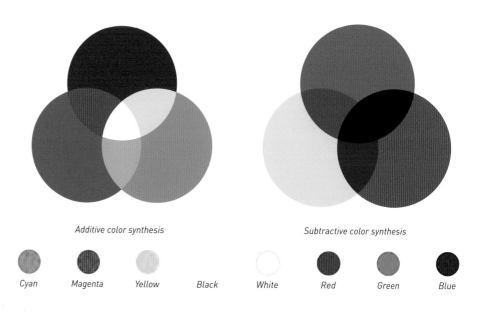

Additive color synthesis　　　　*Subtractive color synthesis*

Cyan　　Magenta　　Yellow　　Black　　White　　Red　　Green　　Blue

SEURAT AND ADDITIVE COLOR MIXING

Some artists have employed the additive system in their work because they believe it adds clarity of color to their work. Seurat, for example, employed the principle of additive mixing by using a series of dots placed next to each other. When viewers look at one of these images from a distance, the dots merge into colored areas. The proximity and size of the colored dots allow the eye to fuse the color: a yellow dot next to a blue dot becomes green, red next to blue becomes violet, and so on. Yet when you stand within close proximity of the painting, it simply becomes a series of juxtaposed dots.

Right: **Georges Seurat's** *Seascape at Port-en-Bessin*, Normandy, 1888. Seurat was so intrigued by the concept of light and color, he believed that the intensity and the clarity of color would be brighter if he imitated the additive process. If his paintings are viewed up close the dots are readily identifiable. If you stand back, however, the color is fused in the eye and a cohesive image is seen.

A second subtractive model is CMYK, which is also referred to as "process color" or "four color" and is widely used in the printing industry. The primary colors in this model are cyan, magenta, and yellow, with secondary colors of red, blue, and green. The fourth color is "key" (black), which is included to enhance the printed color: on their own, the CMY primaries cannot create a rich black.

One can understand the difference between additive and subtractive mixing by experimenting with flashlights and filters. Take three small flashlights, one filtered red, one filtered green, and the third filtered blue, and aim them at the same spot on a wall in a dimly lit room. The resulting patch of light will be white, as all the colors of the visible spectrum are being added. However, if you place all three filters in front of a single flashlight the color of the light patch will become dark gray because the color is absorbed.

Color becomes more complicated when you have to convert from additive to subtractive colors. This is most obvious when it comes to looking at computer systems, where an image seen on-screen uses the additive process, while a printer uses the subtractive process. This has necessitated color standardization and reference systems, so that color consistency is controlled from one device to another.[1]

COLOR VARIABLES: HUE, VALUE, AND INTENSITY Color is an extraordinarily volatile element. While it can be affected by many variables, including light, surface quality, placement, neighboring colors, and design elements, each color has its own personal attributes, which are intrinsic to its nature. Defining these attributes can be confusing, as they are referred to by different names, but there are three key attributes: hue, value (or luminance), and intensity (also referred to as saturation or chroma).

Hue can be described as the property of light that we define verbally or numerically when we see an object ("red," for example). When Isaac Newton refracted light through a prism, the spectral hues of the rainbow appeared including red, orange, yellow, cyan, blue, green, and violet. Even though not always easily perceivable (especially with colors in close proximity), every hue has a position on the visible spectrum. They are represented by a single wavelength, given in nanometers, which is equal to one billionth of a meter. Colors that are not spectral in nature are colors that are mixed with black, white, or any other color. These colors cannot be seen as part of the visual spectrum, but they can be seen as part of a spectral family of its dominant color. For example, a blue-gray can be seen as part of the blue spectral color that shares its dominance.

While his composition paintings originated as trees in the landscapes, Mondrian sought to investigate purity and balance through the use of structural black lines and primary color. A leader within the De Stijl movement, his use of flat colored areas reinforces the creation of balance, strength, and harmony that was the essence of his work.[2]

Another important color attribute is value. Value is the light-to-dark relationship within a color. It is also described as luminance, which refers to the amount of light emitted from a specific area of an object. In the additive process, value is described as the relative brightness of a color. Brightness is the perception that is elicited from the object.

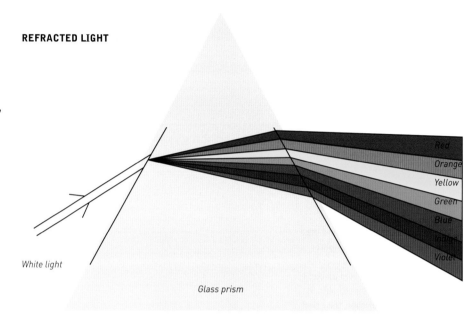

REFRACTED LIGHT

White light

Glass prism

Red
Orange
Yellow
Green
Blue
Indigo
Violet

The third principle attribute, intensity (or saturation/chroma) refers to the maximum purity of spectral color. It can be described as the greatest possible concentration of pigment or dye. When talking about light it is defined as the spectral reflectance, within a defined area.

Theoretically, when dealing with color, maximum saturation occurs when pure pigments exist alone without any binder or medium present. However when we refer to colors mixed with binders (oil paints, for example), they are at their highest intensity when they have not been mixed with black or white or any other colors. Once they are mixed together intensity decreases.[3] Every color has its own intrinsic value at its highest intensity (saturation). Saturated color is a great way to compare color value: some colors, such as yellow and orange, have a much lighter value at their highest saturation point, while other colors have a darker value (such as blues and purples).

If you create color value scales for several colors you will see that the saturation point of each of those colors sits at a different position on the scale. Once that is determined you can add black or white to make them the same value. One way of doing this is to keep one color constant and alter the other color in either direction, or you can shift both of the colors in opposite directions.

Changing the value in a design is a great way to maintain harmony while creating interest and variety. Many interior designers use several values of the same hue to create a feeling of comfort and stability. Changes in textures and materials can be used along with accent colors, preventing a monochromatic (single color) color scheme from being dull. In addition, the same color can be used at its highest saturation to create contrast and interest. Whether it's Buddhist monks creating a mandala, or Mexican women weaving lively tablecloths, rich, saturated color creates a visual feast of excitement for the eye, although the concentration of color that causes us to look at a painting or design may repel us in an interior.

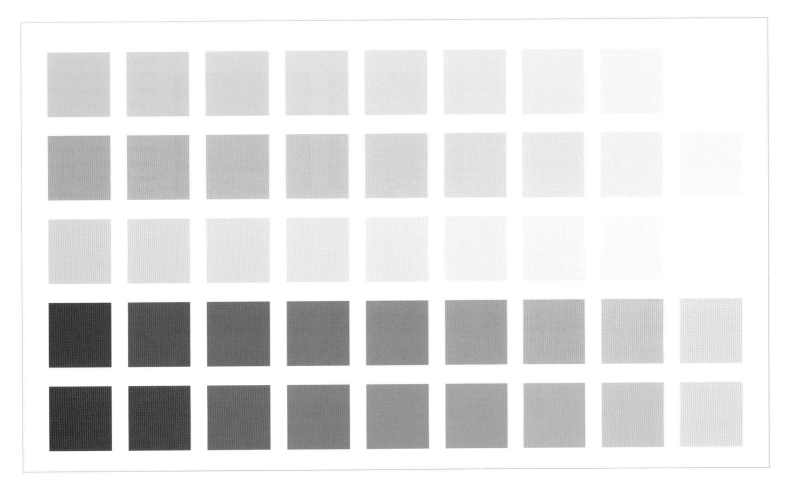

COLOR INTERACTION AND RELATIVITY: SIMULTANEOUS AND SUCCESSIVE CONTRAST

When we begin to study color effects we realize the unstable nature of color's very existence. We understand that each and every color has personal attributes and that these colors appear differently depending on light sources, surface materials, and even the altered experiential perceptions on the part of an individual. What we have yet to consider is the very illusory relationships that colors have with each other. We can see that optical illusions use color and design to "trick the eye" into seeing what is not necessarily there. The work of Victor Vasarely is a great example of color-enhanced illusion. Considered the grandfather of the Op art movement, his pure geometric abstract patterns combined with color, create illusory space and movement.

Color illusion is enhanced because of the theoretical laws of simultaneous and successive contrast, which state that both neighboring color and color, when looked at in a sequence, can be altered. Let us begin by exploring simultaneous contrast. If you stare at a group of identical shapes that are the same purple color and arranged in a pattern on a page, then you look at a blank gray page of the same dimensions, you will not only "see" the shapes of the purple forms, but you will see them in yellow. This illusion is based on the concept that each and every hue has a complement and this complement surrounds the color that you are looking at.

If you choose two colors—a red and a blue for example—and place each of them in a room by itself, with a neutral gray surround, the color will be constant. However, if you place them next to each other, the blue square would appear greener and the red square will seem more orange. This is because, when viewed simultaneously, our eyes see orange on the red and

Left top row: **When two colors are placed next to each other or viewed together they take on the complementary color of the neighboring color. So a red viewed by itself on a gray ground will be seen in its greatest state of purity. If viewed next to a blue, the blue would look greener and the red would appear more orange.**

Left center and bottom rows: Color shifts not only with hue, but also with value and intensity. When you place two colors with the same value together you are shifting only the intensity and hue. If you put two colors together with the same hue, the value shifts and the light color becomes lighter while the dark color becomes darker. If you place an intense color next to a mixed subdued color, the intense color will become more intense and the grayed color will become more subdued. If you place two colors with the same intensity next to each other only the values and hues shift. This is the volatile nature of color that Albers experimented with in his *Homage to the Square* series.

COLOR EFFECTS: HUE, INTENSITY, VALUE

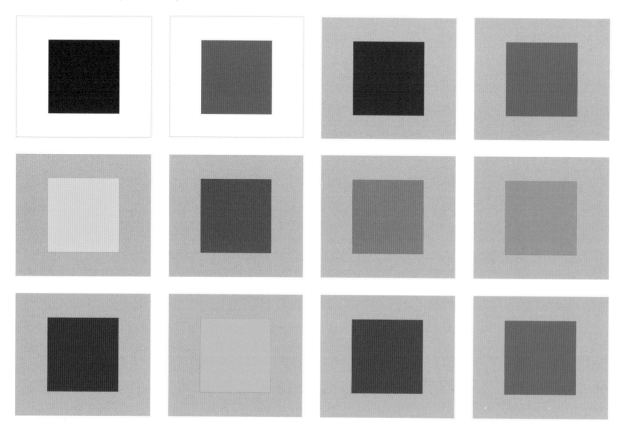

JOSEPH ALBERS

Joseph Albers, a color theoretician, artist, and educator, spent his life studying these relationships. In his book, *Interaction of Color*, he instructed his students to perform relational studies, changing the appearance of smaller colored squares by placing them on larger colored squares.[4] Indeed, the body of Albers' artistic work focuses around a series of paintings named *Homage to the Square*, in which he painted various solid colors within a series of three or four larger squares.

A student of Albers at Yale, Lois Swirnoff also studied color relationships, but in a three-dimensional context. In her book, *Dimensional Color*, Swirnoff expands on Albers' theory by studying the interaction between light, color, and surface in three dimensions, and instructs students to build constructions in which they utilize relational color to create an illusion of altered spatial sensibility.[5]

green on the blue (the complementary of the opposing color). However, when you look at adjacent complementary colors, the effect enhances each color, rather than shifting the hues. So, if you place yellow and purple complements next to each other, the yellow will intensify the purple (by adding the surround color purple), and the purple will enhance the yellow (by adding the surround color yellow).

To make matters more complicated we usually view more than two colors at the same time. In this scenario all of the colors will affect each other to a certain extent. The idea of successive contrast is similar to simultaneous contrast, the only difference being that if you look at a color or a group of colors and then go across the room you carry that complement or group of complements with you. This pattern of relativity can also be experienced relationally with other attributes including hue, intensity, and value. Let's consider a

value shift. If you place two swatches next to each other of the same hue (say, orange), but with different values, the darker color will appear darker and the lighter will appear lighter.

If you placed a dark violet swatch next to a light green swatch they would also appear farther apart in value: the purple would appear darker and the green would appear lighter. At the same time, the hue and intensity will also shift. Yet, if you place a dark violet next to a dark green of the same value, the value will remain constant, so one will not appear lighter or darker than the other—only the hue and intensity would shift. Therefore, the violet would appear redder and the green would appear yellower, but they would have the same value. In this way, you can selectively choose which elements to change, although all three attributes usually come into play when colors are placed next to each other.

Above left & right: *Homage to the Square* by Josef Albers.

COLOR BALANCE Most of the time, we use color with an emotive directive. In interior design we are often looking for color that will create a comfortable, liveable space, while in graphic design we might seek out discordant color to make a statement that will attract attention or motivate an individual. Harmonic and dissonant color combinations are easier to understand in terms of something most of us have experienced—music.

As music has an emotional impact that could be compared to color, musicians have felt a strong affinity to it. The Russian composer, Alexander Scriabin, saw color when playing different notes. As a result he created a "color music" scale based on fifths, in which he associated a color with each note: "C was red, G rosy orange, D yellow, A green, E pearly blue, B the shimmer of moonshine, F# bright blue, D flat violet, A flat purple, E and B flat steely with the glint of metal, and F dark red."[6] In addition, he often conversed with other musicians concerning the nature of color in conjunction with the mood of various pieces. They were often in agreement as to the palette.

Many artists have also felt such an affinity to music. Wassily Kandinsky felt that painting should grow out of "internal necessity," rather than subordinate itself to the material world. He developed a relationship with an atonal musician, Arnold

Schoenberg. After attending one of Schoenberg's concerts in 1911, Kandinsky created *Impression III*, using black to represent the strength of the piano and color as an expression of Schoenberg's dissonant sound.

Yet while there is often dissonance in both music and art, we can also seek harmony. When you think of harmonic music you think of beautiful chords played in unison, utilized to create a melodic sound. Harmonic color palettes can be seen as a beautiful chord that is seen, rather than heard. Harmonic palettes can be based on colors with the same value, or they can be "intensity harmonic" if the intensities of the colors are the same. These harmonies can be used to unify paintings and designs that use a plethora of color.[7]

Opposite: In *Ancient Harmony*, 1925, Paul Klee used "polyphonic" layers of rectangular form and complementary color to enhance patterns, rhythm, and movement, establishing a sense of harmonic visual music.

Right: **Kandinsky's** *Impression III* tries to infuse color and sound together. With reference to Schoenberg's atonal piece, it is an expression of dissonant sound using dissonant design elements and intense color. Kandinsky uses discordant color proportions to reflect Schoenberg's atonal musical influence. For example, the harmonic proportion between yellow and purple is 3/4 purple to 1/4 yellow, whereas in *Impression III* it is approximately 1/4 purple to 3/4 yellow.

COLOR BALANCE

In his book, *Elements of Color*, Johannes Itten, a well-known color theorist, painter, and educator, talks about color harmony and the concept of mathematically derived balanced harmonies. Using the RYB, 12-hue color wheel, he creates different color harmonic intervals. The circle itself consists of three primary colors (red, yellow, and blue); three secondary colors (orange, purple, and green); and six tertiary colors (yellow-orange, red-orange, red-violet, blue-violet, blue-green, and yellow-green). Together, they form a complete wheel because they represent all the colors of the visible spectrum and form a deep neutral gray when mixed together.

From these 12 colors, Itten describes the theoretical harmonies in terms of dyadic, triadic, tetradic intervals, and so on. The dyadic interval forms a pair of complementary colors that are diametrically opposite on the color wheel. The triadic harmony is based on three opposing color points forming an equilateral or isosceles triangle, the most well known being that of the three primary colors, red, yellow, and blue. The tetradic harmony is based on a rectangle or square—an example would be blue-green, red-orange, yellow, and violet.

COLOR WHEEL: COMPLEMENTARY COLORS

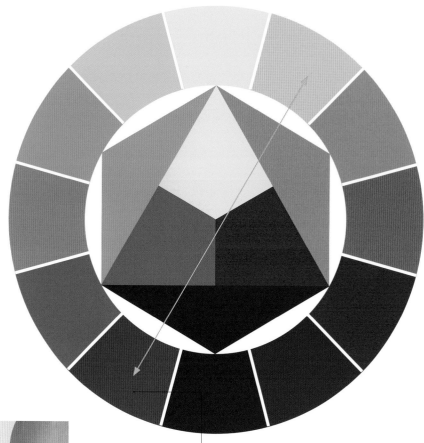

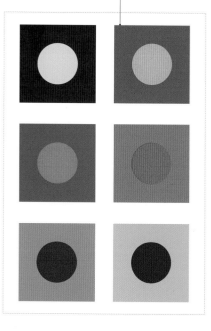

Above & left: **Complements are placed in opposition on the color wheel. When mixed together, they encompass all the colors of the visible spectrum making neutral gray.**

Far left: **This living area is created using a complementary color scheme involving orange and blue. It is harmonious not only because of the color scheme, but also because the proportionate amount of color is carefully chosen. The orange has been carefully chosen as an intense accent color.**

While Itten's simplistic approach uses a closed color system, he sets a standard of theory-based color combinations that are derived mathematically. With the advent of highly complex computer-generated color systems we realize that there are infinite harmonic possibilities. The use of the entire wheel is called "full spectrum color," and because it includes all the colors of the visible spectrum, it puts our eyes and brain in a state of equilibrium. While we can shift these harmonies to create intentional discord, it is the goal of all of these color combinations to create harmony.[8]

Theoretical color combinations control harmony and enhance balance and good design: there is greater ambiguity when speaking colloquially about color schemes, rather than in reference to a theoretical model. These harmonic combinations come in a variety of formulations, and designers define them in the following ways.

The simplest scheme involves two opposing colors, which is a theoretical harmony commonly known as "complementary colors." A split-complementary includes one color and the neighbors of the opposing complement (so three colors in total). A double split–complementary occurs when the neighbors of each complement are used (four colors).

Right: The split-complementary color scheme is readily used in interior design. It involves the use of a pair of complementary colors, however, instead of using the direct opposite color on the color wheel, colors on either side of the complement are chosen. For example, as shown here, instead of yellow and violet, violet has been substituted with purple and deep blue.

Below: Split-complementary colors come in sets of three: one hue combined with the hues on either side of its complementary color.

COLOR WHEEL: SPLIT-COMPLEMENTARY COLORS

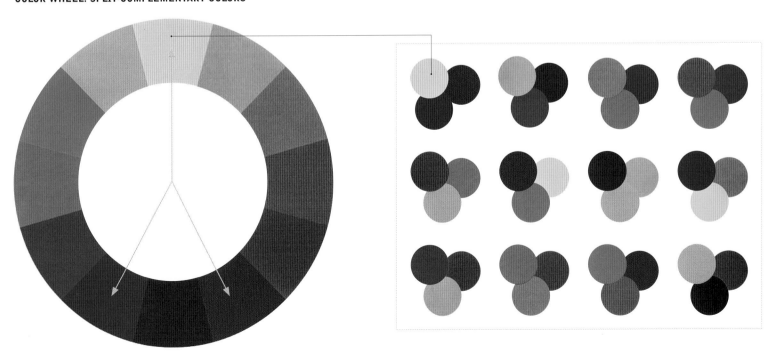

COLOR BALANCE

The alternative to a complementary color scheme is an analogous color scheme that centers around one dominant color and its neighbors. However, the color scheme always appears more balanced if a complementary accent is also used.

Right: **The tetradic color scheme is formulated around a rectangle and involves the use of two pairs of complementary colors.**

Below: **Triadic color schemes involve the use of three colors that form an equilateral triangle on the wheel. The most prominent triadic scheme is the primary scheme of red, yellow, and blue as illustrated in the interiors shot.**

COLOR WHEEL: TETRADIC

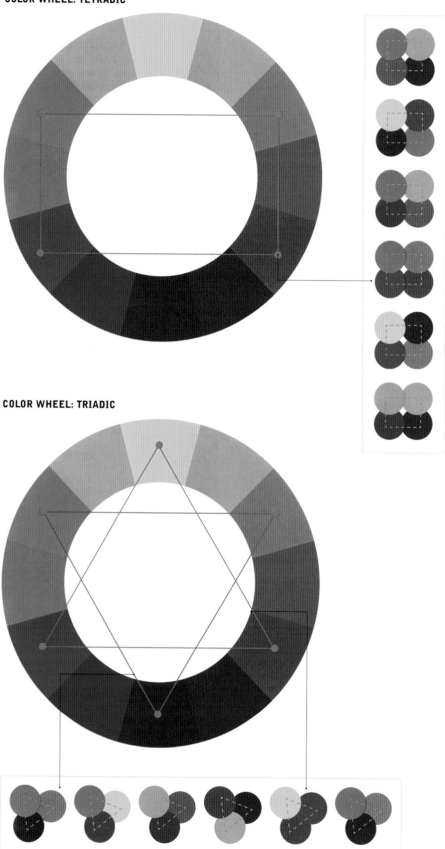

COLOR WHEEL: TRIADIC

Right: An analogous color scheme uses colors that are next to one another on the color wheel. The combination of colors usually match well and create serene and comfortable designs. Analogous color schemes are often found in nature and are harmonious and pleasing to the eye. Here, cushions in an analogous color scheme have been used to punctuate an otherwise white interior.

Below right: Monochromatic color schemes use the shades, tints and tones of one specific color hue. They can be less challenging due to their lack of contrast, however, they are also peaceful and harmonious to the eye. This bathroom works well in a monochrome scheme and is certainly somewhere serene to unwind after a long day.

COLOR WHEEL: ANALOGOUS

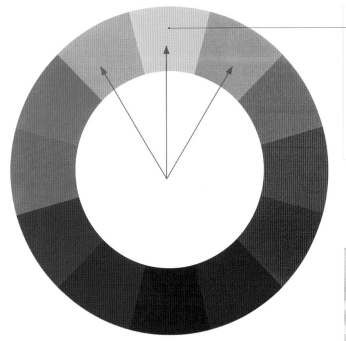

COLOR WHEEL: MONOCHROMATIC

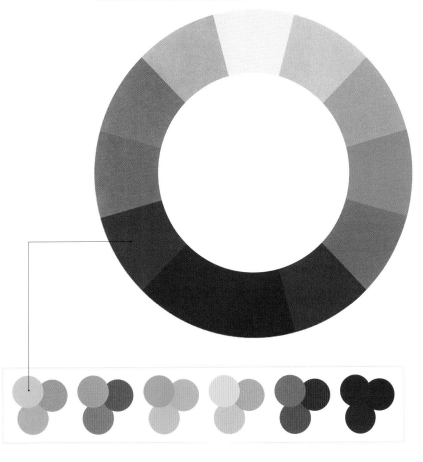

COLOR ALTERATION: PROPORTION, EXTENSION AND WEIGHT; WARM AND COOL,
PLACEMENT At this point, we have a theoretical understanding of how colors can be grouped to create both harmonic and discordant color schemes. We have also seen how colors interact with each other, and we have learned that we can utilize that interaction to enhance their relationships. There are, however, other factors that enhance the design or artistic statement of color in both two- and three-dimensional space. Specifically, this involves the alteration of colors with contrast effects of color proportion, color placement, and color weight.

Have you ever been in a paint store and decided on the absolute perfect color for your living room or dining room, had the store mix it up, and then take the paint home, applied it to a wall, and felt color dismay? This can be attributed to a color relationship called "contrast of extent," which is based on the idea that color needs to work within certain proportional relationships in order to be harmonious. Color gains strength and power when it is increased in extent, so it follows that a color may sometimes appear more harmonious in a small quantity, rather than a larger one: a small amount of a strong color may be pleasing to the eye, but when it occupies a large space it may lose its pleasing quality and its harmony.

Goethe presents some quantitative proportions between colors that enhance its harmonic plausibility. He took pure colors of medium brilliance, placed them on a neutral background, and estimated simple numerical ratios. While this is based on their subjective appearance, rather than objective measurements, it remains useful to explore his proportions. In his *Elements of Color*, Itten discusses Goethe's numerical light relationships, and talks about the strength of each color with respect to its complement, commenting on the complementary pair yellow and violet. If yellow light was three times brighter than violet light, then the relationship would be 3 to 1. Therefore the use of ¼ yellow to ¾ violet would create harmonic balance. Itten went on to describe the relationships between the other complementary pairs: orange is twice as bright as blue (quantitatively, the proportional balance would therefore be ⅓ orange to ⅔ blue), and red and green are equally bright proportionately (the proportional balance would be ½ red to ½ green).[9]

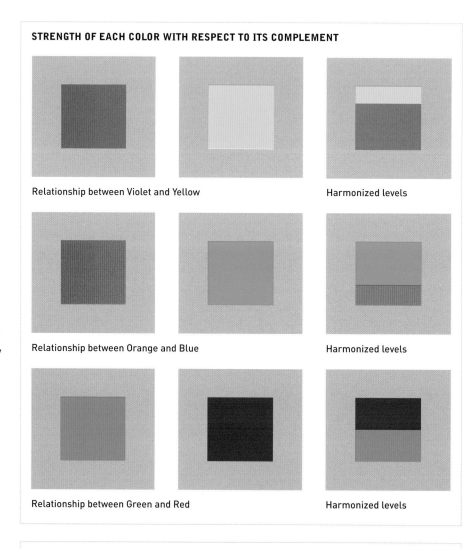

STRENGTH OF EACH COLOR WITH RESPECT TO ITS COMPLEMENT

Relationship between Violet and Yellow

Harmonized levels

Relationship between Orange and Blue

Harmonized levels

Relationship between Green and Red

Harmonized levels

APPEARANCE OF BLACK

Right: Franke Mahnke creates a series of diagrams that show the differing appearances of black when it is placed in different positions in an identical space.

Top view

Center view

Bottom view

Another factor in creating harmonic balance is color placement. In his book, *Color, Environment, and Human Response,* Franke Mahnke creates a series of diagrams that show the differing appearances of black when it is placed in different positions in an identical space. He goes on to talk about how chromatic colors appear when placed in different positions, suggesting which colors might be appropriate for which areas in dimensional space. His description of orange/blue is a clear example of his philosophy: if you use orange on the ceiling it is "stimulating, attention- seeking"; if you use orange on the walls it is "warm, luminous"; if you use it on the floor it is "activating, motion-oriented." If blue is placed on the ceiling it is "celestial, cool, less tangibly advancing (if light), heavy and oppressive (if dark)." If placed on the walls it is "cool and distant (if light)" and "encouraging and space deepening (if dark)." If placed on the floor, "inspiring a feeling of effortless movement (if light), substantial (if dark)."[10] In ascribing locations for colors, Mahnke not only talks about their theoretical strengths and placement, but also of the emotive qualities of colors that impede their positioning. In this way he presents a very important premise of color relationships: that theoretical contrast cannot be singularly felt, but rather must also include of a mix of personal and environmental constraints.

HOW CHROMATIC COLORS APPEAR WHEN PLACED IN DIFFERENT POSITIONS

Orange Ceiling
Stimulating, attention-seeking

Light Blue Ceiling
Celestial, cool, less advancing

Dark Blue Ceiling
Heavy and oppressive

Orange Walls
Warm and luminous

Light Blue Walls
Cool and distant

Dark Blue Walls
Encouraging and deepening

Orange Floor
Activating and motion oriented

Light Blue Floor
Effortless movement

Dark Blue Floor
Substantial

Above & left: **Some colors affect space in different ways. Certain colors placed on the same area in a room can make the space appear very different. The illustrations and lifestyle interior shots shown here support Frank Mahnke's thoughts on how chromatic colors appear when placed in different positions in an identical space.**

Opposite top: **According to Goethe, each pair of complementary colors has a point at which they are in quantitative or proportionate balance. With yellow and violet it is ³/₄ violet to ¹/₄ yellow; with orange and blue it is ²/₃ blue to ¹/₃ orange; and with red and green it is ¹/₂ and ¹/₂. In addition to proportion, placement of color is important.**

Weight can be shifted not only by quantitative color, but also by color choice. We have an intuitive understanding that oranges and reds are more active than blues and greens. Visually, reds and oranges come forward while blues and greens recede. However, spatial color is relative to surrounding color, even with respect to colors in its own family—for example, a yellow-green appears closer than a blue-green.

In his paintings, Hans Hofmann altered spatial relationships by placing areas of flat color on top of or next to each other, changing the scale, hue, and transparency. In his *Memoria in Aeternum* (oils, 1962) he places two rectangles on a low-intensity, multicolored background—a red one at the bottom right of the canvas and a yellow one slightly higher at the left. While yellow would normally come forward, it appears—due to scale and placement—to recede from the red. This kind of color positioning and scale works hand-in-hand with warm/cool contrast to reinforce a contemporary theme of spatial ambiguity in his paintings.

ACTIVE COLOR AND SPATIAL COLOR

Due to our natural sense of perspective, heavier intense colors work better on the bottom, whereas mixed colors that are lighter and less intense feel better on top. Warmer colors tend to come forward while cooler colors tend to recede.

Active colors

Yellows, reds, and oranges come forward

Spatial Colors

Yellow-green comes forward whereas blue-green recedes

Violets, blues, and greens recede

THE STRENGTH, INTENSITY AND WEIGHT OF BLACK ON RICH RED

Illustrating the power of Rothko's painting, *No. 36 (Black Stripe)*. The rich red comes forward and the black stripe recedes until it appears to be a hole in the canvas, creating a feeling of definitive space.

Mark Rothko is another contemporary painter that used color placement to create spatial ambiguity in his paintings. In *Orange and Yellow* (oils, 1956), for example, Rothko softens the edges of his color planes. This lack of hard edges, combined with the positioning of the colors, alters the laws of depth and perspective. While the red-orange is cooler than the yellow, it covers more space quantitatively and adds weight to the bottom of the piece. In his painting *No. 36 (Black Stripe)*, Rothko places a huge black stripe across the center of the canvas. The strength, intensity, and weight of the rich red black moves forward creating a focal point for the viewer and recedes in that it resembles a black whole on the surface of the canvas. Rothko's desire to have the viewer experience purity of color without definitive form is enhanced by his skill in color placement and weight.[11]

Opposite top: **Painters often try to visually confuse us by breaking color principles intentionally. Hans Hofmann, in his painting** *Memoria in Aeternum*, **creates shapes that are defined by color intensity and shape. This makes them appear to float on the low-intensity background.**

Above: *Orange and Yellow*, 1956, by Mark Rothko. The palette here is analogous rather than monochromatic and edges are softly defined so that they blend into the background. In turn, space is perceived ambiguously allowing for greater focus on the color and mood, rather than on the contrast.

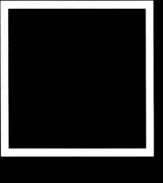

CHAPTER FOUR

COLOR ORGANIZATION

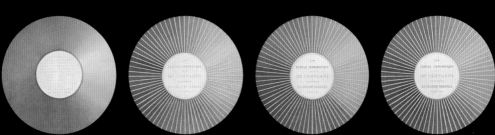

EXPERT: **MARK FAIRCHILD**
Associate Dean of Research & Graduate Education, College of Science, Professor & Director,
Program of Color Science/Munsell Color Science Laboratory, Rochester Institute of Technology, USA

Could you tell us about yourself and describe your role at the RIT Munsell Color Science Laboratory?

I am a professor in the Program of Color Science and Director of the program and the Munsell Color Science Laboratory, as well as being the Associate Dean of Research and Graduate Education for the College of Science at RIT. I am responsible for managing the graduate program in color science and the research and outreach activities of the Munsell Color Science Laboratory. My career began with an undergraduate education in photographic science from RIT. I received both BS and MS degrees in that area many, many years ago. I joined the Munsell Color Science Laboratory at that time, when it was first founded at RIT (in 1983) and started as an instructor in the lab while completing a Ph.D. in vision science from the University of Rochester. My education in photographic science helped me understand the physics and chemistry of color and I completed the picture by learning about the anatomy, physiology, and psychology of color during my Ph.D. I have now been on the faculty of RIT for nearly 30 years.

Could you define color science and talk about the nature of color science education?

I define color science as all the science related to light, materials, and the perception of color. This involves the physics of light sources and illumination, the physics and chemistry of illuminated materials and objects, and the anatomy, physiology, and psychology of human color perception. Color is a perception; light or objects by themselves have no color. Color is created when illuminated stimuli are perceived by an observer, and ultimately described in some way. In our Color Science Program we discuss how light is created and measured, how materials are constructed and their colorants formulated, mixed, and measured, and the function of the human visual system. We do experiments called psychophysics to relate the physical measurements we can make of light and materials to the colors we perceive.

Could you describe the types of research that occur in the laboratory?

At the moment we have two main focus areas for research in the laboratory. One is improving imaging systems through detection and/or production of more than three primary signals. A normal camera senses red, green, and blue signals. Cameras being worked on in the lab might sense six or nine different parts of the spectrum instead of just three. These systems let us better understand objects, such as artwork from a museum and then reproduce it more accurately. The second area is aimed at understanding the differences in color vision between observers. Even observers with what we'd call "normal color vision" vary significantly in their color response. We are trying to understand these differences and build mathematical models to allow the prediction of differences in practical applications such as digital cinema.

Could you talk about how color science and research impacts the way designers utilize color?

This is a little more difficult for me since I am not a designer, but color science is used to create orderly arrangements of color, such as the Munsell Book of Color, that can help designers select useful and pleasing color combinations for design elements. We also work on advancing systems that designers use. For example, a designer using a modern computer display and software is benefiting from color science research that improved the backlight color and efficiency, improved the display primaries and uniformity, defined the color management systems that relate the color values in the software to the displayed color, and taking advantage of sophisticated algorithms that model human color perception when the desired color is reproduced in a new medium.

THEORETICAL COLOR SYSTEMS: SCIENCE, ART, AND SYSTEM EVOLUTION

Anyone who has ever worked with or used color in any way will understand that there is an abundance of color choices. As society has evolved, our capabilities to create a wide range of colors have increased exponentially. While there was a time when we could use words to describe colors, we now tend to rely on numerical notation instead.

Throughout history, people have been fascinated with the idea of color and how we see and interpret it. Ideas about color have come from various areas—from philosophy, art, and science. Many individuals in these fields have felt a need for explanation and organization, and have taken their color exploration, research, and the applied knowledge of their predecessors to create interpretive color systems, each with their own personal directives. The jostling of systems back and forth through the ages has meant that the formal parts of a color system —the number of primaries, their attributes, and the actual shapes and dimensions of various color "models"— have continually been reworked and modified over the years. This has led not only to color organizational "standards" that we use in everyday life, but also to a scientific, artistic, and perceptual understanding of color.

While creativity abounds, there are different thoughts about the theories offered, as the ideas of artistic, philosophical, perceptual, and scientific originators each have different objectives. Artists and philosophers have focused on a more personal approach to color, focusing on the mood and meaning of color, in addition to its properties and attributes.

Several prominent artist-philosophers involved in color system development are Johann Wolfgang von Goethe, Philipp Otto Runge, and Faber Birren. As we have seen, Goethe dealt with color measurement in terms of the numerical proportions of extent, focusing more on the aesthetics of color than his scientifically-oriented color compatriots. He once claimed that "colors are also a product of the self, and we decorate our own personal world with them."[1]

Below left: Greco-Roman theory suggests that there are four personality types. Goethe's "rose of temperaments" (Temperamenten-Rose, left) colorized them, adding red/orange/yellow to choleric, an extroverted excitable type; yellow/green/cyan to sanguine, optimistic type; cyan/blue/violet to phlegmatic, a calm and balanced type; and violet/magenta/red to melancholic, an introverted type.

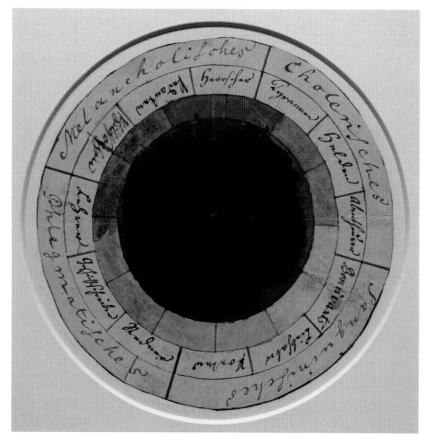

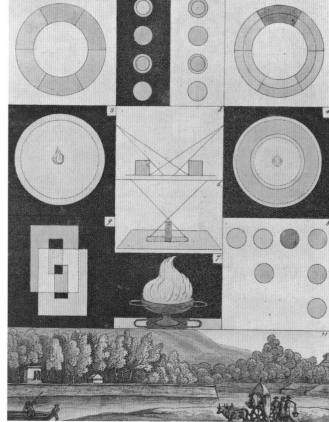

In Goethe book, *Theory of Colours*, he focused on the colors yellow and blue, attaching meaning to them in terms of their lightness and darkness. Of yellow, he said: "In its highest purity it always carries with it the nature of brightness, and has a serene, gay, softly exciting character." In opposition, he says that "blue gives us an impression of cold, and thus again reminds us of shade. Rooms with pure blue, appear in some degree larger, but at the same time empty and cold." Goethe went on to speak about harmonious color as "color in equilibrium,"[2] which he felt would produce a feeling of pleasantness.

Philipp Otto Runge's goal was to create a color sphere involving three basic colors—red, blue, and yellow. The purist colors surrounded the equator with white and black at the top and bottom. He believed an entire color plan could result from the mixture of these three basic colors and black and white. A contemporary colorist, Faber Birren, upheld sociological and artistic orientation toward color, developing a color system that emphasized warm colors over cold, so as to create greater intensity in a work of art.

WARM AND COLD COLOR SYSTEM

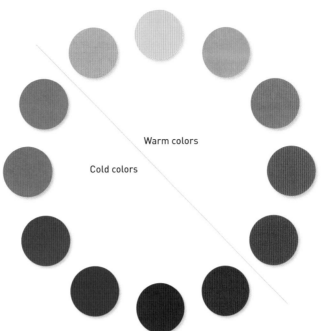

Warm colors

Cold colors

Left: The colorist, Faber Birren, developed a color system that emphasized warm colors over cold, so as to create greater intensity in a work of art.

Opposite right: Goethe's theory of color involves both the physical color, that of light and wavelengths, and the perception of color based on the individual. This image portrays different human perceptions of color and an image of yellow-blue color deficiency (Plate 1 from *Zur Farbenlehre / Theory of Colors*).

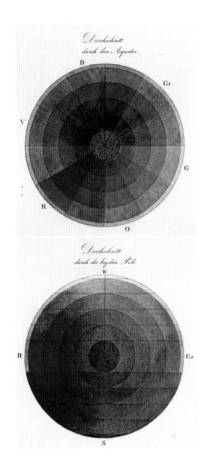

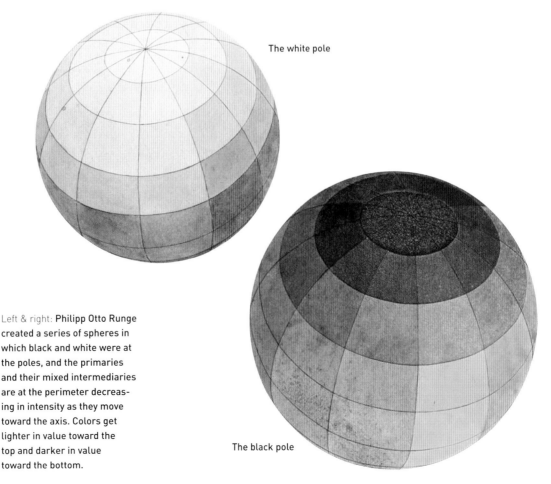

The white pole

The black pole

Left & right: **Philipp Otto Runge** created a series of spheres in which black and white were at the poles, and the primaries and their mixed intermediaries are at the perimeter decreasing in intensity as they move toward the axis. Colors get lighter in value toward the top and darker in value toward the bottom.

Color system theorists were also influenced by the perceptual psychological point of view. Michel Eugène Chevreul, a chemist who worked in carpet manufacturing, observed that the color effect was not the result of each color, but rather the result of the combined influences of its neighbors perceptually influencing each other (as we have noted in the theory of simultaneous contrast). His color circle focused on the relationships between complementary colors.

Despite his scientific leanings, the German physicist, Wilhelm von Bezold, was primarily interested in creating a color system for painters and colorists. He created a color model in the shape of a cone, which was based on human perception, with an emphasis on the blues and violets.[3] Ewald Hering, a German physiologist, was also interested in perception, believing that there were four color sensations that he deemed "psychological primaries": red, green, yellow, and blue. His work lead to the development of the "opponent process theory" of color vision.[4]

In the 1970s, Michel Albert-Vanel created the "planetary system," in which he tried to encompass all of the original color attributes and expand them to include active light/passive pigments, transparency/opaqueness, and matte/gloss. He followed in Hering's footsteps by suggesting that color sensations viewed perceptually cannot be treated in isolation.[5]

Finally, there is a group that seems to have a greater affinity with creating color systems that rely on math and science. Several examples are the work of Isaac Newton, John Maxwell, and Hermann von Helmholtz. As we have seen, Newton refracted white light to view the visible light spectrum. At the same time, he created a color circle based on a color's intensity and spectral hue, reflecting his feelings about the nature of light. A contemporary of Newton, James Maxwell created a triangle based on the three light primaries: red, green, and blue. He is known as being the individual initially responsible for quantitative color measurement, which is more commonly known as colorimetry. In his study of hue, saturation, and brightness, von Helmholtz determined that there was a difference in the ways that colors "appeared and behaved" in light versus pigment (additive versus subtractive).[6]

Opposite: **These are segments from Michel Eugène Chevreul's color sphere as described in his work, *The Law of Simultaneous Contrast*, written in 1839. It portrays a color oder system that is scientifically organized establishing a relationship between numbers and tones.**

Below left & right: **Ewald Hering believed that their were four psychological primaries that had no relationship to each other, basing them on perception rather than pigments. He created his system around red/green and yellow/blue components.**

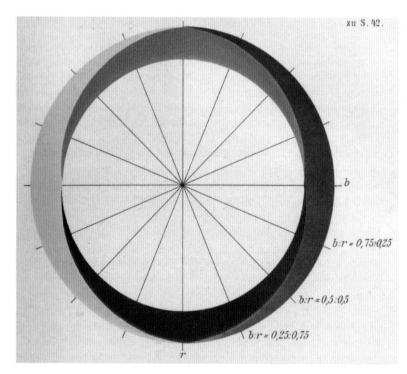

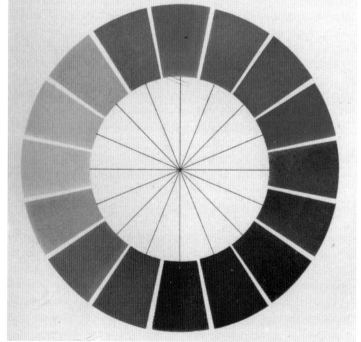

THE "GOLD STANDARD" COLOR SYSTEMS In this complex, interconnected world in which we live, with the development of global manufacturing, marketing, and trade, the overriding need for color standardization is apparent. With designers in New York, manufactures in the far east, and marketing people dispersed throughout, all working in multiple languages, there needs to be a way that everyone can achieve color commonality. Color standardization is part of the design process that can be universal. In the previous section, we looked at various ways of understanding and organizing color, which includes phenomenological, perceptual, and scientific approaches. We have explored what color is, how it is perceived, and how it might be organized. However, in order to utilize it with efficiency, dimensional, numerically based systems have evolved that designers, artists, and scientists all look toward for communication and color standardization. Consequently, there are many systems to choose from in today's world, depending upon need.

The reasoning behind any color system is to provide a way in which color can be seen, identified, and utilized within a relational context of its personal attributes. While additional characteristic attributes and relationships have come into play, many designers still rely on a core system utilizing hue, value, and intensity. One of the most widely used color models is the Munsell color system, created by artist, educator, and painter, Albert H. Munsell. It is pictured as a color tree containing 10 basic hue families: red, yellow, green, blue, and purple being the major, and then orange, yellow-green, blue-green, purple-blue, and red-purple. These colors comprise the Munsell hue circle that rotates around a light-to-dark axis representing value: colors fan out from the central gray scale to their highest intensity at the outer color circle.[7] Many standardized systems have been influenced by the development of the Munsell system, including the ISCC-NBS System of Color Designation developed by the Intersociety Color Council and the National Bureau of Standards. This system expanded on Munsell's to include 13 basic color categories and 16 intermediate categories, which were further subdivided into 267 named categories. In 1976 the organizations created a publication named The Color Universal Language and Dictionary of Names that became the definitive source of the system.

MUNSELL'S COLOR TREE

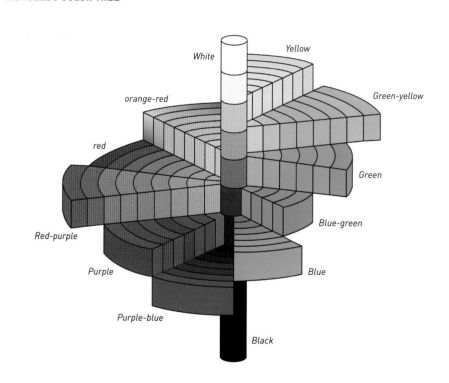

Above: **Munsell believed that there were better ways of describing color than verbal notation, so he used paint chips to create a numerical system of identification. Many interior designers work with color systems based on Munsell's pragmatic approach. Often referred to as Munsell's Color Tree, the central axis is white to black from top to bottom, and the colors move out from the axis increasing in intensity. There are five primary colors and five intermediary steps.**

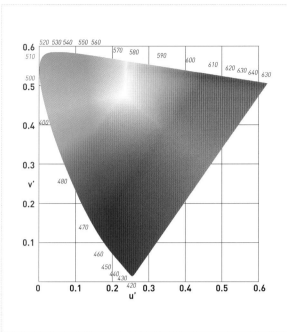

A system widely used in color specification is the Pantone system. The Pantone Reference system comes in different palettes dependent on design direction and in addition to color specification Pantone Inc. provides trend-forecasting information. Pantone has both a digital and material component, which helps demonstrate what a color looks like in the material it is intended to be used in, whether that is paper, plastic, or fabric. The Pantone system offers a wide variety of color palette options—for graphic design it comes in solid or process colors, neons, and metallics. For fashion and home it is offered in cotton, nylon, and paper. Pantone Inc. has also created specific palettes for companies such as Lowes and Sephora.[10]

Left: The CIELUV chromaticity diagram is a two-dimensional graph of the chromaticity coordinates of spectral color (380–770nm). The diagram represents a quantitative relationship between the physical wavelengths and visual perception, allowing the designer/artist to define color on the screen and in print.

Below: Pantone Plus Fandecks establishes consistency throughout the design and print process because all parties involved have a standardized reference palette.

Another system that is widely used today is the Natural Color System (NCS) created by the Scandinavian Color Institute. The NCS system is based on the idea that people can see and identify color without depending on color measurements or samples. Based on a series of color triangles, one for each hue, the system relies on four chromatic sensations (red, yellow, blue, and green) plus black and white. The hue is defined by how much blackness or "chromaticness" it has, in other words, how chromatically strong a color is. The system is commonly used in architecture, design, and fashion.[8]

With the advent of the computer, systems of numeric identification became commonplace. The Commission Internationale de L'Eclaire de France, an international authority on light, illumination, color, and color spaces, created a color specification and measurement system that would be intelligible to the "standard observer." The CIE system developed out of a need to organize color objectively and standardize it. The original system created in 1931 created a visual link between wavelengths in the visual spectrum with color perceived by the eye.[9]

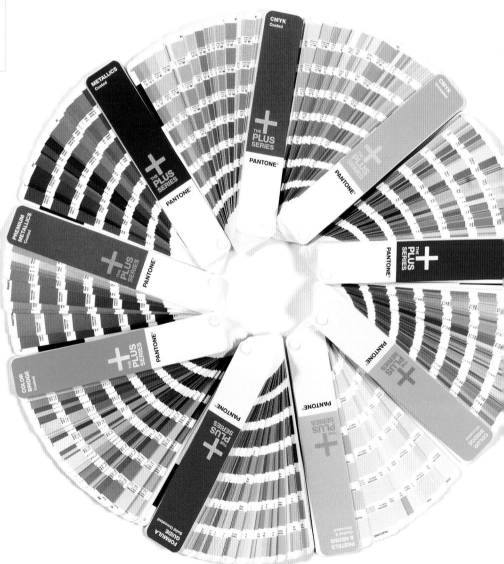

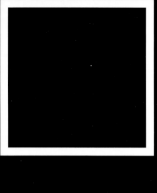

CHAPTER FIVE

PIGMENTS AND DYES: CHEMISTRY

EXPERT: DR FLORICA ZAHARIA

Conservator in charge, Department of Textile Conservation (DTC), The Metropolitan Museum of Art. The DTC is involved with the conservation, preservation, and research for the Museum's textile collection.

Could you tell the readers a little bit about your background?

Since 1988 I have been a textile conservator in the Department of Textile Conservation at The Metropolitan Museum of Art in New York City. My education includes an MA with specialization in tapestry and textile structure, and a PhD in Visual Arts with a focus on textile materials and technologies, and their impact on artifacts' aesthetic qualities. As few decades ago there were fewer formal training programs for conservators, my major hands-on training in conservation came from my work at the Museum.

What was involved in the conservation of the *Emperor's Carpet*?

The *Emperor's Carpet* is an outstanding example of the classical Persian carpet produced in the 16th century. It was purchased by The Metropolitan Museum of Art in 1943. The conservation of this piece was performed over a three-year period by a group of the DTC's conservators, and it was completed in 2010 for the reinstallation of the Museum's Islamic galleries, now called the Art of the Arab Lands, Turkey, Iran, Central Asia, and Later South Asia (ALTICALSA). For successful conservation, the understanding of the carpet's historical/cultural background, technical characteristics, as well as its condition was crucial. The curators study primarily an artifact's history, its design, and iconography. From the technical perspective conservators look at the artifact's manufacture including fibers, woven structure, and dyes. For dye identification, conservators work in collaboration with the Museum's scientists from the Department of Scientific Research. The *Emperor's Carpet* is made of a silk foundation and a fine wool pile, asymmetrically knotted. The carpet's weaving structure, especially selvages, needed an in-depth investigation, because of their poor state of preservation and their complicated weave. For this purpose, a loom was set up and the selvages' structure was recreated. The carpet's overall condition was good, although small damages were distributed throughout the whole piece. The carpet's ends were especially in very poor condition, probably a result of exposure to high foot traffic. We suspect the piece was folded and stored folded for many years because the marks of the folded areas are visible. Over 700 patches were applied during previous campaigns of restoration. Although these patches stabilized the fragile areas of the carpet, they also caused distortions. The patches were documented and removed. After regaining its original shape, the carpet needed stabilization to a back support. Wool fabric dyed in the appropriate color to match the carpet's original background colors of green, red, and yellow was used as support and as compensation for missing areas. Minimal stitches attached the fabric to the back of the carpet. Couching stitches were used for stabilization of fragile areas. Because the carpet will be displayed flat, we were able to minimize the number of stitches used for its consolidation.

When restoring a piece, do you have dye formulas that can match the old color or do you match it to the new color and expose it to light after that?

When supporting material is needed for a consolidation treatment, and for compensating for the missing areas, appropriate fabric is chosen and dyed to match the original. Natural dyes are never used for conservation purposes because they will fade very quickly. We use synthetic dyes, a variety of metal complex dye that will be stable for approximately 400 years in a museum environment.

PIGMENTS: ORGANIC AND INORGANIC, NATURAL AND SYNTHETIC

When it comes to the non-digital color world, using color involves choices between pigments and dyes. In order to work with them successfully it is important to understand the inherent physical qualities of these substances and the differences between them. When you see a colored material, you are not viewing the pure pigment or dye—what is seen is the pigment or dye and the material that it is bonded to or mixed with. This material, which is known as a binder, varies depending on the end product: if it is paint, it could be linseed oil, or if it's plastic, it could be an acrylic resin, for example.

The major distinction between a pigment and a dye is that pigments do not dissolve when mixed with binding materials, whereas dyes do. Whether it is chromatic, achromatic, or fluorescent, a pigment is particulate matter, which maintains its chemical integrity while suspended in a binder solution. On the other hand, dyes dissolve and lose their integrity when combined with the binder material. In other words, pigments retain their structure, while dyes do not.

While pigments maintain their integrity, other factors may still cause the color to differ between pigments of the same name. The hue and value may change if the binder material contains color of its own, for example, or if there are other pigments added. The intensity may also change depending on the quantity of binder that is added to the pigment: increasing the quantity of the binder, decreases the relative quantity of particulate matter, leading to a decrease in color intensity. This is sometimes the reason why lower-grade paints are not as effective or attractive as higher-grade paints—they may both be the same color, but the manner in which this color has been achieved may be very different.

Accurate color systems are therefore important, as they establish consistency between the buyer and the manufacturer. A number of paint companies promise that sample swatches are identical in composition to the paint, by using the same pigments and binders for both the samples and paint. The use of the exact same pigments is paramount, as even if two pigments have the same name, there may be differences in quality due to where they were resourced or manufactured.

Pigments come from a variety of sources, and can be categorized as either natural organic, natural inorganic, synthetic organic, or synthetic inorganic. The development of pigments can be traced through history from Paleolithic times. In these times, it has been determined that artists used pigments to tattoo themselves, tan hides, preserve food, and create decorative cave paintings.[1] The colors used were umbers, red and yellow ochers, charcoal black, lime white, and manganese oxides: these are considered natural inorganic pigments, as they come from the earth and carbon materials that result from fire. Because of terrain differences, some pigment variation existed and it is interesting to note that even in early times artists traveled distances to find pigments.

In the mid- to late-Minoan period (c. 2100–1100 BCE), artists applied water-based pigments directly to a fresh lime surface to create beautiful frescoes on the island of Crete. Using wet plaster allowed pigments of metal and mineral oxides to bind well. These fresco artists had to work within the time limitations of the drying plaster, which caused them to work quickly, with fluid lines, creating natural scenes with brightly colored patterns that are energetic and intuitive.

Below: Henna, a dyestuff that is used as a temporary skin and hair dye has been used since antiquity. The use of Henna as a decorative element is an integral part of the traditional Hindu wedding.

Right: **For millennia artists and craftsmen have used natural organic materials that surround them to add color to their clothes, their environment, and their artwork. They took materials and ground them into powder or boiled them into dyes. The famous Altamira cave paintings (dated between 14,000–20,000 years ago) are a fine example. The artists responsible for them used charcoal and ocher or haematite to create the images, and diluted these pigments to produce variations in intensity, creating an impression of chiaroscuro.**

Bottom right: **This Minoan fresco from c. 1500 BCE is known as the *Toreador Fresco*, and was found in the Knossos Palace, Crete. It was created using pigment mixed in water and applied to wet lime plaster.**

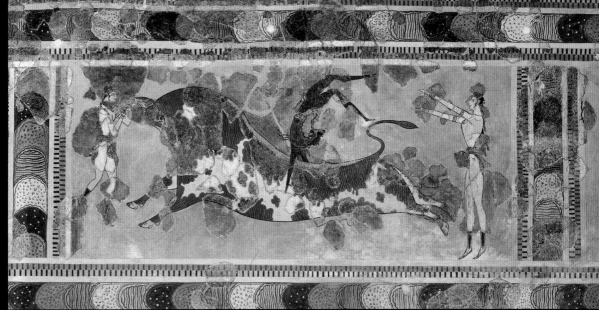

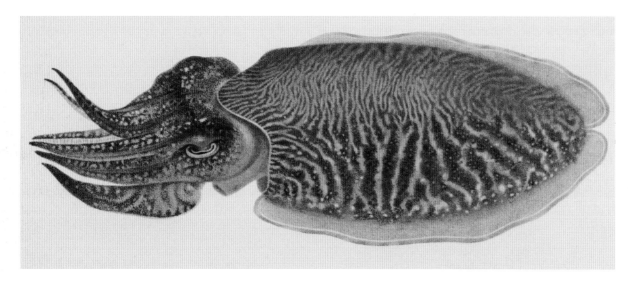

Left: **The dye known as sepia comes from the ink sacs of cuttlefish.**

Right: **In *Girl with a Pearl Earring*, c. 1665, Dutch painter Johannes Vermeer used ultramarine—from the precious stone lapis lazuli, imported into Europe from Middle East—to create the girl's oriental turban.**

Below: **Around 4000 BCE, the development of glass allowed the ancient Egyptians to create the first synthetic inorganic pigment, known as Egyptian blue. Used throughout the time of the Roman Empire, Egyptian blue was produced by grinding and heating a mixture of lime, sand, copper, and iron. "Egyptian blue" ceramic ware, New Kingdom (1380–1300 BCE).**

Through time, the availability of colors has increased due to cultural innovation and the evolution of synthetic pigments. Around 4000 BCE, the development of glass allowed the ancient Egyptians to create the first synthetic inorganic pigment, known as Egyptian blue. Used throughout the time of the Roman Empire, Egyptian blue was produced by grinding and heating a mixture of lime, sand, copper, and iron. Today, synthetic inorganic pigments are made using chemical processes, rather than grinding and washing minerals and clays from the earth. It was not until the mid-1800s that many more synthetic inorganic pigments were manufactured on a large scale, including cadmiums, zincs, cobalts, and iron oxides. These pigments were cheaper than the natural inorganics, and had greater steadfastness and purity.

Pigments that stem from organic materials (as opposed to minerals), are described as natural organic or synthetic organic pigments. Natural organic pigments are derived from animals—fish skeletons, for example— and a great variety of plant matter, including tree roots, flowers, berries, and peat. Colors derived from these pigments include indigo and madder, Vandyke brown, sap green, carmine, sepia, and Indian yellow.

Many organic pigments have interesting origins. For example, coming to India from Persia in the fifteenth century, Indian yellow was made from the urine of cows that had fed on mango leaves (the cows were malnourished and laws eventually prohibited the practice). Sepia, meanwhile, comes from the ink sacs of cuttlefish, while Vandyke brown is a combination of organic and inorganic material stemming from clay

iron oxide and decomposed vegetation.[2] However, many natural organic pigments are in fact dyes that have been changed into pigments by precipitating the dye with a metallic salt. This process results in a "toner," which is the most concentrated form of organic pigment. The toner is often bound with an inert compound such as alumina hydrate for bulk.

Synthetic organic colors are carbon-based pigments manufactured from such substances as petroleum products. They are deemed "organic" because they contain carbon atoms, which have the flexibility to be combined with many other compounds. Synthetic organic pigments originated in the mid-1800s, when William Henry Perkin, a student at the Royal College of Chemistry, was trying to synthesize quinine. Instead, he produced "mauve"—the first synthetic organic pigment—from a purplish aniline dye combined with potassium bichromate. These pigments are very saturated and include quinacridones, phthalocyanines, perylenes, pyrroles, and arylamides.[3]

DYES Have you ever marveled at the beautiful colors of an Afghan or Persian rug? If you have, then your enthusiasm and delight stems in part from the lush dye-colored yarns that have been used in the rug's creation. Ever since man discovered how to color cloth, we have been searching for flowers, roots, trees, and even small insects from which to extract dyes. It is the evolution of dyestuffs, and the process of dying yarns, cloth, paper, and other materials, that has made so many options available to us in terms of creative inspiration and, in turn, beautiful end products.

As with pigments, dyes are also classified as either natural inorganic, synthetic inorganic, natural organic, or synthetic organic. Each dye is further categorized by its dyeing properties, usage, and origin. While pigments are used mostly for paints, cosmetics, and plastics, dyes are used primarily for textiles, paper, wood, and food products. There are also dyes made for specific applications, such as the contrast dyes used for magnetic resonance imaging (MRI).

Many of the dyestuffs that we use fall into the category of organic. Due to material degradation, we do not have records of dyes prior to 6000 BCE, but we are able to trace seeds from archaeological digs to this time period. Weld, for example, is an herbaceous plant that grows to be about five feet tall (1.5 meters), and this was used for dyeing from the Neolithic age until the advent of synthetic colorants.

From the Middle Ages until dyes became chemically manufactured, weld was used with indigo to create beautiful and rich green dyes. True indigo—one of hundreds of indigo plants—grows mostly in Asia and other warm climates, and is a bristly shrub that produces small violet flowers. For indigo to become a dye, it must go through a fermentation process in which the leaves are piled into a bucket with other varied ingredients (in Morocco, it was combined with various fruits, such as dates and quicklime to ferment). Once fermented, the dye vat is ready.[4] Organic dyes have been readily used throughout time for the very simple reason that almost any shade or color can be produced using plants.

With the exception of a few very expensive dyes, such as indigo, madder, weld, and cochineal, the colors of natural organic dyes were not especially bright, light, or particularly water-fast: muted tones dominated.

Below left: **Large hand-made ceramic dye pots are used to ferment a colorless compound named indicant from indigo plants. In Africa, dyeing indigo is used to create beautiful blue plaid and patterned textiles, and dates as far back as the fifteenth century.**

Below: **Tika or tikka pigments—often used in spiritual rituals—are sold in market places across India. The pigments are used to paint faces or worn as a mark in the center of the forehead—a Hindu symbol that represents the third eye; one that sees beyond normal vision.**

However, as the dyeing process became increasingly more efficient and less costly, the desire grew for dyes that had greater strength of color and intensity. With the birth of the industrial revolution, fabrics were created that could be printed upon, increasing demand for a better dye-processing system. In 1759, a Frenchman, Christophe-Philippe Oberkampf, perfected the process of block-and-roller printing with newly designed machinery.

In the mid-nineteenth century, with the growth of manufacturing, scientists found ways to develop synthetic dyes by extracting color elements: the chemist Henry Perkin extracted mauvine, which he began to manufacture. Soon, other aniline derivatives were being manufactured, and, with the discovery of the carbon molecule, development of synthetic dyes flourished.

Today, there are many dye groups, including acid dyes, basic dyes, direct dyes, mordant dyes, vat dyes, reactive dyes, disperse dyes, azoic dyes, and sulfur dyes. Different dyes are more receptive to different materials: some require acids (as in basic dyes), some require salt or other compounds (as in direct dyeing), and some of the most organic dyes require a mordant, which acts as a fixative for the dye, and is responsible for an altered color appearance.[5]

Left: The *Emperor's Carpet*, thought to have been produced in the second half of the sixteenth century in the eastern Iranian city of Herat, is identified by its purple and red background, green and blue border, with flashes of yellow. The carpet is decorated with animals, floral patterns, and arabesques.

Below left: After wool is sheered from sheep it is washed, carded, and hand-spun into yarn. It is then dyed and laid out to dry in the sunlight.

Below: Traditional hand-weaving with hand-dyed yarn in Peru. In the Andes mountains, women use traditional methods of weaving. Wool and alpaca, in browns, grays, blacks, whites, and other natural dyes are woven on back-strap looms.

RECIPES Paint can either be manufactured or made by hand. Purists at heart will take great delight in the making of paint materials and dyestuffs. The process is quite interesting and there is much to be learned about pigments and dyes by learning how they are derived and bonded. While recipes can vary by region, culture, and historical time frame, insight into the paint- and dye-making process broadens our understanding of how paints work and how they can be best utilized.

While modern technology has provided us with flexibility in the use of materials, it has also led us to experience how colorants behave differently in relation to binders due to the varying compositions of binder materials. The ultramarine blue pigment, for example if originating from the same source, remains constant, but its appearance can be altered by changing the type of binder used, and the relationship of pigment to binder. Artist pigments—a particulate substance suspended in a binder or binding medium—can be prepared in several ways. They can be ground naturally or precipitated from an aqueous solution. Artists today have a variety of painting materials to work with that include everything from watercolor, gouache, and tempera, to milk paint, acrylic, or oils. In addition, there is a variety of media that can be utilized to enhance the painting process and even change the characteristics of the paint, such as its texture. But it is the combination of pigment and binder choices on the part of the artist that results in the creation of a personal color vision.

How to Grind Pigments
Pigments, previously made from raw ingredients, are now often found in synthetic powdered form. While pigments come in particulate form, it is a good idea to re-mull them with a glass or marble muller before mixing with a with a binder to form a stiff paste. There is variability in terms of assimilation between paint and binder dependent upon the specific pigment. Place the pigment on a non-porous surface and grind it. Once a suitable paste is made, it should then be ground thoroughly in a series of batches in a circular motion until each batch is completely smooth and of the same consistency. Dependent on the type of paint that you are making, make a mound of the pigment and pour water or linseed oil to create the paste. Mull again and once smooth add the preferred binder.

Pigments to Paint
Once a pigment has been ground or precipitated it can be combined with different binders to create different types of paint. One paint category is tempera. Tempera, a translucent paint, is created with different kinds of emulsions defined as a stable mixture of a water-based solution with an oily, fatty, waxy, or resinous substance. Two great examples of this are egg tempera, in which whole or parts of the egg are used, and milk paint, which has a casein base and is often used on furniture.

Below: *Turban Squash*, 2007, by Douglas Racich. A hard surface is best used when painting with egg tempera, so Racich uses ¼" thick untempered hardboard sealed with Gamblin rabbit-skin glue He uses a warm orange -based black on the background to enhance continuity throughout the painting.

Right: *Bucket of Tarts*, 2003, by Douglas Racich. In addition to egg yolk and water, Racich uses various pigments from Gamblin, Sinopia, and Winsor & Newton. His wonderful capacity for rendering illumination is enhanced by the glossy surface.

DOUGLAS J. RACICH

Left & below: *Squash and Apples*, 2011, drawing and painting by Douglas Racich. When comparing the drawing with the painting, the difference in the way the background space is defined becomes apparent. While the drawing suggests the objects are sitting in an ambiguous space, the addition of color in the painting creates a contrast between the rich dark background and the textured wooden surface, establishing a spatial context.

01.05 pigments and dyes: chemistry / recipes

Artist Douglas Racich, describes preparing the surface, which includes choice of surface and sizing preparation. He says:

"The first step in my process is to select and prepare the support. My preferred support is ¼" untempered hardboard, cut to size, which I prepare with a traditional chalk gesso. The gesso is necessary because the weak binding strength of the tempera paint requires a slightly absorbent ground. The ground is relatively inflexible, which necessitates the rigid support of the hardboard. To size the panel, I apply a layer of rabbit-skin glue, which acts as an isolating coat and helps bind the gesso to the support. I use the same rabbit-skin glue to make the gesso, combining it with Fredrix marble dust and water. (Acrylic gesso is not as absorbent and is not chemically compatible with egg tempera.) I typically apply four to five coats of gesso over the initial sizing, lightly sanding each layer after it has dried to produce a smooth surface for painting."[6]

Because of the nature of the material the egg tempera must be refrigerated and has a time frame in which it must be used. The paint has a translucent quality and is therefore applied by multiple layerings.

EGG TEMPERA BINDER

Douglas Racich explains how he makes egg tempera:

"To obtain the egg medium, I crack open a raw egg, allow the white to drain off, then place the egg yolk sac on a paper towel; this helps remove any remaining egg white and allows easy handling of the yolk sac, which I pierce and allow to drain into a container. Then I mix in a small amount of water before adding pigment. The amount of pigment used depends on the type of pigment, as some colors need more to achieve the desired effect."[7]

CASEIN-BASED TEMPERA

Another product in which the binder is derived from food that is extraordinarily strong and often used on furniture is casein-based tempera, a milk-based product. Casein is a series of proteins mostly found in mammalian milk. Casein-based tempera is a quick-drying water-based paint used by painters and decorative artists .

Ingredients
- 2½ oz. (80g) casein powder
- 9 fl. oz. (approx. 250ml) cold water
- 1 oz. (32g) crystalline borax
- 9 fl. oz. (apr. 250ml) hot water by volume

[1] Soak casein powder in cold water in a covered container overnight.

[2] Dissolve borax powder in hot water.

[3] Add borax solution to the casein solution and stir.

[4] Hydrolysis will start right away and must be completed before the next step (wait approx. two hours until no more swelled casein particles can be seen and the yellowish mass is evenly translucent).

[5] Heat the solution in a double boiler until it becomes liquid (140° F).

[6] Once the solution has cooled, it will return to a syrupy consistency and is ready to be used as a pigment binder.

[7] Important: thin resulting mixture with water in a 1:1 ratio. The full-strength glue is too strong and will crack after application.

[8] Mix two parts of casein to nine parts cold water.

[9] Mix two parts crystalline borax with nine parts hot water.

[10] As with all water-based media, the chosen pigment has to be wetted first.

[11] Add small amounts of water to the dry pigment. Then using a palette knife or spatula, work the water into the pigment until it retains a paste consistency.

[12] Add the casein solution to the color paste sparingly. The casein-to-pigment ratio cannot be described in exact proportions. The amount of pigment will vary according to the desired opacity.

[13] The amount of binder (casein solution) varies according to pigment. Before use, apply small amounts to a piece of cardboard to make sure that there is a sufficient amount of binder. If the pigment comes off after a gentle rubbing, add more casein solution.

[14] Once pigment and binder have been combined to the desired consistency, the resulting paint can be thinned with water.[8]

GUM ARABIC

Ingredients

• 300 grams (10.5 oz) Gum Arabic powder

• 3 drops clove oil, wine, vodka, or denatured alcohol (optional)

• 1 liter (2.1 pints) of boiled water

Preparation

[1] Boil water and pour over the powdered gum with a ratio of 1 part gum to 2 parts water, stirring to make sure there are no lumps.

[2] Allow the mixture to soak for 24–48 hours for full absorption.

[3] Add drops of the clove oil or alcohol to extend shelf life of the gum in wet form. Prepared Gum Arabic must be stored in the refrigerator to deter mold growth, but this can make long-term storage hard. It is advisable to make small batches so the solution will be fresh, rather than storing larger quantities for an longer period of time.

GUM TRAGACANTH

Ingredients

• 15 grams (0.5 oz) Gum Tragacanth

• Vodka or other alcohol to moisten the Tragacanth

• 3 drops clove oil (optional)

• 1 liter (2.1 pints) of water

You can use Gum Tragacanth as an alternative to Gum Arabic for watercolors.

[1] Mix the Gum Tragacanth in your mixing vessel with enough alcohol to create a very soft paste.

[2] Add the water and shake well. This will swell into a gelatinous suspension. You may wish to filter it through cheesecloth to be sure there are no remaining inconsistencies.

[3] Add drops of clove oil to extend shelf life. As with Gum Arabic, prepared Gum Tragacanth must be stored in a refrigerator, so you might wish to make it in small batches.

Above: Prior to being mixed with binders, pigments resemble piles of colored sand. Since nothing has been added to the color, it is at its highest possible intensity.

WATERCOLOR AND GOUACHE

Ingredients

- Prepared Gum solution (Arabic or Tragacanth)
- Honey (Acacia is preferable) in a 10% proportion to the weight of gum solution used
- Pigments

[1] Mix all the ingredients and crush them on a glass plate using a spatula to obtain a paste with a thick, creamy consistency.

[2] Finish the mixture by crushing it with a glass muller (available at art supply stores).

[3] Transfer your paints to saucers for painting. When creating your initial gum, you can add Glycerin as a plasticizer to prevent cracking and brittleness. The ratio would be 1 part Glycerin to 5 parts of your prepared gum solution. Add the Glycerin after gum has been completely dissolved but while still warm.

[4] Since gouache is opaque watercolor, if you would like to make gouache instead of watercolor just add whiting chalk at 15% the volume of the pigment.[9]

Watercolor and Gouache

In its pure form a watercolor is made with pigment and gum-based preparations. Water is the only vehicle, so that it is transparent. Each pigment differs in the amount of binder that it needs. The binder in watercolors is water-soluble; usually plant-based gums such as Gum Arabic or Gum Tragacanth. Here are several recipes for binders and the creation of pan watercolors. For long-term storage it is recommended to place them into individual cups that can be used with a watered brush.

Above & below: Watercolor can come in the form of cakes in a pan or in tubes. Once water is added it can be used to create a transparent surface. 100% rag content watercolor paper is the best choice as a result of its absorbency and textural ability to hold color.

Pastels

Pastels create the purist color because the ratio of pigment to binder is very high. Pastels were hand rolled as crayons as early as the fifteenth century. While they have been used since then by many artists including Degas and the color is beautiful, they are mostly powder based and will wear off the page if a fixative is not applied. Today many artists employ the use of oil-based pastels. Earth Pigments suggests that the key to making good pastels has to do with the hardness or softness of the pastel because the degree of hardness affects its ability to bond with the paper. The paper should have a textured surface such as a cansen pastel paper so that it will hold the pigment.

Above: **Pastels, made of powdered pigment and a binder, usually come in the form of chalky sticks, although the consistency varies. Due to their powdery nature, they tend to transfer unless fixed with fixative.**

Above: **One can really see a magnificent use of color by Edward Degas in his dancer pastels. The ability to apply the color freely by hand allows for an immediacy of application resulting in freshness and** elasticity of mark making. In the painting, Degas created areas of color that crossed the delineated lines of the figure, enhancing movement in the piece.

BASIC PASTEL RECIPE

Ingredients

- 1 part Gum Tragacanth
- Alcohol or wine
- 30 parts distilled water (approx)

Preparation

[1] Prepare gum by placing it in a covered glass bottle or container.

[2] Begin by pouring a small amount of alcohol (grain or denatured ethyl) to moisten the gum, then add water and shake the container.

[3] Leave this solution for one or two days. Tragacanth can't be rushed. It will not dissolve, but instead will form into a gelatinous solution.

[4] When ready to mix with your pigments, warm the Tragacanth and strain it through cheesecloth.

[5] Mix the pigments with distilled water to make a paste.

[6] You may wish to use the pigments alone, or mix them with chalk, for example, in a 1 part pigment to 2 parts whiting chalk ratio.

[7] Crush the pigment paste with the gum solution until smooth and evenly distributed.

[8] Spread the wet pastel onto absorbent paper to help pull excess moisture from the mixture.

[9] While it is damp before completely drying, cut or break into shapes to work with.

[10] Test to see if the proportions are correct. If the pastels crumble in your fingers, there is not enough gum. If they slide on the paper without leaving color and texture, there is too much gum.

[11] Linseed oil or wax can be added to your preparation to make pastels last longer.[10]

Oil and Acrylic Paint

The most common binder for oil paints is linseed oil. Once the pigment is ground on a non-porous surface it is mixed with a spatula with the linseed oil. It does not take much oil, maybe a tablespoon or so. Once the linseed oil and pigment are combined to form a paste, the paste can be mulled again to even out and smooth the mixture. Various media can thicken or thin oil paint. These media consist of various combinations of stand oil, linseed oil, thickened linseed oil; gloss, matte or Damar varnish; and some sort of odorless solvents. They come prepared or you can mix them yourself dependent upon need. Acrylic paint involves the use of pigment combined with acrylic resins.

Above & below: **Oil and acrylic paints most commonly come in tube form and are pigments mixed respectively with linseed oil and acrylic resins. Acrylic paint dries a lot more quickly than oils, so isn't as malleable in terms of working into the color over time. However, acrylic paints are water-soluble when wet, so can be diluted to give the effect of watercolor. Oils need to be diluted with a solvent such as turpentine or white spirit to vary the viscosity of the paint.**

PART TWO

THE PSYCHOLOGICAL AND CULTURAL CONTEXT OF COLOR

CHAPTER ONE

COLOR AWARENESS AND

EXPERT: Karen Schloss

Assistant Professor (Research) department of Cognitive, Linguistic and Psychological Sciences, Brown University Providence, RI. She is the Principle Investigator at the Visual Perception and Cognition Lab, and has published extensively in the field.

Could you tell me about yourself and how you became interested in color?

I've been interested in color since I was a child, when one of my favorite activities was organizing my crayons using different color ordering systems. During college I formally studied color any chance I got. In a Judgment and Decision-Making course I wrote a paper on color preferences; in a Human Learning and Memory class I studied how color-coding facilitates memory; and in my architecture design studio I explored how color-coding can be used to document changes in structure. I then went to graduate school at UC Berkeley to study under Professor Stephen Palmer. We developed a large-scale project on color called the Berkeley Color Project (BCP), where the same set of participants came to the lab for eight sessions and did several experiments on a single set of colors, the BCP-37. Experiments included preferences for single colors and color combinations, color harmony, color similarity, color-emotion associations, and color music associations. The results have formed the bases for several published journal articles (including two in the Proceedings of the National Academy of Sciences) and laid the foundation for several other articles/book chapters and ongoing research.

Could you talk about your work on color preference including the study on color and emotive expressions?

The goal of our studies was to understand how color preferences are formed. We formulated the Ecological Valence Theory (EVT), which posits that preference for a given color is determined by the combined valence (liking/disliking) of all objects associated with the color. The idea is that people generally like colors that are associated with positive things and dislike colors that are associated with negative things. We found that 80% of the variance in average color preferences can be explained by such preferences for associated objects. The theory further suggests that such color preferences can act as

steering function that guides people to approach beneficial objects (e.g., ripe fruit, members of one's own social group) and avoid harmful objects (e.g., rotting fruit, members of an antagonistic rival social group).

Could you talk about synaesthesia and your work with color and music/sound?

Music-to-color synesthesia is a condition in which listening to music (or sounds) causes people to experience colors either in their mind's eye, or projected in space. We were interested in whether people who do not have synesthesia still have strong music-to-color mappings. In our initial study we asked participants to listen to 18 selections of classical music and click on the colors they felt fit with the music. Another time, we asked them to judge how much they associate colors with each of a set of emotions, and did the same for the music and emotions. We found that people associate lighter, yellower, and more saturated colors with faster music in the major mode, and darker, bluer and less saturated colors with slower music in the minor mode. We also found a strong relation between the emotional content of the music and the emotional content of the colors associated with music: people like "happy" colors to go with happy music and vice versa.

With respect to color-emotion associations, we found that happier colors are lighter and more saturated and sad colors are darker and desaturated. After accounting for lightness and saturation, yellower colors were no more happier than bluer colors (contrary to popular belief). In a separate study where I controlled for lightness and saturation, I found that yellows are just as sad as blues if they are dark and desaturated, and just as happy if they are light and saturated. This is an important point, because people often talk about color-emotion associations in terms of hue (e.g., yellow is happy; blue is sad; red is angry), and I have seen design websites say that yellow is happy, and if it is too bright for you, you can tone it down. But, toning it down makes it less happy.

COLOR COGNITION: COLOR ATTENTION AND MEMORY We have established that light enters the eye and the retinal sensors perceive it. We also know that electrical impulses convey information from the retina through the optic nerve to the brain. What we must explore further is what happens to those impulses once they arrive at the cortical areas in the brain. The concept of color perception and response has been the subject of much research by scientists, psychologists, anthropologists, designers, and artists alike. Questions that researchers have considered in their work have covered many topical areas. Their questions are varied and the reasons for asking them are based on differing intentions and directives. These are the concerns of the study of cognitive color. In other words, cognitive color is a way to understand the human color response with respect to "thinking, knowing, remembering, judging, and problem-solving."[1]

One area of interest concerns what happens inside the brain when color is perceived and recognized by the brain. Questions arise as to whether the brain sees the accurate color or a color altered by an interfering variable. Elizabeth Loftus, of the University of Washington, did a study with college students to determine if misleading information could alter color recognition. Students watched a slide presentation on a car accident involving a green car. When the students were asked questions, the researchers referred to the color of the car as blue in some cases and green in others. On color recognition tests, students who were told the car was blue shifted to believe the car was blue while students who were given accurate information remained true to that original color.[2]

Another question that researchers have asked concerns color memory. They questioned whether each time a color is seen is it as though for the first time or is there color memory? If there is color memory, how long can the memory persist and which colors are remembered the most. In an article, "Memory Color Effect Induced by Familiarity of Brand Logos," Kimura et al. discuss their study of the relationship between color memory perception of an object and its actual color. By using a variety of logos with different familiarity levels, they determined that "memory color increases with the familiarity of objects."[3]

Not only do familiar colored objects enhance color memory, but color itself can act to enhance personal memory. It has been determined by researchers at the University of Toronto that color enhances visual memory for images in the natural environment. By comparing both color and monochrome grayscale images by a group of participants it was found that

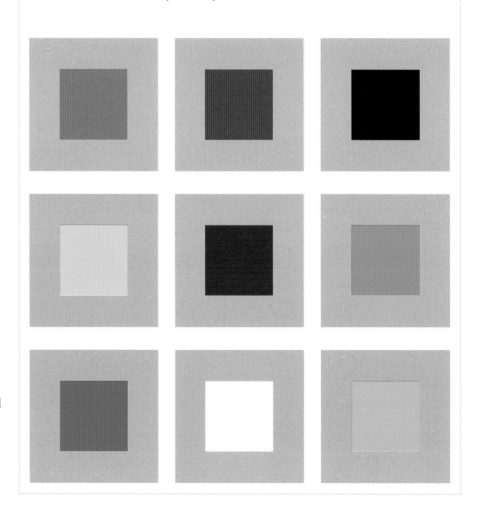

STRENGTH OF EACH COLOR WITH RESPECT TO INDIVIDUAL HUMAN PERCEPTION

Look at the nine color swatches below individually. Cover them up and say their names. How many can you remember and in what order do you remember them? Choose one of the colors and decide whether you like it or not. Describe that color with words. What does this color reveal to you about yourself?

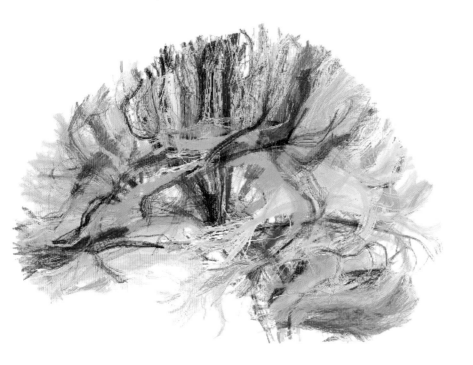

FRIEND	DOOR	MUSIC
COPY	FUTURE	

THE STROOP EFFECT

BLUE	GREEN	YELLOW
PINK	RED	ORANGE
GREY	BLACK	PURPLE
TAN	WHITE	BROWN

color bound to an image of natural scenes early on enhances recognition memory by helping to process the image.[4] Lynnay Huchendorf, a graduate student at the University of Wisconsin, La Crosse carried out another study into whether color enhances memory. Called *The Effects of Color on Memory*, a group of 115 students were given a packet that contained a list of 20 words, several mathematical tests, a blank recall sheet, and a demographic questionnaire. Some of the packets had the information placed on red and yellow sheets, others received green and blue sheets, and some received packets on white paper. The students were then asked to recall the words from the list. Those with the red and yellow packets recalled more than the others.[5]

Many researchers have explored the relationship between language and color, a huge and complex field that combines linguistics, semiotics, and cognitive science. They concern themselves with naming and the similarities and differences of color names within different cultures. Although not specifically dealing with the direct relationship, one can see the complexity of language and color by studying the Stroop Effect. Named after John Ridley Stroop, it "demonstrates the interference that the automatic processing of words has on more mentally challenging tasks as naming the color." Participants taking the Stroop test,

a neuropsychological test, are asked to name colors of the words presented in different colored inks. They are also asked to name the color of the ink not the word. There are many other variations of the test, which is used to determine cognitive flexibility and processing speed.[6]

Color awareness can also increase or decrease cognitive behavior. Researchers have found that people have different reactions to interior spaces dependent upon the color chosen. They have determined that some colors such as red cause agitation and excitement. This is apparent in research comparing red and blue. Researches from the Saunder School of Business at the University of British Columbia in Vancouver, found that red and blue stimulate different motivations and can enhance performance on different types of tasks. They believe that different associations with red or blue can induce alternative motivations. Because red activates an avoidance type of behavior it makes people more vigilant. As a result it might enhance detail-oriented tasks. Blue on the other hand is often associated with peace and tranquility. It was felt that this environment might be conducive to innovation, creativity, and risk-taking.[7]

Above left: **Colors stimulate receptors that send messages to the brain. The brain interprets these messages differently according to an innate response combined with age, gender, and cultural/environmental experience.**

Above top: **Color can help or hinder individuals from interpreting words. It has been found that it can make words easier to memorize.**

Above: **Color can inhibit visual processing. The Stroop test is given to individuals to determine cognitive flexibility.**

COLOR RESPONSE AND PREFERENCE Researchers are interested in the concepts of color preference and response for a variety of reasons that range from understanding shopping tastes to bettering the health and well-being of Alzheimer's patients. It is important to understand what makes us prefer one color and dislike another. While most of us can agree on a color name, we vary in how we feel about it. When you go into a friend's or colleague's home you either feel comfortable or ill at ease with their personal taste and color palette. Color preference and response is due to a combination of personal and environmental factors. While you might look at a muted orange and be reminded of the clay soil of the desert southwest, someone else might think of it as the color of dirty water coming out of a faucet. As a result you might describe the orange as romantic and spiritually calming, calling it "Sedona red," while the individual who thought it looked like dirty water might be sick to his stomach and name it "rusty-nail red."

If we are to determine what causes us to respond to color in a certain way, we must look at physiological, psychological, and cultural responses to color. We understand that sensations of certain colors create arousal in the brain and stimulate metabolic activity, while others decrease it. This is especially evident with bright red, which has been known to make your blood pressure rise. Oddly enough pink has been used in prisons to keep prisoners from rioting.

In a study on the biological components of color preference in infancy, conducted by Anna Franklin, newborns demonstrate spontaneous preferences to chromatic over achromatic color. She also determined that red was preferred to green: She recorded infants'

Right: **The color red elicits both an emotive and physiological response. It has a variety of meanings such as blood, anger, and fire, and it can act as a stimulant, increasing your heart rate. Pink, however, has the opposite effect and has been used in prisons to stop prisoners experiencing feelings of aggression. The "pink cell" in Attendorn prison in Germany is protected by special security features to isolate prisoners who are in danger of hurting others or themselves. The color is believed to calm the prisoners and shorten the time they spend in the bare room.**

Red acts as a stimulant.

Pink has a calming effect.

eye movement in response to a presentation of eight color stimuli varying only in hue. The infants looked longest at the reddish and shortest at the greenish hues. Only half were attributed to background interference.[8]

Understanding that there might be a physiological component to color choice, we can also see that there might be a developmental aspect to color preferences. In his book *Color, Environment, and Human Response*, Frank Mahnke talks about color with respect to his Color Experience Pyramid." The biological reactions to color lay the groundwork for more sophisticated color response. Above the biological response base is a level that he names as the collective unconscious from Jungian Psychology. Mahnke says this is "a point of shared collective unconscious which

is not controlled by intellect or conscious rational thought which act as inherited experiences."[9] These color preferences change as people develop conscious awareness and symbolic understanding.

Below: Colors can have both positive and negative connotations, and color preference and response is due to a combination of personal and environmental factors. While you might look at a muted orange and be reminded of the red clay of the Sedona desert, someone else might think of it as the color of dirty water coming out of a faucet.

ADULTS' COLOR PREFERENCE

In an independent online study participants were asked to specify their favorite color.

Men were found to prefer blue, while women prefer red, purple, and pink.[10]

COLOR RESPONSE

Orange

Negative response

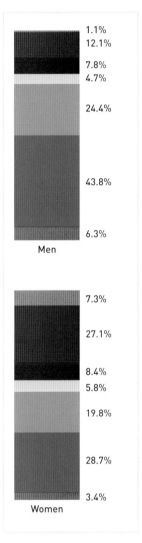

Men

1.1%
12.1%
7.8%
4.7%
24.4%
43.8%
6.3%

Women

7.3%
27.1%
8.4%
5.8%
19.8%
28.7%
3.4%

Positive response

Left & below left: **Research** seems to indicate that color choice is in part cultural. More research has to be done in order to determine how much is physiologically based and how much is environmental. South Korean photographer, JeongMee Yoon, started *The Pink and Blue Project* when her five-year-old daughter couldn't get enough candy-colored possessions. This made her realize that this preference is the result of cultural influences and the power of pervasive marketing, which says pink is for girls and blue is for boys. *Tess and her Pink Things*, 2005 (top) and *Hojun and his Blue Things*, 2007 (bottom).

Opposite left & right: **According** to Faber Birren, people who feel an affinity toward the color red tend to be "aggressive, vigorous, given to impulsive moods and actions." If you are drawn to green you "probably dwell in the great forest of humanity."

In an article from the *British Journal of Developmental Psychology*, "Pretty in pink: The early development of gender-stereotyped color preferences," Vanessa LoBue suggests that there is no evidence that girls naturally prefer pink to blue. In fact, there is actually information that suggests that all children prefer blue. She performed a study with girls from seven months to five years in age. By the age of two and a half, the girls have a preference for pink over other colors, and boys show a greater dislike of pink. This may be due to a learned response. LoBue talks of the "social convention" of color. She says in the article:

Dressing girls in pink and boys in blue was first noted in the early 1920s. More recently, observations of parents and their infants at suburban shopping malls revealed that 75% of infant girls were wearing pink, whereas 79% of infant boys were in blue (Shakin, Shakin, & Sternglanz, 1985). Children are aware of this differential dressing patterns quite early on: by the time they enter preschool, they make decisions about gender identity based on color."[11]

Color awareness comes not only from developmental awareness but also from personal color associations. The article, "An ecological valence theory of human color preference,"[12] published by psychologists Stephen Palmer and Karen Schloss, in the proceedings of the National Academy of Science of USA, suggests that people's particular aesthetic responses to a color are a reflection of their response to objects and situations that they have previously experienced. So people who have positive color experiences with an object/situation tend to like the color and people who have negative experiences with objects/situations dislike the color.

Cognitive color preference or color choices made on a conscious level can be universally or individually characteristic. If your beloved, grandmother wore a magenta, orange, and gold scarf, even if it's not a particularly attractive combination, you will always have positive experiences with those colors due to previous personal experience. If a childhood enemy always wore a distinct shade of blue no matter how wonderful the color is, your personal response might always be negative.

Scientists are also interested in knowing whether color preferences are personal, and if they are what do they reveal about the individual and his or her personality. Faber Birren talks about different personalities of people who have a specific preference for a color. He suggests that if you prefer the color red, "the interest in your life is directed outward. If you love red, the intensity is natural to your spirit and you belong in the midst of life. You are aggressive, vigorous, given to impulsive moods and actions." He goes on to say of a preference for green: "Cool fresh and comforting green has wide appeal. The sign of balance and normality, it has the universal attraction of nature. Love green and you probably dwell in the great forest of humanity. You are: respectable neighbor, homebuilder father or mother of spoiled children."[13]

We can say that much more research has to be done to determine specific causal effects between color and preference/response. We can understand that color response is both personal and environmental. It is individual and universal. It is regional, national, socio-economic, and a result of individual, personal experiences, associations, impressions, and symbolism.

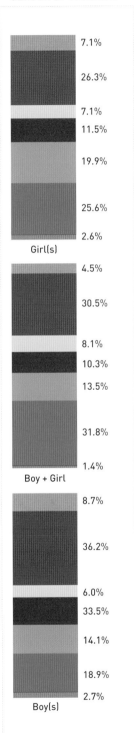

WOMEN'S COLOR PREFERENCE BY GENDER OF CHILDREN[14]

7.1%
26.3%
7.1%
11.5%
19.9%
25.6%
2.6%
Girl(s)

4.5%
30.5%
8.1%
10.3%
13.5%
31.8%
1.4%
Boy + Girl

8.7%
36.2%
6.0%
33.5%
14.1%
18.9%
2.7%
Boy(s)

COLOR AND EMOTION: THE COLOR AND MOOD EFFECT, SYNESTHESIA

In Carlton Wagner's book *The Color Response Report*, he says response to color is inherited. Response to color is learned. Response to color is geographic. Response to color is regional. Response varies with light, climate, and income. What he leaves out is that response to color is emotional. We live in a world filled with colorful expressions and meanings. The constant color input from our homes, our clothes, the things we buy, and the advertisements that we see in magazines and on television; it is obvious that the impact of color on us is unmistakable. It has led us to redefine what color is and how we should relate to it. The color that we experience every day is entangled with human feelings and moods. It is color that evokes emotion. Evocative color comes from our complex personal responses to our environment and those around us.[14]

When we talk about the preference or response to color, we are talking about a person choosing a color or an object because it is a color that they like. This refers to a response that individuals have to a specific color or group of colors. When we are talking about color and mood, we are talking about how colors themselves elicit an emotive feeling. In other words, it is the color itself that elicits the response. It is important to consider if color can evoke emotion—can colors used in certain ways elicit specific feelings or moods? If this is true, artists and designers can use these colors to bring on a specific response.

If we take a step back to talk about the commonality between music and color in terms of the desire to create both harmonic music and design, we can also talk about the emotional impact of both. There is new research that actually suggests that when experiencing color choice with respect to music, the associations are tied to emotions. In another article published by Palmer and Schloss, music-color associations are mediated by emotion, they state: "US and Mexican participants chose colors that were most/least consistent with 18 selections of classical orchestral music by Bach, Mozart, and Brahms. In both cultures,

faster music in the major mode produced color choices that were more saturated, lighter, and yellower whereas slower, minor music produced the opposite pattern (choices that were desaturated, darker, and bluer). There were strong correlations ($0.89 < r < 0.99$) between the emotional associations of the music and those of the colors chosen to go with the music, supporting an emotional mediation hypothesis in both cultures."[15]

Now that we see that research suggests that the music-color relationship evokes emotion, we can continue to explore the emotional effects of color by studying emotional color and painting. Painters and designers throughout time have attempted to express emotion and create feeling through the use of color. This is readily obvious in the work of Edvard Munch. His paintings *Despair*, *Anxiety*, and *The Scream*, reflect upon his personal angst and the misery of the times. In the painting *Anxiety*, Munch expresses these feelings through the lonely sorrowful individuals crossing a bridge. The gray muted tones in combination with the electric red oranges of the sky, and the yellow orange colors of the face, enhance the feeling of discomfort in the piece.

Right: *Anxiety*, 1894, by Edvard Munch. Munch expressed himself artistically through color and distortion. His feelings of isolation are rendered through faces on a group of individuals and atonal disproportionate color. While the colors appear to have some red commonality they are not harmonic and they are used disproportionately.

Feelings and emotions are elusive, but research has determined that color is the most readily seen design element. When designers try to convey an important emotion they will utilize the colors that evoke that feeling. Many people have tried to qualify emotion in terms of color, and there are wheels and charts that attempt to represent it. Color inspiration for interior design palettes is often based on emotion. In *Colors for Your Every Mood*, Leatrice Eiseman talks about eight personal color moods: whimsical, nurturing, contemplative, romantic, tranquil, traditional, dynamic, and sensuous. She describes whimsical as: a "fun-loving, spirited, and joyful set of colors."[16] "Whimsical" colors include red, yellow, and blue, orange, green, and purple.

The graphic world is very clear on the fact that emotive color attracts attention. It will often play on the effectiveness of mood color and association to sell products or promote events. Often the color of a logo color can elicit positive associations and feelings for the product. Emotive color can also be used as an attention getting device. This is often the case in packaging. It can be said that emotive color is one of the most powerful tools an artist or designer can have to hand.

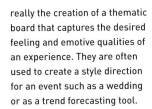

Opposite, right, & below: In the design world part of the design process is the creation of what is known as a mood board. In these instances colors are chosen to support the emotive feeling of the board. This is really the creation of a thematic board that captures the desired feeling and emotive qualities of an experience. They are often used to create a style direction for an event such as a wedding or as a trend forecasting tool.

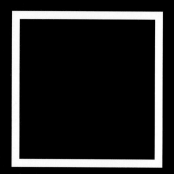

CHAPTER TWO

CULTURAL RESPONSE, SYMBOLISM, AND MEANING

   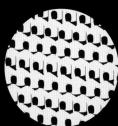  

EXPERT: **LEATRICE EISEMAN**
American color specialist assisting companies in their color choice in a range of areas, including packaging, logos, and interior design. Director at Eiseman Center for Color Information and Training. Executive Director of The Pantone Color Institute. www.colorexpert.com.

Could you tell me a little bit about your background and how you got to be Executive Director of The Pantone Color Institute and the principle of your own business?

My educational background is a mix of design and psychology, a good combination because psychology is such an important part of learning about color. It helped to answer questions and understand better why people are drawn to specific colors and what it means when they react to colors in a particular way. I had been involved in the color world and written a book which has been reissued as *More Alive with Color: Personal Colors— Personal Style* (2007, Capital Books) and Lawrence Herbert, founder and CEO of Pantone, Inc., asked whether I would be interested in talking to him about the possibility of starting another arm of Pantone that would be dedicated more to responding to people's questions, people's concerns about color that weren't of a technical nature, but were more about the how and why of color or if you will the psychology of color.

I just finished reading your and Keith Recker's book, *Pantone: The Twentieth Century in Color*, and I wondered, when you make a color design decision, do you rely on history, geography, or culture?

Well, it is all of the above when you are making a decision. For example, I love to point out to everyone that just before versions of my book came out in Chinese, I was told that we had to be cautious about using white in China. That was fascinating to me because in the early nineties I had been to Taiwan, where most people are from Chinese extractions, and I noticed that in pictures of young brides in the photography stores, they were all wearing white gowns and white veils—alongside another picture of them in red gowns. I went to the people who had sponsored my trip and asked why brides in Taiwan would prefer to wear white, the color of mourning. They said it was because they all wanted to look like the western brides. They thought that it was very romantic and beautiful to wear a veil and a very pure color like

white. This younger generation was not bogged down by old concepts, traditions, and roles. In order to keep the grandparents and parents happy they also often wore a red gown, the traditional color of weddings in China. The bottom line is that you really have to be up to date and not just accept old ideas as given, but be aware of what is really happening now. This is not to say that culture does not play into it. If you were raised by the ocean, it wouldn't be unusual for you to love blue. You may not be aware of the culture or the geography in which you were raised but it is buried in the psyche. This positive response remains unless something happened on a personal level that caused a negative reaction. However, if you are going to be putting out a product that needs to travel well, you have to deal in generalities and judge the color by the majority response.

What is the process involved when you're picking the Pantone color of the year?

There is always a calculated risk when you choose a color, but it will help if you do your homework and have a professional sense of where color has been in the recent past and examine the zeitgeist of the consumer public. We look at it with respect to how accepted we think it would be from the standpoint of public mood, what is the public looking for in the way of color? Travel is also important. You really need to look at it from an international standpoint. Other considerations include looking to the entertainment industry. Films such as *Frozen* that have the most spectacular usage of color are going to be very influential because they have an audience of millions of people worldwide. The wonderful orchid color worn by the sisters in the form of a cape was outstanding against all the blueness and the coldness in the location. Even if you weren't paying attention to it, the color seeps into the marketplace or people start to look for that color in the marketplace.

GEOGRAPHICAL AND REGIONAL COLOR

Associations and inherent meanings can influence how individuals interpret a design. Color can be a key element in creating context or making a statement. From a design standpoint, the use of local/native colors can be beneficial because familiarity provides comfort and as a result stimulates sales. On a larger scale, color can contribute to reinforcing a region's identity.

While palettes might vary, the colors do not necessarily differ from one region to the next, rather they have different regional interpretations. A good example of this is a national flag. In his article "Three cheers for Red," John Bergen talks about how the colors for the United States flag were of particular importance in the initial design concept. Charles Thomson, then secretary of congress, talked about the meaning behind the color palette of the flag. "White signifies purity and innocence; red, hardiness and valor; and blue signifies vigilance, perseverance, and justice."[1]

Red, white, and blue are used for many national flags, but while the colors remain the same, differing regional and cultural color interpretations make the meaning of the colors significantly different. For example, while blue signifies vigilance, perseverance, and justice in the American flag, in the Chilean flag it symbolizes the sky, while the blue of the Laotian flag is represents both the Mekong River and prosperity.

Similarly, while the white of the United States flag represents purity and innocence, for Chile it represents the snow-covered Andes, and for Laos, the full moon over the Mekong River.

Red represents hardiness and valor for the United States, but for both the Chileans and the Laotians it references blood spilled during the fight for independence. In addition, for the Laotians red also symbolizes a bright future.[2]

In order to identify the color palette of an area it is important to research local culture. When studying geographical color, Jean-Philippe Lenclos (designer, colorist, and founder of Atelier 3D Couleur, a Paris-based studio specializing in color palette development and application), talks about what is required to gain an understanding of local color. In the recipe of local color determination he includes the light and environment, and the socio-political behaviors of the inhabitants, as well as the customs and material culture.

Below: While the colors red, white and blue have been used for the national flags of various countries, it is the evolving design that enhances the color choices and distinguishes them from one another. When reviewing the history of the national flag of the United Kingdom—commonly known as the Union Jack—it reveals the fact that the design is a composite of various regions of the United Kingdom.

Right: With regard the Chilean flag, blue symbolizes the sky, while the white represents the snow-covered Andes, and the red signifies the bloodshed of the fight for independence.

CAMINO DE ALTA
MONTAÑA EXTREME
PRECAUCIONES

CHILE

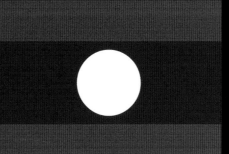

Left: The American flag started with 13 stars and grew to include a star for each state. The white disk in the center of the Laotian flag reflects unification and solidarity under the leadership of the Lao People's Revolutionary Party.

With his archeologist wife, Dominique, Lenclos traveled the world in search of sites to intensively study local color, visiting and documenting locations throughout the world. Their extensive research focused on architectural construction—floors, walls, roofs, doors, and shutters—and terrain samples. It also included cultural symbols and decorative surfaces.

This scientific approach to palette development reveals a specific color identity and diversity with respect to the various regions studied. The Lenclos' book *Colors of the World: A Geography of Color* includes color charts portraying the dominant chromatics of the regional architecture, as well as illustrations in colored pencils that are compared with color guides and divided qualitatively into a "synthesis chart." The process also features substance boards. In-depth research is a key process in developing an accurate color picture.

An exemplary study of color palettes was conducted by Lenclos in the modern state of Lesotho, South Africa. South African people consist primarily of tribal groups and Dutch immigrants descended from the Sotha and the Ndebele tribes. The study revealed the color palette for homes as being a combination of clay masonry combined with two pigment families: tinted grays made with natural pigments, and red and orange tones made from organic pigments. Blues and greens are used for the doors. With these pigments, colorful geometric and figurative patterns are painted on homes and community buildings. Traditional ochers and browns and some bolder contemporary colors are used in murals on the walls based on prayers to the ancestors.[3] What we might ascertain from the Lenclos' methodology is that studying local resources for evidence-based inspiration is important if you want to establish geographic color association.

When talking about geographic color we can refer to everything from a continent to a country, a region, or even a neighborhood, and with basic research techniques and color-matching identification we can get a sense of local color. In designing the identity for the Rhode Island Museum of Science and Art (RIMOSA), it was decided that a regional color palette should be used. Photographs were taken extensively throughout the state: color samples were taken from wildlife, architecture, and landscape, and a color palette was developed that included rich greens for the vegetation, blues and greens for the waters of the "Ocean State" (as it is referred to), and grays for the sky, the grayed shingles on homes, and the wood from the docks. Oranges were chosen from the fall leaves, and violets and pinks for the spring flowers.

As the museum focuses on appealing to an audience aged 12 and upward, the intensity of the color palette was heightened to make it appear more youthful and festive, with the green taken from the vegetation becoming lime, and sky blue becoming cobalt. In a similar way to the Lenclos' investigation, the colors for a museum based in Rhode Island came from the structures and landscapes of the area, enhancing the community ties and allowing the museum to stand as an institution that is readily identifiable with the state and the region.

Regional color can be beneficial in defining cultural identity, and in an article in *American Demographics* magazine (Feb 2002, Vol. 24), Pamela Paul presented a poll on how taste shifts occur due to age, sex, and ethnicity, which is subsequently reflected in regional color. The study showed that cultural and ethnic background shape color preference, and Paul suggests that demographic diversity lends itself to a richer and more varied color palette. As in the diversity resulting from a multi-cultural environment there are great benefits to regionally based color identities. The loss of local color to globalization would be a great design and creative limitation, creating color uniformity throughout the world.[4]

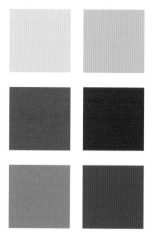

Below: The exterior of a traditional "modern style" Basotho house, near Phuthaditjhaba, Free State Province, South Africa. The design is in line with Lenclos' findings in that it is made up of grays, reds, and ochers, and the pattern is fairly geometric.

Above & right: The cultural colors of Mexico, its artworks, its fabrics, combined with the warmth of the climate extends to the neighborhoods in which people live. The intense light allows for strong colors, which are then bleached in the sun.

SOCIO-POLITICAL COLOR

SOCIO-POLITICAL COLOR In addition to geographic association, color can have socio-political implications. As noted, color preference can differ due to age, sex, and ethnicity, so it would follow that different palettes could motivate groups of individuals in different ways. In her article, "Wearing your Politics on your Sleeve: The Role of Political Colours in Social Movements," Marion Sawyer, of the School of Social Sciences at the Australian National University (Social Movement Studies Vol. 6, No. 1, 39–56, May 2007, Routledge),[5] suggests that color plays a role in social movements not only to establish symbols, but to also bolster the emotional life of the movement.

Sawyer goes on to discuss the ever-present party colors that stem from ancient Greece and the rise of political symbolism in the nineteenth century. While color choice has many other contingent factors, it has been especially important in motivating individuals politically. Colors chosen for their historical and psychological implications are used in politics for a variety of purposes—from inciting and rabble-rousing to calming and unifying.

Throughout history, these kinds of color sentiments have not only been utilized to make socio-political statements, but a variety of governmental archetypes have been attached to specific colors. Black, for example, has associations with anarchy and fascism; blue is linked to conservatism; gold and green can both suggest capitalism; and we have long equated red with both socialism and communism. Indeed, the color and the identity of a political movement can become so strongly integrated that the color or colors themselves become representative of it.

One of the most obvious examples of this is the case of the "green movement," an environmentally based movement that has actually taken on the name of the color. Though it encompasses every color from teal to lime, green in this context has developed a personality. As such, many brands use green to associate themselves with the movement or to state that they are eco-friendly, with the "green" brand not only signifying eco-friendly products and services, but also representing companies that utilize green practices in their manufacturing or construction. In our environmentally conscious world, green is not only an adjective, but it has gained such presence as to become a noun and a verb—the phrase "go green" has become synonymous with saving our planet.

Yet while green is universally positive and accepted by all, other colors in politics stand for less positive and perhaps more provocative feelings of defiance and social unrest. Red is a good example of a color that is readily used as a socio-political motivator.

It is widely known that red stimulates us in such a way as to cause our heart to beat faster and our brains to work slower. By using the color red as a subtle threat cue, researchers were able to determine that participants who viewed red showed a decrease in heart function and that in turn showed a decrease in brain function.[6]

For centuries, red has been tied to man's "fight or flight" mechanism, with many meanings for the color being attached by various cultures. Red is the color of the elements of fire and sun; it is both aggressive and bold, and has been the color of royalty and revolution.[7]

By the late nineteenth century, red was synonymous with the socialist revolution and continues today to serve as a political statement in Russia. Social advocacy posters in Russia and around the world use red to suggest socio–political change. In the show *Graphic Advocacy: International Posters for the Digital Age* (2001–2012), at the Massachusetts College of Art, posters for the Occupy Wall Street movement used red to show strength and power. One of the poster designers, R. Black, describes his piece in the show:

"This has been the most controversial of my posters because I used the image of Wang Weilin, also known as *Tank Man* or the *Unknown Rebel*. Reaction was very polarized, with people taking sides on whether it was accurate to compare the Tiananmen protests to the Occupy movement. For me, this represented the kind of success I think any poster artist wants—to make people think and provoke debate, whether in agreement or not. I believe Wang Weilin is a hero, an icon, and a martyr, and I wanted to convey the idea that, if everyone had the same courage and conviction about standing up for their beliefs, despite the sacrifice, real change can occur. Some observers suggested that I made the people of the movement look like clones, as I replicated Wang's image to create the crowd, but I see it as a metaphor: we are him, he is us, we are one, and change happens through solidarity."[8]

Opposite top left: **Political color varies over time, space, and geographical location. Since the mid-1800s, the color red has been associated with the socialist movement. It is also considered a symbol of revolution: it was the color of the French Revolution in 1789, the Bolshevik revolution in 1917, and, later, the Chinese Revolution of 1949.**

Opposite top right: **The color green's association with nature has been extended to cover everything from organic produce, to energy efficiency. "Going Green" has become a lifestyle direction suggesting taking a stand and living for a better earth.**

Opposite bottom: **Colored ribbons have been used symbolically to express social and political awareness for many generations. For example, the red ribbon is used to symbolize people affected by or living with Aids. The yellow ribbon has been tied to troop support. It is interesting to note that a color change on a simple ribbon design can have so much impact and significance.**

In R. Black's poster (right), the dominating presence of red clearly stands for revolution, but also for power and solidarity. Against this red, three black tanks stand out menacingly, but they are overpowered by the presence of white in the lower half of the poster, depicting individuals standing in resistance, the strength and solidarity of the movement emphasized by their numbers overflowing the bounds of the picture plane.

There are, however, other symbolic meanings attached to the color red. It is the color of passion and our hearts, and as such is representative of Valentine's Day. In China, where the color red represents good fortune and joy, women traditionally wear red on their wedding days, and the New Year is celebrated with red dragons. Egyptians used red ink to record important events, and we also use red ink to draw attention to changes in a text document.

While the power of red is undeniable, especially with respect to advocacy, other colors are also used to represent political ideas. Blue is a color often chosen by corporate America because it symbolizes both trust and stability. It is also a color intrinsically tied to the resources of air and water. In the powerful global-warming awareness poster on the page opposite, a blue color palette depicts of the rise of the water level. Leo Lin talks about his poster:

"Global warming is a critical issue, a warning signal from our Mother Earth. Increasing temperatures result in rising sea levels with potentially catastrophic consequences for low-lying shore communities. Some island nations will be submerged if the sea level continues to rise. I try to express these concerns in my work, appealing to everyone to take care of our environment and love this planet we live on."[9]

Posters are just one form of political expression. Solidarity can be expressed by the use of a colored item, with colored ribbons playing an important role in the creation of visual symbolism in America, to establish a collective identity of support behind a particular cause. One such example was the use of yellow ribbons during the Iran hostage crisis (1979–1981) as a symbol of support for the hostages and the plight of their families.[10]

Yellow ribbons became synonymous with military plight and were used again during the Gulf War, but other colored ribbons have also been used to raise awareness or show support of a specific cause: red ribbons (the "color of passion") were used in the

fight against Aids, for example, while pink ribbons are still used today to support breast cancer patients (although the latter was originally conceived as a peach-colored ribbon).

Flags have been employed in a similar way to express causal identity. One such flag represents gay pride—the rainbow flag has become one of the most widely used and recognized symbols of the gay pride

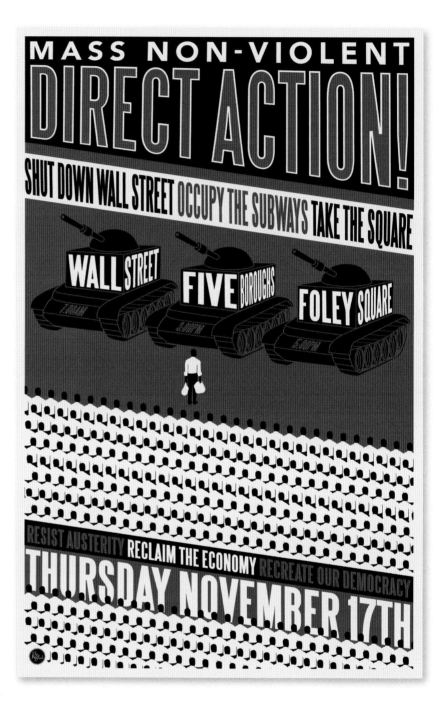

Above: This poster references the idea of red as suggesting revolt. Its design is purposely anarchic. The perspective is on a diagonal and combined with military tanks in a line, promotes solidarity and action.

G L O B A L   W A R M I N G

other colored ribbons have also been used to raise awareness or show support of a specific cause: red ribbons (the "color of passion") were used in the fight against Aids, for example, while pink ribbons are still used today to support breast cancer patients (although the latter was originally conceived as a peach-colored ribbon).

Flags have been employed in a similar way to express causal identity. One such flag represents gay pride—the rainbow flag has become one of the most widely used and recognized symbols of the gay pride movement and LGBT unity. Artist and civil rights activist, Gilbert Baker, designed it to represent the diversity of gays and lesbians around the world. He says: "pink stood for sexuality, red for life, orange for healing, yellow for the sun, green for nature, turquoise for art, indigo for harmony, and violet for the soul."[11] The design of the flag, combined with the color palette, suggests a rainbow coalition. Rather than indicating difference, it uses positive color intonations and meaning to unite individuals and give them a sense of self-respect.

Above: The idea that global warming is raising the earth's water level is referenced here using the old adage "barely keeping your head above water." The simple design and use of blue transmits the idea that we are to drowning in our own environment effectively.

Above right: It is interesting to note that the Pride flag encompasses the visible spectrum promoting the idea of both inclusion and diversity.

CHAPTER THREE

COLOR, A HISTORICAL PERSPECTIVE

EXPERT: **CLARK SCHOETTLE**
Executive Director, Providence Revolving Fund.

Could you describe the analytic process that you go through when trying to recreate the original color scheme of a building?
We typically start by doing a paint scraping in an area that has paint build up to try to determine the original colors. Usually you can find original traces of color behind downspouts or in protected areas like porches or inside corners. This may involve magnification if there are many layers and it is difficult to determine the order. If the colors are not that interesting we will use the information to at least determine if the trim was darker or lighter than the body color.

Could you talk about the process of developing a color palette that is historically correct?
We also know generally by the age and style of the house whether the trim would have been lighter than the body. Usually Federal and Greek Revival and Colonial Revival would have off white or cream trim and a medium-density body color. Italianate, Queen, and Victorians between 1870–1900 could go either way.

Many of the old pattern books of house designs also included a spec sheet on materials and often included recommended paint combinations for each house design. We have studied those combinations as well for guidance. I typically start with the Historic Color palette from the paint company (Benjamin Moore or Sherwin Williams) and then add to it, including different hues and intensities.

How does historic color enhance neighborhoods?
Through the Providence Revolving Fund we have helped select the historic colors for over 400 houses in the Elmwood and Broadway Armory historic Districts. By working off of a similar historic pallet for all of the houses, we have created a harmonious combination of colors, which has helped to unify the neighborhood visually. In a similar way, we have chosen over 100 historic paint combinations for Brown University historic buildings. Again working off the same palette for all buildings has created a harmonious effect that contributes to the continuity of the campus.

COLOR IN A HISTORICAL CONTEXT Throughout time, color has been used to enhance designs that direct individuals in cultural and religious life. The Greeks and the Romans both associated color with universal harmony. In Greek mythology, sunlight was divine, and as a result, Athena—the goddess of wisdom, courage, and inspiration—wore a golden robe. Hindus and Buddhists have also recognized the sacredness of the color yellow.

With the advent of trade, commerce, and technology, color palettes evolved and expanded beyond their original geographic region. In addition to gaining different meanings from new cultures, as colors traveled through time and place they also became encumbered with new historical, cultural, and technological associations.

Color that makes an identifiable statement with respect to the material culture and design of a particular time can be referred to as "period color." Period color is the passion and curiosity of many historians, anthropologists, and archaeologists because the architecture and material culture provide an insight into the people of a particular era. Indeed, period color can be so significant that it becomes an identifier for a specific point in time.

In his book, *Color and Meaning: Art, Science and Symbolism*, John Gage talks about the colors of indigenous tribes of Central America in the pre-Columbian era. He explains how the dyestuff cochineal red (named "puca" by the Incas) was so highly valued by the Incas that it was used as a currency from 750 CE.[1] When Hernán Cortés invaded Mexico in 1519, he found Moctezuma II in beautiful robes dyed in brilliant red from the cochineal. Cortés brought the dye back to Spain, where the Spanish used it to create scarlet. Because of its scarcity, scarlet became associated with wealth and power, finding uses in cardinals' robes and military jackets for the British Army. Reds and oranges still permeate Latin American culture today.[2]

Below: **Buddhist architecture, Bangkok, Thailand. Color symbolism is an important part of Buddhist art and ritual.**

Opposite top left: **Ming dynasty, Hongzhi mark and period, 1488–1505. This porcelain dish was painted in under-glaze blue with yellow over-glaze enamels. The yellow glaze, added to previously glazed dishes enhances the blue motifs making them stand out from the background.**

Opposite top right: *Virgin of Belén*, **Peru, Cuzco School, circa 1700–1720. The robes portrayed in this painting would have been dyed using cochineal red, popular as a dyestuff across the whole of Central America.**

Opposite bottom left: **The brilliant polychromatic glazes used on vases during the late Ming period are more complex in design, content, and color than the earlier monochromatic pieces.**

Opposite bottom right: **Mantle made from alpaca fiber in plain weave with stem stitch and loop stitch embroidery. Peru 200 BCE–CE 200. Here again, the richness and vibrancy of the predominant color red would have been achieved using cochineal dye.**

Another example of period color is "Ming dynasty blue," also known as "Hongwu" after the first emperor of the Ming dynasty. Although the earlier Yuan dynasty potters had introduced copper red and cobalt blue into their pottery, it did not become popular until the Ming dynasty. "Hongwu" was originally imported overland from Iran, in cake form. It was then ground and turned into a pigment that was painted onto the porcelain, which was subsequently glazed and fired.

Because of the lumpy consistency of the pigment, early Ming pottery was characterized by the unrefined use of thick lines and uneven wash tones. The quality of the paint improved when it was mixed with native cobalt oxide. Cobalt oxide was also used alone and modified for more delicate use with copper oxides. Additional decorative glaze colors used were celadon, red, green, and yellow. Creating beautiful pottery to glorify the dynasty and its benevolence, the potters used decorative design elements of dragons, flowers, and birds. Together, the design and color became representative of a great period in Chinese history.[3]

India is another nation whose colors geographically identify its culture. However, unlike the blue of the Ming dynasty, India's colors are not identified with a specific period in history. While the bright pinks, oranges, and reds that are found in tapestries, clothing, and architecture are ever-present in the culture, the idea of colorfulness is deeply rooted in historic ritual.

A prime example of this is Holi, a seasonal festival of colors that celebrates the rites of spring. Originally called the festival of Holika, Holi is a festival of merrymaking based on legends and mythology from India's history. It is a joyous celebration that brings people together regardless of caste or religion and includes the smearing of paint and throwing of pigments on each other.[4]

Right: **The Holi Festival is celebrated with great enthusiasm and positivity. The pigmented color intrinsic to Indian culture is pure and at its highest intensity covers the crowds that spew it. The mixing of colors suggests national pride and casteless unity.**

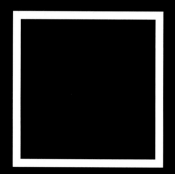

CHAPTER FOUR

TRENDS IN COLOR

EXPERT: **LESLIE HARRINGTON MBA PhD**
Executive Director of the Color Association of the United States, Leslie Harrington gained her degree
in Interior Design from The International Academy of Merchandising and Design, and her MBA from
Stern School of Business, New York University. Leslie Harrington is the principal of LH.Color.

**Could you talk about your career path and how you
ended up as head of the oldest color association in
the United States?**

My mother worked at Benjamin Moore Paints and I began
working there part-time, then full-time, before I went to
interior design school. After graduating, Benjamin Moore
asked me to return and become the color person for
Canada. In the 1980s the emphasis was on "preserve
and protect" rather than color choice, so I went across the
country lecturing to designers and architects on color
and trends, creating mood boards and promotional
material by hand. I talked about the emotional content of
color but I wanted a better basis for understanding color,
so I went to business school. Business school allowed me
to communicate with the business community. It gave me
a toolkit and a slightly different perspective with which I
could approach color, backed by business practices.
After that I studied for a Ph.D on the impact color and
emotion has on business sales. At this point I started my
own consulting firm creating color forecasts, so instead
of one product line I had to deal with everything from
fashion to pharmaceuticals. Because of my background
I could define what was happening and the reasons why
it was happening: we wanted colors that sell, not colors
that build inventory. I then became head of the Color
Association of the United States.

**Could you talk about how someone gets into the field
of color forecasting?**

If you want to be in the color field it is not only a matter of
learning about color in school, getting basic information,
or an internship. There are few jobs in color forecasting
because it is a small part of design marketing, so it's also
about the experience behind you and learning on the job.
Get a job with a trends organization like Stylesight or a
retailer like Target. Most companies have a marketing
person, or a designer, or a product development person,
but they usually don't have a color person on staff.

What does the color forecasting process entail?

Initially, color forecasting involved gathering information.
With technology and data, color forecasting today is not
what it will be in the future and the field will evolve to
meet people's demands. Part of what I do is to develop
what future forecasting will entail.

The forecasting process is intuitive. It benefits
from a collective rather than singular perspective, so I
bring together individuals from a variety of industries
each year and create mood boards consisting of what
they see around them. Then we pool the information
into various "buckets": the "Social Bucket" (pop culture,
red carpet films, music, TV shows, and so on); the
"Technology Bucket" (computers, cellphones, iPads,
and so on); the "Political Bucket" (conflict, political events,
campaigns, bills, and so on); and the "Economic Bucket"
(indexes, stock markets, inflation, and so on). Once we
have gathered everyone's information and hear their
conclusions, the big question to answer is why they
come to these conclusions.

From this information we can cut across all the
buckets for specific geographical regions or brands
or product lines for example fashion intimate apparel
Look at something globally and try to explain what is
happening, you will find that there are commonalities.
We also explore things that pop up that are uncommon.
We then we pull it altogether and look at it. it. Seasoned
veterans are more accurate in there forecasts because
they know how it pulls together. They are more aware
of what the population can feel comfortable with at the
time of the forecast. Timing is everything.

In order to be good at forecasting you must
have a world view and an understanding of what the
marketplace will bear. You must be able to translate
information to a particular product line, determining what
consumers will want. The work will include everything
from providing just colors, through to a color story or
theme, complete with full palette development.

THE 1940s AND 1950s The color palettes of an era are a reflection of the sentiments of the period. We have explored how the socio-political and historical environment can influence popular color choices, but these colors can become so intrinsic to cultural history that they establish themselves as identifiers of the period itself. However, color palettes evolve over time, so just as history does not stop precisely on a decade marker, so it is with color. As a result, period color palettes naturally include some of the colors from the previous decade, adding new ones to the mix and discarding some of the older ones.

This was the case with the colors of the 1940s and 1950s, whose color palettes stemmed from two earlier design movements: Art Deco and Mid-Century Modern. The style of the 1940s was defined by extreme circumstance. It was both tumultuous and prosperous, and could be characterized by satisfaction and doubt. 1940s color was also a time of color evolution. Although not as pronounced, the Art Deco palette of the 1930s still lingered, including the gold, silver, and copper that stemmed from Art Deco architecture, the mauves and apricots of its decorative arts, and the browns and greens taken from nature.[1]

Above: **Models sporting Berketrex Utility wartime Fashions designed by Norman Hartnell.**

Left: Poster by Austin Cooper produced by the railway companies to advocate cutting back on train travel for the good of the war effort.

Right: **This wartime poster perfectly illustrates the predominant colors in the US during the Second World War: khaki, red, white, and blue.**

Are you a girl with a Star-Spangled heart?

JOIN THE WAC NOW !

THOUSANDS OF ARMY JOBS NEED FILLING !

Women's Army Corps
United States Army

The Second World War changed perspectives and production. With rationing and war, color and design styles were conservative and clothing became simple and utilitarian. The demand for military goods changed production directions, leading to shortages and rationing—the American textiles industry was monitored by the government and voluntarily self-limited the production of goods. The color palette became dominated by the war, and was based on a palette of khaki, olive greens, grays, and patriotic blues—bright colors such as red and orange were used mostly as an accent.[2]

Left: The green/gray khaki "dress blues" palette reflects the military attire of the Second World War. The War effort influenced clothing and its design, expressing frugality and subdued color. Money was put toward the War effort, and even food was rationed during this time.

At the end of the war and the beginning of the post-military boom, color returned to design, although it was still somewhat restrained. The color palette began to shift to what became known as Mid-Century Modern, picking up with the introduction of brighter colors and deeper tones. Greens, purples, cool blues, yellows, and warm reds were added to the palette.

Prefabricated homes started to be manufactured, and paint companies flourished, pointing buyers in the direction of the apricots and mauves from the recent past, but with the addition of light yellows, grass greens, and off white for their interiors.

Christian Dior, the famous French design house, created a new look that spared little when it came to color and fabric, in order to express affluence. Dior used light, feminine hues that were far removed from the art deco colors of the pre-war days and introduced two-piece outfits comprised of curvaceous, bell-shaped skirts and waist-cinching jackets. Corsets and hip pads were used to accentuate the bell shape, and dresses were soft and romantic.[3] Although McCarthyism and an outright fear of communism loomed, the 1950s were characterized by optimism and the rise of equality. Color-wise, there was a return to innocence, with pastel colors of pink, turquoise, mint green, pale yellow, and blue becoming popular. Prosperity was also reflected in the advent of gardening colors: white ginger, fully saturated pale pink, sea foam green, and kingfisher blue. While the palette was soft, the idea was to use color combinations that created contrast and interest.[4]

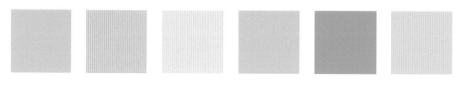

Top right: **Marlene Dietrich** in a Dior dress circa 1950. The pastel pink/peach of her dress was a signature color of the early 1950s.

Right: With the advent of new materials and technologies pastel colors—pink, pale yellow, mint green—were applied to the home. With the end of World War II people now had the means to have their own home and suburban life flourished.

Opposite top left: **Television** stars such as Lucille Ball became trendsetters. Her personality and striking looks embodied the bright spirit of a modern woman in the 1950s. Modern colors were clean and bright and included vibrant yellow, deeper oranges, and grass greens. Brightly colored Fiestaware became popular too.

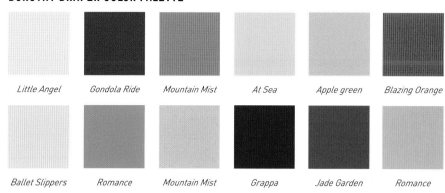

Little Angel	Gondola Ride	Mountain Mist	At Sea	Apple green	Blazing Orange
Ballet Slippers	Romance	Mountain Mist	Grappa	Jade Garden	Romance

Color also began to be applied to everyday products such as Tupperware and Fiestaware, which came in rose, chartreuse, gray, and forest green. Bold designs such as stars, stripes, checks, and polka dots came into vogue, while atomic graphics inspired by space and science, as well as fruit, flowers, and abstract designs were everywhere. Chrome and vinyl dining sets were created in pink and blue; kitchen cabinets went from primary colors to pastels; and pink and black were often seen in bathrooms and kitchens.

The Mid-Century Modern palette continued to be of influence with its yellows, apricots, and grass greens, but other popular interior colors were navy blue, red, and white. The Scandinavian color palette—which included shades of brown, cream, gray, and green—was also often used on the exterior of houses.

A great designer of this period, who relied on the modern palette of deep tones and bold colors, was Dorothy Draper. An accomplished columnist for Good Housekeeping Magazine, as well as an author, and a textile designer for Schumacher, Draper was one of America's greatest trendsetters. Her designs included the interiors of TWA jets and the Packard automobile for Chrysler, the restaurant at the Metropolitan Museum of Art, New York (nicknamed "The Dorotheum"),

and The Greenbrier in White Sulphur Springs, West Virginia. With the design of The Greenbrier, Draper was asked to redecorate with "romance and rhododendrons," which she did using vibrant, "splashy" colors in never-before-seen combinations, such as aubergine and pink with a "splash" of chartreuse and a touch of turquoise blue. She used cabbage rose chintz, paired with bold stripes; her "dull" white and "shiny" black checkered floors.[5]

Above: **Dorothy Draper**—thought of as the founder of interior design—used incredible bold colors and flowery prints in her design projects. Her palette, referred to as American Baroque, reflected growing delight in deep reds and greens. One of her greatest achievements was The Greenbrier luxury resort in West Virginia.

THE 1960s AND 1970s The Abstract Expressionist art movement that developed through the 1940s and 1950s was a clue to what was going to occur in the 1960s. The artists' utilization of color to express personal emotions and their desire to free themselves from the classical ideology could be seen as the beginning of the breakup of the conventional conformity of 1950s society.

An anti-establishment feeling had bubbled up in the 1950s, but it exploded in the 1960s. This tumultuous period became synonymous with the breakdown of idealism, and disillusionment with irresponsible excess and inequality. Playing a key part in this were the "flower children," or hippies, who created their own style of dress, music, art, and lifestyle. The hippie look consisted of ethnic prints, with Indian saris used as bedspreads, curtains, and wall hangings. Colors were inspired by nature, with green, gold, orange, and yellow being found on everything from clothes to home decor. Combinations such as fuchsia pink and tangerine orange were placed side by side, while bright, metallic vinyl wallpapers were also popular. The desired effect was a striking, provocative look—it was an age of heightened awareness and the colors and design of the era reflected it.[6]

The pastels of the 1950s gave way to bright and daring colors, seen in Marimekko fabric designs and the work of Pop Artists such as Andy Warhol and Peter Max. Marimekko's simple and bold graphic style related well to the Pop Art movement, which borrowed brightly colored graphic images from ordinary household products. Andy Warhol's work used bold primary colors straight out of the tube, in a similar fashion to the Fauvists. Rather than emotion, however, Warhol's non-representational colors reflected the pop culture that inspired him. In brilliantly colored images of Marilyn Monroe, Warhol experimented with screen printing, adopting commercial processes that were devoid of the human hand and personal originality.

Bold, non-representational color was also important to Peter Max, whose unique symbolism and vibrant color palette have continued to inspire new generations of Americans throughout the decades. Although environmental causes and animal rights were the subject of many of his paintings, his psychedelic, counter-culture imagery became so popular that in addition to painting, he designed everything from postage stamps to airplanes.

The 1970s were no less tumultuous. This era of independent thought and continued experimentation saw the growth of environmentalism, which was reflected in the color palette of the time. Pumpkin oranges and avocado greens joined harvest gold. The Native American movement expanded the period colors to include a natural palette of rich rusts and golds, gray-greens and teal, and in the late 1970s the punk movement shifted the color palette once again, with the inclusion of hot pinks and bright oranges, yellows, and blues.

Opposite left: **The idolization of the Kennedy clan turned Jackie Kennedy into a style icon. Many tried to emulate her, particularly, her use of color. She was a huge fan of Marimekko dresses.**

Opposite: **The 1970s were a time of experimentation and boldness. The art of Peter Max, an artist and designer known for his bright spectral color, exemplifies countercultural feeling and the psychedelic movement.**

Above right: **English model Twiggy sits cross-legged in an exotic tent constructed in Justin de Villeneuve's home, early 1970s.**

Right: **One trend that characterized the 1960s and 1970s was the back-to-nature sentiment reflected in color palettes—harvest gold, rust, pumpkin, and avocado became very popular at the time.**

THE 1980s AND 1990s The final decades of the twentieth century saw increased conservatism, which led to deregulation and laissez-faire economics. While President Reagan and the Republican Party preached less government interference, strong international relations led the United States to expand its realm of influence.

The pluralism of the 1980s affected color choices. Yuppies—baby boomers with a college education, who entered the job market with well-paying jobs and expensive tastes—adopted a conservative look based on gray, beige, and olive. Fashion designer, Ralph Lauren, added forest greens, crimsons, and golds to the colors of the era, while Laura Ashley, a Welsh fashion designer, developed a line of small prints where muted colors—blues, grays, mauves, and soft pinks—dominated the color palette.

These conservatively elegant palettes contrasted strongly with the colors of the Memphis design collective and the clothing designer Yves Saint Laurent, who both utilized intense color in their designs. Memphis—a Milan-based design collective founded by Ettore Sottsass in December 1980—consisted of both architects and designers who created postmodern furniture, fabrics, ceramics, glass, and metal objects throughout the 1980s. Often made with plastic laminates, the furniture used gaudy colors, kitsch motifs, and asymmetric shapes that lent it a feeling of playfulness. Some pieces resembled sculptures covered with patterns such as green and yellow "snake-skin" or brown "tortoiseshell." Colors were primary with some light blues, tans, and black.

Algerian fashion designer Yves Saint Laurent came of age in the 80s, introducing the world to colors influenced by his North African background. As a result, magentas, oranges, and pin-based tans, as well as greens, became popular.

Right: **The 1980s began to see a rise in pluralism—grays, violets, and mauves became popular, such as this outfit by Yves Saint Laurent, 1981.**

Opposite left: **A piece by the Memphis Group, whose work was often made from plastic laminates and playfully kitsch. Colors were usually primary, however, patterns such as faux green and yellow snakeskin and brown tortoiseshell were favored.**

Opposite right: **In the 1990s, global warming became a very real issue and was brought to the forefront of public debate. This, together with an increasing awareness of other climate change issues, saw the environmental movement grow at a staggering rate, embraced wholeheartedly by the counterculture movement. A byproduct of this was the predominance of greens in fashion and design.**

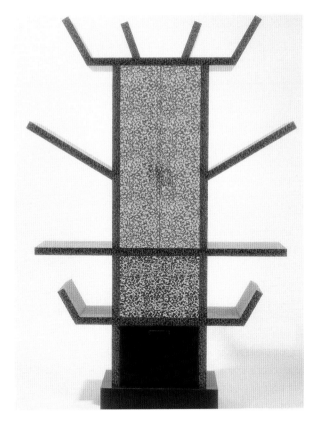

In the 1990s, design and color in the United States very much paralleled social developments. Republican attitudes strengthened, with an expansion of preppy values. The magentas, mauves, pinks, and greens of the 1980s continued to be in the color forefront, but color and design influences from other cultures brought bright, rich, warm colors: earth browns and yellows from Africa and hot reds, purples, pinks, grass greens, and bright yellows from Mexican products and merchandise.[7]

At the same time, the anti-materialistic "grunge" movement arose, that encouraged the wearing of thrift store clothing, plaid shirts, and denim jeans. It was an unkempt look that saw black, grays, dark browns, and reds permeate the cultural color palette.[8]

The green environmental movement also grew in strength, with lime green and chartreuse becoming popular, as well as colors of spiritual quietness, such as pastel yellows, greens, and turquoise.[9]

THE TWENTY-FIRST CENTURY Life in the twenty-first century is evolving and expanding in a world faced with both celebration and trauma on a near-daily basis. It is a time of rapid change, accompanied by the problems and pleasures that are part of the process.

In a world of pluralism and globalization, differing ideologies create conflict and unrest. The earliest part of the twenty-first century saw terrorist actions on a global scale, and dramatic governmental reorganizations, especially in the Middle East. It was a period of renewed conservancy, which saw crusade-like religious fervor and radical extremism.

The start of the twenty-first century was an era of emerging economies, with a variety of cultural outlooks and increasing disparity between the one percent upper class and what remained of the middle classes. China rose to become a superpower, while the Brazilian, Russian, and Indian economies also expanded. As a result, ethnic brights from emerging countries saw sunny yellows, true turquoises, warm oranges, teal, and reds becoming part of the palette popular at this time.

Green came to fore, in environmental sense and in people's yearning for calmness and tranquility. Outdoor life and exercise became important so simple, earthy colors became prominent: stone and other earth colors; blues matching the color of sky and water; and botanical greens. Organic and pearlescent finishes become popular because of their natural look.

While the economic crisis looms large in much of the Western world, cooled-down, grayed-out browns and grays satisfy our urge toward classic colors in an economically-challenged time. They offer a softer option than black, which seems harsh, and brown, which doesn't seem strong enough.

The times are culturally and socio-politically complex, with a desire to commune with nature—as long as personal technology is also available. The colors become a mix of faded vintage and neon bright—it is both minimal and full spectrum as past, present, and future live together and geographical lines are blurred.

With the rise of internet communications everyone is exposed to design culture everywhere, and while we have yet to see what the future holds for the twenty-first century, this eclectic period of change and opposites is sure to reveal many possibilities in terms of directions, lifestyles, color, and design.

Below left & right & oppsite top left: With increased travel and international exposure the Chinese, Brazilian, and Indian economies continue to expand. Colors with punch, such as yellow, turquoise, orange, teal, and red become the mainstream palette, and bright neons are contrasted with blacks and grays.

Opposite bottom left: Environmentalism continues to grow and getting back to Mother Nature is very much in vogue. As a result, greens and earth tones are very popular.

Opposite right: Cool grays and browns are ever popular and offer a softer option to black, which seems stark in comparison. Office chic becomes more casual.

PART THREE

APPRECIATING COLOR

CHAPTER ONE

THE HISTORY OF COLOR IN PAINTING

EXPERT: **NANCY FRIESE**

Professor Nancy Friese's paintings and prints have been exhibited nationally and internationally. The recipient of several prestigious competitions and awards, Friese was elected to the National Academy (Museum and School in New York City) and received two National Endowment for the Arts Fellowships and the Japan-US Friendship Commission Creative Artist Fellowship. Friese is represented by Cade Tompkins Projects.

Could you talk about your background in terms of how you became interested in painting and what you do now?

I started art school when I was 25 and was immediately committed to being an artist for life. I went to The Art Academy of Cincinnati, Yale University Summer School of Music and Art at Norfolk, and The University of California at Berkeley Graduate Program before getting my MFA from Yale University School of Art. I enjoyed art as a child and took painting lessons where we copied masterworks. My family was nature-oriented and I became a landscape painter-printmaker. Initially I tried to be expressive in color, and through the years I have moved more toward naturalism.

Tell me about your work.

I work in open air and follow the trajectory of historical landscape artists around the globe. The experience of observing and translating the natural world is revelatory and exhilarating from ordinary locales to sites on travels. Each sitting brings changes in color. I work in oils, large-scale watercolors, and in printmaking.

What is your painting process?

I start with broad color areas covering the canvas or paper and deepen the tonal range slowly. I am always trying to re-invent the way the color sits in a place—by stretching the underlying hue or corollary hue of an object or space. My works begin bright and intense, and slowly move toward more balanced and integrative color. How much of one color can I use in intensity and still keep it within the plane it sits? How do I isolate my looking so I can paint in smaller shapes of flat pre-mixed colors? How do I use peripheral vision responses of color and give a focus as well? These are things that I think of when I am organizing shapes and lines into spatial reading and dynamic meetings.

My readers would be especially interested in how you make color choices. Could you elaborate on this?

After reading about, looking at, and trying various colors, I slowly move my work forward. All my past experience of art affects my color choices in combination with my particular sight and propensities. Choice of media also affects my approach to color. I want to keep the watercolor luminous so use very little solidly opaque color, while I enjoy laying down areas of opacity in oils. I work my way from bright colors to balanced colors. I think in turn about light/dark, bright/dull, warm/cool, and complementary/analogous colors. I like to surprise myself with broader areas countering a multitude of smaller color events. Broad planes can carry ten colors connected almost at any location or can be swathed in a broader singular color. The piece slowly comes together and moves me to a certain point of synthesis. After I am inside, I look at the piece, recognize what I did, and may add some heightening or dulling to hold the piece together.

How do you think that your color choices influence the content, in other words what role does color play in your work?

I see color and form as the content of my work within the role of landscape. How an artist thinks is so clear through the color choices that he or she makes. One can figure out the intention through the color. It is a big, long color stream moving constantly from genre to genre and from era to era.

Which great colorists influence your work?

I can look equally to the past with interest at Gwen John's color as well as Ernst Kirchner's color. When I was at Giverny as an artist-in-residence, I spent the six months reading and looking carefully at Claude Monet's paintings and that time to more deeply look into one artist's color choices was very special.

COLOR AS LIGHT At the time of the French Revolution and the onset of the Age of Reason, artists found it within their scope to choose their subject matter freely. This led to painters such as the Neoclassical French painter Jacques-Louis David (1748–1825) and Spanish painter Francisco Goya (1746–1828) discarding the established traditions in lieu of personal choice. The content of Goya's work was not idealized, but rather true to life, reflecting the concepts of immediacy and reality that were hot topics in Parisian cafes of the time.

J. M. W. Turner (1775–1851), a British landscape painter, is often referred to as "the painter of light," and may be credited as one of the greatest influences on Impressionist painting. Turner believed that nature was a reflection of human feelings and emotions, so wanted to imbue his paintings with motion, color, and light, making them both striking and energizing to the eye. What came out of this new irreverence was the ability of an artist to choose not only what he painted, but also how he expressed it.

Below: *Keelmen Heaving in Coals by Moonlight*, 1835, by J. M. W. Turner, the British landscape artist commonly referred to as "the painter of light."

Édouard Manet (1832–1883) was both a Realist painter and an Impressionist. While he preferred to paint from life, he disregarded traditional modeling and perspective, focusing instead on modern urban subjects. His paint application differed from traditional painters in that he abandoned glazes and blended brush strokes. Rather than build up colors in layers, Manet preferred to choose a color that would create the desired effect and apply it directly on the canvas, placing discrete areas of color side by side. Working in this way meant artists were no longer subject to long periods of drying between layers, enabling a faster painting technique that was better suited to capturing light quickly— something that was crucial to the Impressionist movement and its philosophy.

Key figures in the Impressionist movement included Eugène Boudin (1824–1898), Camille Pissarro (1830–1903), Edgar Degas (1834–1917), Paul Cézanne (1839–1906), Alfred Sisley (1839–1899), Claude Monet (1840–1926), Berthe Morisot (1841–1895), and Pierre-Auguste Renoir (1841–1919). These artists shared an interest in modern subjects, "plein-air" painting, and bright colors, which was made available in part through the development of paint tubes by artist John Rand (1801–1873).[1]

The movement got its name from Monet's painting *Impression, Sunrise* (1872). In his painting of Le Havre harbor in the early morning, Monet was particularly concerned with the pictorial representation of light, which he tried to capture with color. The

Below: *Impression, Sunrise*, 1872, by Claude Monet. The harbor in Le Havre captured in the early morning.

COLOR AS LIGHT

artists sought to capture the appearance of fleeting momentary images rather than create a precise replica of nature, so color takes precedence and the style relaxes the boundary between foreground and background in pictorial space. However, in doing this, the resulting lines and contours caused their paintings to appear "unfinished" to many other artists of the time.

Monet painted many landscapes in this way, including his *Haystacks* and *Water Lilies* series. He yearned to paint what he experienced, and when he was introduced to the concept of plein-air painting by Boudin, Monet left the studio to paint on site. He often worked outside directly on large-scale canvases, before returning to his studio to re-work and complete them. Influenced by Japanese prints, Monet abandoned conventional color application, believing that a painting changes when the light changes, so it must be handled with quick brushstrokes. He used light-colored grounds of white, light gray, or yellow. Colors were often used straight from the tube and mixed on the canvas, with wet paint applied on top of wet paint to blur the image. He built up texture through his brush strokes, creating vibrant surface grays and darks using complementary colors; browns and blacks were removed from his palette by 1886. According to James Heard in his book, *Paint Like Monet*, analysis of Monet's paintings shows that he used lead white, chrome and cadmium yellow, viridian, emerald green, French ultramarine, cobalt blue, Rose Madder, and vermilion.[2]

The concept of capturing color and light was carried further by artist Georges Seurat (1859–1891). Seurat painted in the late nineteenth century using the Impressionist method, but employed his studies of color vision to create a style known as "pointillism," in which a picture is created using small dabs of juxtaposed color. Rather than combining on the canvas, the color is fused by the eye: when a painting is viewed up close a series of dots appears, but viewed from a distance a coherent image is created.

Seurat's palette consisted of flake white, cadmium yellow, vermilion, Rose Madder, emerald green, cerulean blue, Prussian blue, French ultramarine, and cobalt violet.[3] Although his paintings became areas of color without linear definition, Seurat was able to render simplified representational forms, little realizing that the ideology and technique that he employed would remain integral to art and design today.

Left: *A Sunday Afternoon on the Island of La Grande Jatte*, 1884, by Georges Seurat. It is interesting to note the contrast between the bottom third and the top two thirds of the painting in terms of light. The bottom third is cast in a shadow where the grass is a combination of mostly blues and violets, whereas the sunlit grass contains mostly yellows and oranges.

FEELING COLOR When the early Impressionists threw out the use of realistic color and structured drawing, they had no idea how far their free painting style would lead their descendants: Manet was unaware that his use of flat areas of color might lead to a flattening of space on the modernist canvas, for example. Those who wished merely to paint an impression with respect to light and color did not foresee that painters and sculptors alike would not only personalize what they saw and felt, but that the painting itself would become modified or absent of any detectable figuration.

Great colorists such as Vincent van Gogh (1853–1890), Paul Gauguin (1848–1903), Edvard Munch (1863–1944), and Henri Matisse (1869–1954) took these concepts to heart and created a link between the Post Impressionists and the German Expressionists. Their distortions of figure-ground relationships, and their ability to discard the actual color of an object for emotional preference and feeling made them strong predecessors to the movement.

Van Gogh was known for his use of bold color and the textural application of paint—he used the pure-color brush strokes of the Impressionists to express personal emotional fervor. His painting, *Starry Night* (1889), was a subjective expression of the evening sky outside of his sanatorium room window at Saint-Rémy-de-Provence. Its swirling rich blues, intertwined with golden yellows, move around the canvas over a seemingly quiet village. In this whirling gestural landscape, van Gogh exposed the viewer to his feelings, his experiences, and his own personal vision. While the colors of *Starry Night* are predominantly blue and yellow, the colors of the artist's palette included yellow ocher, chrome yellow, cadmium yellow, chrome orange, vermilion, Prussian blue,

ultramarine, lead white, zinc white, emerald green, red lake, red ocher, raw sienna, and black. Another painter who based his work on personal expression was Paul Gauguin. While he began his career as an Impressionist, his wanderlust caused him to travel to the hinterlands of Tahiti where he was immersed in its primitive culture and art. His travels encouraged him to create works with strength and intensity of feeling, with the application of simpler, flatter forms, and strong color patches. The influence of the tropical landscape and the culture caused Gauguin to paint with a greater freedom than the French color palette allowed, with the ability to utilize distortion in his images. The artist's use of color was bold and expressive, and sometimes uncomfortable. In his paintings we see characteristic blues, yellows, bright reds, oranges, and olive greens, which are often combined with heavy black lines. Gauguin's color choices, their disproportionate use, and his focus on expression over beauty, made him a forerunner of the Symbolist movement, which set out to express emotions and ideas, rather than realistic images.

Left: It is interesting to note van Gogh's interest in combining both natural and artificial light in this painting, *Starry Night*, 1889. The sky, portrayed by light values of sky colors is lit up with the light from the moon and the stars; while within the village below the windows are aglow from internal illumination.

Right: Paul Gauguin's *Fatata te Miti (By the Sea)*, 1892, was painted during his first trip to Tahiti. The painting depicts two women by the sea, about to bathe, and a figure of a male fisherman with a spear in the distance. Gauguin has combined three-dimensional sculpting of the human figure with flat two-dimensional rendering. He has captured a romanticized view of Tahitian life and the landscape.

FEELING COLOR

A key Symbolist painter, Edvard Munch used color and design to depict psychological feelings and moods: "In an age wracked with anxiety and uncertainty, my sufferings are part of my self and my art. They are indistinguishable from me, and their destruction would destroy my art."[4] Munch believed that the artist is not someone who represents nature, but someone who conveys his experience with it. *The Scream* (1893) is one of Munch's most famous works, and in it he was able to convey immediate emotion with expressive color, swirling movement, and distortion.

Another movement of the period that was involved with non-representational color was the Fauvist movement, led by Henri Matisse. In its desire to "liberate color from the natural world," this anti-materialist movement wanted not only to free color, but also to simplify form. To this end, Matisse created paintings that expressed emotion using wild colors with no regard to reality. Although he maintained some sense of figurative representation, Matisse often flattened his images creating a series of patterns rather than three-dimensional forms.

In his painting *Purple Robe and Anemones* (1937), Matisse flattened the image by defining the structures with bold black lines. His complementary color palette and bold black brushstrokes weave the figure and ground together, while the intensity of the color further flattens the images. Although there is figurative reference, the color line and form play a far more significant role.

Left: *The Invocation*, 1903, by Paul Gauguin. Through his color choices and focus on expression instead of beauty, the artist became a forerunner of the Symbolist movement.

Right: *The Scream*, 1893, by Edvard Munch. A focal area surrounding the figure is created by a vertical stripe painted on the right edge of the canvas meeting a diagonal formed by the rail both painted with an intense orange color. The figure's head is contrasted by a dark blue swath.

COLOR AS CONTENT: GEOMETRIC ABSTRACTION, SHAPED CANVASES, MINIMALISM

While taking on different orientations throughout the twentieth century, the Expressionist movement has played an integral role in modern art. Characterized by freedom and rebellion from established academic art, the movement utilized intense personal expression, portrayed through simplified or distorted forms and exaggerated, sometimes discordant color palettes.

Expressionism has included both abstract and figurative work. Early figurative work is characterized by German Expressionists such as Franz Marc (1880–1916) and Ludwig Kirchner (1880–1938). Franz Marc was influenced strongly by van Gogh's use of emotive brushstrokes and expressive color, form, and composition to create images of contemporary life, as well as by the work of Wassily Kandinsky (1866–1944). Marc believed that nature offered spiritual redemption, and that there was "godliness" in animals. This was demonstrated in

his series of painting of horses, in which the rounded shapes of the animals interact with each other and the background. Marc painted the horses using each of the three primary colors to evoke some sort of metaphysical symbolism. He expressed his feelings on color: "yellow, a 'gentle, cheerful, and sensual' color, symbolized femininity, while blue, representing the 'spiritual and intellectual,' symbolized masculinity."[5]

Another German Expressionist painter and printmaker, Ernst Ludwig Kirchner, used intense color

and simplified forms like Marc, but he preferred to paint mostly nudes, urban nightlife, and portraits. Kirchner used rough brush strokes, angular forms, and clashing colors to portray personal angst. In *Street, Dresden* (1908), Kirchner used awkward perspectives and exaggerated emotional color to convey feelings of anxiety and alienation in relations to urban living. The disproportionate amount of pink enhances the perspective, pulling it forward and making the figures look as if they are resting against the ground rather than standing on it. Only two or three faces are distinguishable and they are painted in orange and muddy green. They are looking forward rather than at each other enhancing their loneliness.

The influence of European art and the German Expressionist movement on the Abstract Expressionists was made possible by a plethora of new shows at the Museum of Modern Art and the Museum of Non-Objective Painting (a predecessor of the Guggenheim) that featured cubism, abstract art, Dadaism, surrealism,

and an important retrospective of Matisse. The focus of the art world shifted from Paris to New York, and many great European artists of the time—Piet Mondrian (1872–1944), Fernand Léger (1881–1955), and Hans Hofmann (1880–1966), for example—relocated to the United States.

On his arrival in the United States, Hofmann became an influential teacher of modern art. He believed that art was spiritual and that nature was a source of inspiration. Hofmann's intense use of color and design stemmed from the influence of the cubists and the fauvists. Working with color and spatial relationships, Hofmann studied the structure of the picture plane, placing rectangular areas of intense color next to each other to create a spatial dynamic between them. By changing the proportion, placement, and scale of the shapes he altered spatial reality and classical perspective. His students included many Abstract Expressionists such as Joan Mitchell (1925–1992), Wolf Kahn (1927–), Helen Frankenthaler (1928–2011), and Frank Stella

Left: **Franz Marc's painting,** *The Little Yellow Horses,* **1912. According to James Harris MD, in his article "Art and Images in Psychiatry," yellow represents the feminine qualities of "cheerfulness and sensuality while the blues represent masculinity." In this painting, the curvaceous lines of the horses themselves could seemingly represent femininity surrounded and encompassed by a blue background.**

Right: **In Ernst Ludwig Kirchner's** *Street, Dresden,* **1908, the singularity of light value on the figure in the foreground enhances her seeming self-absorption in her own thoughts. She stands out from the crowd and creates a focal point to express Kirchner's personal dismay.**

(1936–), as well as Lee Krasner (1908–1994), a painter in her own right and wife of Jackson Pollack (1912–1956).

Troubled by the lack of humanity they saw in the world, young artists in America in the 1940s and 1950s felt compelled to express their concerns. The American Expressionists chose to do this using monumental canvases and spontaneous gestural painting. They were influenced by both primitivism and the Jungian idea of the "collective unconscious"—they wanted to paint timeless and powerful subject matter with directness and immediacy.

Both Lee Krasner and Jackson Pollack worked with gestural painting, with Pollock abandoning his brushes in favor of "drip painting"—a radical technique that involved placing the canvas on the floor and throwing and pouring paint across it. Pollock wanted to create "pure painting" with emotional intensity, capturing it's fleeting quality with vigor and strength.[6] Pollack's knowledge of physics allowed him to understand the way in which colors would flow, realizing both spontaneity and control.

Lee Krasner saw the importance of the personal expression that her husband employed, but her approach was slightly different—the grids of Mondrian and the colors of Matisse influenced Krasner's painting style. In her Little Image series (1946–1950) she utilized small, highly textured squares to create compositions in a semi grid-like fashion. The grid is more obvious in some paintings than others, but the brightly colored surfaces are filled with the movement of layered, interlocking brushstrokes to create an intimate modeled surface.

While gestural painting was explicitly about capturing emotions and personal expression, there were Expressionists who believed that emotions could be portrayed in ways different to the wild gestures of Pollack. These painters remained interested in creating fields of modulated color, but worked purely with the expressive potential of color, rather than with thick, gestural strokes.

While their paintings were large in scale (like those of the gesture-based Expressionists), the Color Field painters focused on a contemplative spiritual experience that was devoid from memories and associations. The paintings were to be felt as an experience that enveloped the viewer, freeing them from the materiality of everyday life.

Mark Rothko (1903–1970) explored the concept of spirituality, as a result of which he was asked to design a series of canvases for a chapel in Houston, Texas. The chapel was funded by Houston philanthropists, John and Dominique de Menil, and is a tranquil and meditative place. It is designed in a circle, so the worshiper can sit on benches surrounded by Rothko's work, which consists of floor to ceiling rectangular paintings on every wall. In order to complete the project, Rothko hired two assistants to apply the paint in quick strokes in several layers, comprising brick reds, deep reds, and black mauves.

For much of his mature work Rothko explored the emotive, spiritual qualities of color and shape. Placing colored rectangular shapes horizontally on vertical canvases, he created a spatial dynamic for studying the relationship between warm and cool colors on the flat picture plane. Rothko explored the compositional potential of color and form on the human psyche, and his personal philosophy intertwined with the Chapel's mission statement as "a place to inspire people to action through art and contemplation, to nurture reverence for the highest aspirations of humanity, and to provide a forum of global concerns."[7]

At this time, colorists were exploring other techniques of visual expression. Helen Frankenthaler, an abstract expressionist whose works spanned six decades, painted directly onto unprimed canvases so that the material could absorb the colors. In her piece Canyon (1965), which she painted in acrylics, she created a large stain that flowed outward from a boldly colored center. While concerned with formal issues of the color-shape relationships, the large red field is surrounded by a blue-green area, which suggests a reference to nature. This staining process would influence the work of Morris Louis (1912–1962), a second-generation Color Field painter and part of the Washington Color School.

Right: Lee Krasner, *Composition*, 1949. It is interesting to note that while she applied pure color pigment, at its highest intensity with spatulas and sticks, because of mixed colors on the canvas surface some grays and low intensity color resulted. In addition she applied white thickly on top to create hieroglyphic like structures.

SECOND-GENERATION COLOR ABSTRACTIONISTS

Following in the footsteps of Rothko, abstract painters of the 1950s and 1960s continued to try and rid their work of any sense of gesture, pictorial depth, or illusion, but still working predominately with color and form. Sub-movements within Color Field painting were established including the Washington Color School and Hard-edge Painting. In addition to fields, these movements utilized stripes, washes, and geometric forms. Artists of this time period focused on a linear approach, their goal being to apply color to flat surfaces to create a sense of overall uniformity and consistency. They expanded their possibilities with new techniques, such as using unprimed canvases, synthetic mediums, and staining.

Morris Louis, considered a member of the Washington Color School, utilized Frankenthaler's technique of stain painting to create large-scale paintings on unprimed and unstretched canvas, in which blank areas were contrasted with areas of color. He made his stain paintings by tilting the canvas while he poured a mixture of paint and turpentine directly onto it. In *Blue Veil* (1958–1959), the translucent layers of paint mix and blend their colors on the surface, with purer, unmixed areas about the edges.

Ellsworth Kelly (1923–) combined the spirituality of Rothko with hard-edged painting. Differing from other abstract artists he believed that abstracted works should be derived from observed reality. In his piece *Spectrum V* (1969) he created thirteen evenly painted panels in different colors, which when hung on the wall together created an almost architectural feel.

Hard-edge painters were also sometimes considered to be part of the Op Art movement, which is based on the idea that optical effects are part of the perceptual process. Within an optical illusion, perceptual ambiguities can be created through the use of color, line, and shape. These ambiguities create a different perception than the reality of the work, allowing motion and color to "shift" as a result of element placement. Prominent artists of this movement include Victor Vasarely (1906–1997), Carlos Cruz-Diez (1923), Yaacov Agam (1928–), Julian Stanczak (1928–), Richard

Below left: Richard Anuszkiewicz's, *Iridescence*, 1965. One can see Albers' influence here. The underlying structure resembles the Homage to the Square series, but instead there are linear elements that lead the eye in to the central area. While Albers often stays within the same palette family, Anuszkiewicz uses complementary colors and value contrast.

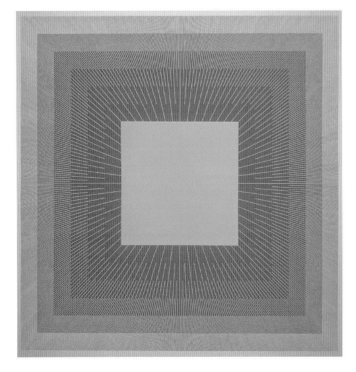

Left: Julian Stanczak's *Filtered Yellow*, 1968. In this optical painting Stanczak uses simple shapes and linearity to convey color light relationships and perception.

Above: Morris Louis's *Blue Veil*, c.1958–59. While this is a large-scale painting/installation piece there is softness to the staining process that gives the piece a drapery-like feeling and adds dimension, form, and movement.

Anuszkiewicz (1930–), and Bridget Riley (1931–), based on theories stemming back to the teachings and work of Joseph Albers (see page 41).

Two direct disciples of Albers were Julian Stanczak and Richard Anuszkiewicz. In an interview with the artist, Stanczak talks about color and his work. He says: "My primary interest is color—the energy of the different wavelengths of light and their juxtapositions. The primary drive of colors is to give birth to light. But light always changes; it is evasive. I use the energy of this flux because it offers me great plasticity of action on the canvas. Color is abstract, universal—yet personal and private in experience. It primarily affects us emotionally, not logically as do tangible things. Color is non-referential. By itself, it cannot easily be measured or quantified. For our sense of order and self-preservation, we grasp for measurements, fixed entities, and control in order to formulate our relationship with our environment. Sizes and locations are scrupulously observed and remembered to satisfy the logic of the brain, which inquires, 'What is it that I am looking at?' and 'Where is it in space?' So I ask, 'How can I dish out colors—colors that create beautiful melodies—without forms that will contain them?' As a colorist, I have to have the means to measure the density of the actions of one color against another. I must have form. Yet in the end, I do not want form for form's sake. I want to shout or whisper through colorants acting against each other and create experiences that are more than they are factually. That is how visual poetry can be achieved."[8]

Anuszkiewicz was also interested in color and juxtaposition, and studied the illusions that were created by attaching high intensity complementary colors to the same structure. It is interesting to note his Monet-like concern with how the light and time of day affected his sculptures.

DESCRIPTIVE ART Whether figurative or abstract, color and light were a preeminent force in the creation of art in the twentieth century. While new realism appeared to put content before form, and abstractionists put form as content, art of this time period, regardless of its direction, had both psychological and perceptual underpinnings.

Both abstraction and figurative art rely on the formal elements that include line, shape, color, volume, texture, and perspective. Many modern artists followed the direction of abstraction in their work, but there were others who kept true to the idea of seeking content from observation. Rather then making color, line, and form the subject matter and content of their work, they chose to continue to render what they saw.

Impressionists and Post-Impressionists of the late-nineteenth and early-twentieth century began to treat traditional subject matter in new and different ways, both in terms of technique and content. Rather than create an idealistic formalized rendition, these artists preferred to paint what they saw in everyday life. They painted landscapes, urban scenes of the city, workers on the farm, and bathers in the tub. Technically, they strived for immediacy and did away with classical layering. In the early twentieth century a type of contemporary figurative style was evolving in America. It was based on celebrating democratic ideals and creating paintings that were accessible to the masses, praising the contemporary life of rural, small town and urban America. This form of American realism includes such artists as Edward Hopper (1882–1967), Charles Burchfield (1893–1967), Reginald Marsh (1898–1954), and Jacob Lawrence (1917–2000), who each painted scenes of typical American life, yet with their own personal view of the world.

Hopper stated: "One of the weaknesses of much abstract painting is the attempt to substitute the inventions of the human intellect for a private imaginative conception." He painted what he saw around him, but it was his inner vision that created the uniqueness of his work. He believed that painting was the result of "subconscious expression" on the part of the artist. With oils, watercolors, and etchings, Hopper used balance and geometric form to suggest a narrative and create a broad emotional response from limited number of elements.

Both Hopper and Burchfield's greatest strength was their understanding of color and light. *Empty Barn and Sheds* (1917) portrays Burchfield's sophisticated understanding and ease of color application.

Thematically similar in content to Burchfield, Hopper's work revolved around a combination alienation and beauty of every day life. His use of light and shadow gave great strength and volume to his images. He stated: "We recognize visual form only by means of light and light only by means of form, and we further recognize that color is an effect of light in relation to form and its inherent texture. In nature light creates color; in painting color creates light."[9]

One can see Hopper's brilliant use of color and light in *Chop Suey* (1929), a painting of two women having a conversation in a restaurant. Hopper focuses on the way light hits the subjects, spilling in through the windows and highlighting areas with the intense warmth of yellows and oranges. The only other light area of the painting is done in the achromatic color of white, placed on the table and an angular shaped form coming from another window. The interior is contrasted with the complementary color of deep blues and greens.

Intensity of color was also important to Jacob Lawrence, whose paintings depicted visual narratives of important African Americans. He was known for his use of geometric figures and bold color, with his painting technique enhancing his ideology. Lawrence

Above: *The Migration Series, Panel No. 1: During World War I there was a great migration north by southern African Americans*, 1940–41, by Jacob Lawrence is one of 60 pieces painted simultaneously about African-American migration to northern industrialized cities. This image depicts flatly colored figures crowding together to form a surface pattern that suggests activity and motion.

Right: Edward Hopper's *Chop Suey*, 1929. Hopper uses both intensity and value in this painting to portray highlights. He uses bright yellows and oranges depicting the light that surrounds the figures in the foreground separating them from the remaining parts of the image.

created a visual storyboard on gesso hardboard panels, systematically applying flat areas of color, one at a time, starting with black and moving to increasingly lighter colors. In order to maintain consistency he would use colors out of the tube, only adding white paint. Using up to 60 panels, which could be viewed simultaneously, he would paint so as to create vertical and horizontal rhythms. In addition, he would use symbolic icons and words to represent the struggles of the African-American people.[10]

Milton Avery (1885–1965), whose work included portraits, still lifes, and landscapes, also painted areas of flat color. Because Avery stood staunchly outside the parameters of the art world, his independence of vision allowed him to bridge the gaps between abstraction and realism with his own personal aesthetic. While his figurative subject matter resembled realism, his technique combined the simplified forms and flat colors of artists such as Matisse with gestural brush-strokes and the use of a palette knife—and even his fingers—to create areas of modulated color in the style of the Expressionists.

Georgia O'Keeffe (1887–1986) is another artist whose work hung between reality and abstraction, also remained true to nature while using color and light as a tool to create beautiful organic forms. Whether it was a flower or complete abstraction, she was able to create depth through gentle shifts in the value and intensity of color. The concentration of hue varied in her paintings—some had bright, intense color, while others were muted—but she always worked with a limited palette. In the painting *Oriental Poppies* (1928), O'Keeffe uses color, shape, and texture to explore abstraction, while maintaining the figurative aspects of the subject. The poppies have no background. Instead, the floral color bleeds to the edge to enhance the abstracted nature of the image. An earlier piece from 1927 (which she aptly named *Abstraction White Rose*) integrates the foreground and background even further, losing some of the planar distinctions with the use of muted colors.[11] The paintings of Wolf Kahn show his involvement with nature and landscape, and his understanding of color and light. Arguably a landscape painter, Kahn is also considered a Color Field painter, whose use of radiant color and light evokes a sense of time and place. His color and spontaneity stemmed from Hans Hofmann's practice of using nature as a starting point. In his painting, *Cotton Barn at Beech Island, S.C.* (1998), Kahn uses intense pinks, violets, and oranges with muted greens to lend the painting an intensity of spirit combined with the quietness of contemplative nature that surrounds the barn.

Opposite top: *Cotton Barn at Beech Island, S.C.*, 1998. Using a complementary pair of colors Wolf Kahn creates a structure that is clearly depicted, but also dissolves into the landscape. By placing yellow on the bottom half of the farm building and carrying it into to the grass below, he defies the distinction between structure and landscape.

Opposite bottom: O'Keefe's *White Flower*, 1929, features a mostly monochromatic palette. This subtle use of color features in many of her works, including *Oriental Poppies*, 1928.

Left: In *Porch Sitters–Sally and March*, 1952, Milton Avery uses flat, simple shapes and ordinary everyday scenes to express his sophisticated color understanding.

TWENTY-FIRST CENTURY COLORISTS

Art in the twenty-first century is boundless in both material and direction. Technology has given artists the ability to create everything from paintings to installations, to crowd-sourced events. What used to be available only to museumgoers and private collectors now can be see on YouTube.

Approaches to visual expression have taken various directions that range from super realism to abstraction and much in between. Artists themselves are not pigeonholed and have expressed themselves in many directions. Collective artwork has become possible, bringing different points of view and styles together. Super-realists, such as Richard Estes and Janet Fish, use color and light to create reflection, transparency, and translucency, infusing their works with rich detail. Richard Estes' subject matter never seems to stray from the urban street scenes of New York City. His attention to shadows and the reflective and translucent qualities of glass allows him to create complex, but believable intertwined spaces. While Estes prefers dealing with urban landscapes, Janet Fish concentrates on still lifes. Her work is an interweaving of layers of transparent and translucent objects that are intertwined in such a way as to cohesively have an effect on one other.

Other contemporary artists have less involvement with accurate representation and focus more on graphic relationship's of form and color. Alex Katz, an iconic American modernist and figurative artist, well known for his portraiture depicting family and friends, creates flat planar elements to represent figures. Another artist working figuratively is British artist Chantal Joffe. Working mostly in large scale and depicting women and children, Joffe uses fashion photography, family snapshots, and advertising as inspiration. She works in oils and introduces distortion into her interpretation of the source images. Often Matisse-like in her approach to pattern, Joffe flattens the backgrounds in her paintings, but the figures themselves maintain their dimensionality and psychological emotions. The intensity of color that surrounds and contrasts the figure enhances the eeriness of the expression.

While some artists such as Joffe are able to depict strong emotive qualities through figurative work, others prefer to express themselves with pure abstraction. Japanese artist, Tsuruko Yamazaki, was part of the Japanese avant-garde art movement known as Gutai—meaning "concrete" and "embodiment." Yamazaki's preferred medium was tin, due to its malleable and reflective qualities.

The German artist and one of the pioneers of the New European Painting, Gerhard Richter has over the years adopted many different stylistic approaches to painting including abstraction. At the turn of the century, Richter became increasingly focused on abstract painting. One of his recent explorations of abstraction and color takes the form of stripes. *Strip*, 2011, is a digital print on paper mounted between aluminum and perspex. It "presents dozens of long horizontal stripes of varying thickness spanning a width of three meters. It is a tantalizing taste of what is still to come from one of the world's most prolific and respected living artists, whose insatiable desire to explore the languages and possibilities of painting and image-making continues to keep him at the forefront of developments in contemporary art today."[12]

Right: *Work*, 2009. Dye, lacquer, thinner on tin. 47.5 x 47.5cm (18 3/4 x 18 3/4 inches). © Tsuruko Yamazaki. Courtesy of the Artist and Almine Rech Gallery. Yamazaki's experimentation with industrial fabricated synthetic materials such as vinyl, tin, and mirrored surfaces allowed her to create beautiful abstractions by combining them with pigments and dyes. Using tin she created colors of indigos and magentas that came from the oxidation process itself.

Below: *Strip*, 2011 by Gerhard Richter. A digital print on paper between aluminum and perspex is one of the artist's recent explorations of abstraction and color.

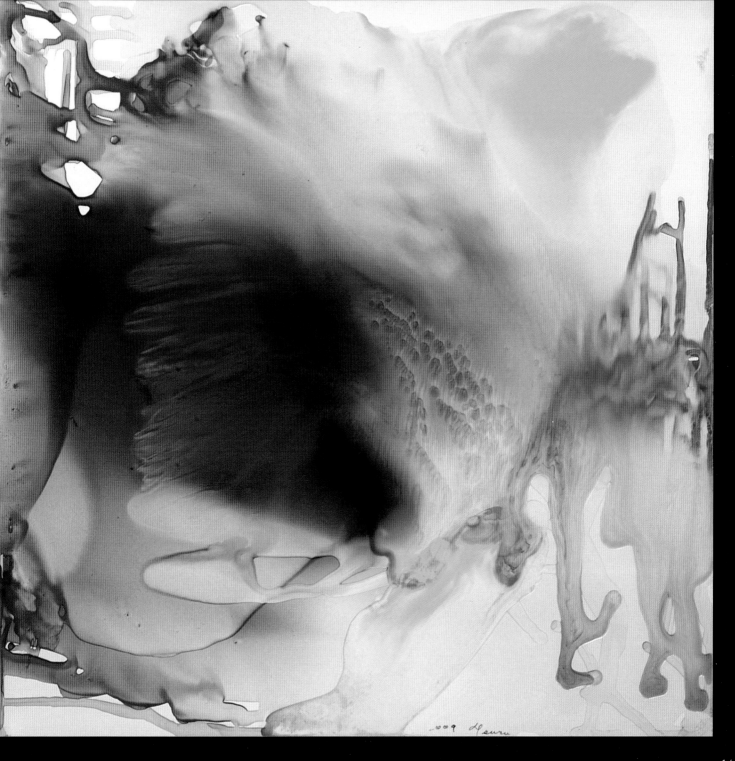

COLOR IN PHOTOGRAPHY

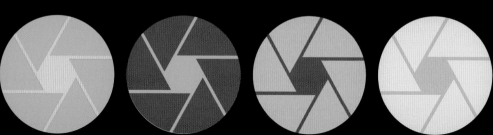

EXPERT: **JOHN ROHRBACH**
Senior Curator of Photographs at the Amon Carter Museum of American Art and the author of *Color!*
American Photography Transformed.

Could you describe your job and your involvement with the *Color! American Photography Transformed* exhibition October 5, 2013–January 5, 2014?
I am Senior Curator of Photographs at the Amon Carter Museum of American Art. I initiated and assembled the show *Color! American Photography Transformed*.

What was the inspiration and reason for putting together the show?
My inspiration was Eliot Porter. He committed himself to making color photographs in the late 1930s, yet that act made him an outcast among his fellow artist-photographers. I asked the question why? The second point is that my colleagues tend to think that fine art photographers first took up color in the 1970s and color became acceptable only in 1976 with William Eggleston's major exhibition at the Museum of Modern Art. I kept finding other color photographs that were made well before the 1970s. I began to ask who else was working in color before the 1970s, what instigated that work, what ideas underlie it, and how do those points relate to both the Eggleston show and what came after.

Do you think that the addition of color to photography has given added meaning to the images and giving the photographers more creative freedom as a result of it?
Most definitely.

How do you think that the show itself contributed to the growing prominence of color photography?
It highlighted the diversity and the importance of color through the early and middle decades of the 20th century, well before the Eggleston show. It also built an argument for the interweave between fine art and color photographs created for advertising and documentary practices. Ideally, my project will instigate further conversation and new projects on color by others.

What do you think about photography as part of installation pieces? There are some photographers who actually do an installation piece, have a photograph of it and have them relate to each other. What are your thoughts on that kind of thing?
Including photographs in installation pieces is simply another step in the medium's evolution, a symbol of the embrace of photography by artists working across the board.

Do any photographers employ color techniques that were particularly interesting to you in the work that you have used for the exhibit?
Certainly the shift from analog to digital has opened broad new vocabularies for using color. When one can change colors down to the pixel, and when one recognizes that the image is not a record of the world as much as a translation of it, digital technologies open new avenues for blending reality and fiction in remarkable new ways. Gregory Crewdson and Alex Prager are only two of many photographers exploring this new purely photographic reality. We also see photographers as diverse as Robert Bergman, Sharon Core, and Todd Hido drawing explicitly from the vocabulary of painting.

Is there anything else that you would like to comment on that maybe I didn't cross that might be an interesting thing to add to our conversation?
One thing that really astounded me in my early research was how much the debates about color prior to 1976 reflected misgivings about photography's place in the arts. Color offers a means for reflecting the world with ever more exactitude even as it opens a door to a new language of sight. We still deal with that dichotomy, especially in museum settings.

COLOR PHOTOGRAPHY The first lasting color photographic image was produced in 1861, the result of a collaborative effort between physicist James Clerk Maxwell and photographer Thomas Sutton. Based on the Young-Helmholtz theory of trichromatic color vision, Maxwell understood that mixing the primaries of red, green, and blue could create every possible color. Maxwell asked Sutton to illustrate a lecture on color vision with three separate black-and-white photographs of a multicolored ribbon—one taken with a red filter, another with a blue filter, and the third with a green, filter. Maxwell superimposed the three images, using projectors fitted with filters of the same colors, to produce a single, full-color image. This color separation process was to be used for the next 100 years.[1]

However, it was not until 1907 that the first mainstream method of color photography was created. Discovered by the Lumière brothers, Auguste and Louis, the Autochrome Lumière process used a glass plate coated with an emulsion containing a mosaic of small grains of colors dyed red-orange, green, and blue-violet to simulate the trichrometric vision of the eye.

In 1912, Rudolph Fischer, a German inventor, developed a subtractive color process that used "couplers" embedded in three emulsion layers sensitive to red, green, and blue colored light. Although the use of multiple layers of emulsion was an advance in the color photographic process, leakage between the layers resulted in poor color quality.

This was remedied in the 1930s, when Eastman Kodak developed Kodachrome film, "a positive black-and-white film that reproduces color by using identical red-, green-, and blue-striped filters over the camera and projector lenses." The process involved three emulsion layers that were used to produce colors that were complementary to the red, green, and blue primaries. Kodachrome did not incorporate dye couplers into the emulsion layers—instead they were added during processing. In this way, the camera imitated the visual perceptual system, with each emulsion layer correlating to a visual receptor in the cones. The use of multilayer emulsions is still used in film today.[2]

The question as to whether to take photographs in black and white or color is ever up for discussion. Throughout the development of photography, purists have felt that color is a distraction, taking away from the focus of the image rather than adding to it. Indeed, some professional photographers prefer to work in black and white, believing that monochrome better portrays depth and intricacies of form and shape. In addition, black-and-white photography distances the subject matter from reality, enabling a "timeless" image to be recorded—as we saw earlier, color can sometimes suggest a specific era.

However, color can be advantageous, as it can be used to enhance emotional content—color harmony and color discord can create a psychological response, evoking a specific feeling or a mood. In addition to creating emotional feeling, color can also enhance design principles, such as emphasis, proportion, extension, weight, placement, and movement. As a result, photographers can alter hue, value, and intensity to increase or decrease contrast in their images, using these properties to alter relationships between elements in the photographs.

Left: The first color photograph taken by professional photographer Thomas Sutton for a lecture given by Maxwell. The image of a tartan ribbon was created using three individual filters that were the same colors as the red, green, and blue receptors in the eye and then superimposed each of the three images to create a colored photograph.

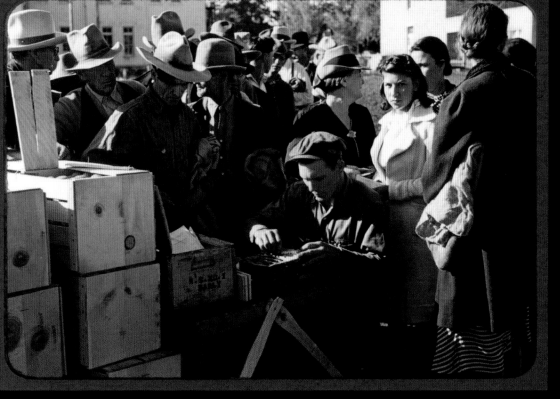

Left & below: *Distributing Surplus Commodities*, St Johns, Ariz, 1940, by Russell Lee (top) and *Street in San Juan, Puerto Rico*, 1941, by Jack Delano (bottom). Both Lee and Delano were employed by the Farm Security Administration Photographic Documentation Project established by President Franklin D. Roosevelt. They photographed images of everyday life, including both rural and urban areas.

FINE-ART PHOTOGRAPHY The relationship between photography and the fine arts has always been one of interaction and response. Although they were largely limited to black and white until the 1930s, there were photographers that responded to—and were tied to—various art movements throughout the twentieth century. Several movements of consequence to both photographers and artists were Cubism, Pop Art, Surrealism, and Photo-realism.

Cubism, originating with the works of Picasso and Georges Braque, fragmented recognizable everyday objects and reconstructed them, dealing head-on with the modern paradox of flattened space on a two-dimensional canvas. A catalog of the 1981 show, Cubism and American photography, 1910–1930, held at the Sterling and Francine Clark Art Institute in Williamstown, Massachusetts, suggested that Cubism triggered the formation of modern photography by providing an art style that it could understand and utilize.[3] Included in the exhibition were works by Edward Steichen and Paul Strand. Steichen thought of himself as a craftsman who used the mechanical medium of photography, believing that photography needed to understand and emulate art movements of the time.

In the same Cubist vein, Paul Strand created a series of abstractions taken on a Connecticut porch. The images consisted of free-floating, ungrounded shadows that break up the pictorial space. Their beauty lies in the simple abstracted forms created by altered perspectives of the porch taken bathed in light and shadow. The Cubist style is also readily apparent in the works of Charles Sheeler, who used its principles in both his paintings and photographs. With an urban focus, Sheeler created the photograph *Millyard Passage*, and a companion painting, *Manchester*. His photographic technique merged two images into one to create a sharp, angular look that forces the viewer to look at two perspectives at once. For *Manchester*, he simplified the shapes and tonal qualities of his photograph to create a series of flat planes. These were combined with a monochromatic purple palette that imitates a black-and-white photograph, putting the emphasis on value.

The use of Cubist style in photography transcends time. Two contemporary artist-photographers—David Hockney and Randy Scott Slavin—used the cubist ideology to create their photo collages. Naming them "joiners," Hockney coalesced different time frames and different perspectives of the subject into one image. While some of the collages are based on the overlapping of varying sized images and others are designed in a grid, it is the juxtaposition of differing viewpoints with the same color palette that establish an overall unity in his work.

Hockney's photo collage, *Pearblossom Hwy., 11–18th April 1986 (Second Version)*, (route 138), is a huge work, measuring 78 x 111 inches (1.98 x 2.82m)—it is so large in scale that it feels as if I it can be entered. The collage's reality as a complete image is reinforced by the variety of colored pieces of the same image that collide together to create perspective and space. The slight choppiness caused by the images lends movement and light to the piece, and implies the transience of the moment. In addition to the juxtaposition of similar colors, an overall harmoniously and proportionately balanced complementary orange and blue palette is utilized. This combination was also used by Hockney in his water landscapes and pool paintings,

Hockney's fellow Pop Artist, Andy Warhol, also used photographic images as the starting point for his screen prints, picking popular images and creating them in multiples on the same piece in a variety of bright colors. Utilizing the mass-production process of silk-screen printing, Warhol's art became part of an assembly line process in which photographs were transferred onto silk. Taking the work out of the hand of the individual artist allowed the photographic image to be printed with different colored inks, producing a vibrancy of layered color. Warhol created several "mass-produced" images in this way, from photographs of celebrities such as Marilyn Monroe, Elvis Presley, and Jackie Onassis.

Below: It is interesting to note in *Pearblossom Hwy., 11–18th April, 1986 (Second Version)*, how David Hockney uses intense color and out-of-scale signage to enhance the idea of dual perspective, seeing the highway from both the driver's and the passenger's perspective.

Right: In a series of ten screen prints entitled *Marilyn*, 1967, Andy Warhol did not alter any elements of the photograph beyond the color palette. The color—bright, flattened, and unrealistic—gives the photograph a sensibility that is both impersonal and dehumanized.

SURREALISM AND POST-SURREALISM Surrealist photographers wanted to express creativity and imagination. While the Cubists freed themselves from the idea of traditional perspective by taking fragments of images and combining them together to create a new reality, Surrealist artists and writers—backed by the Freudian ideology of the time—tried to release the imagination by creating images that were dreamlike or irrational. Although they had similar roots in Dadaism—a nihilistic response to the atrocities of war—Pop Art and Surrealism diverged at that point. While Pop Art reacted to the post-war period and excessive materialism with art that reflected the realities of everyday pop culture, the Surrealists escaped into a dreamlike world by using mundane objects in an incongruous contextual environment.

In a similar way to Cubist photographers, who merged multiple images from various perspectives into one cohesive photograph, Surrealism juxtaposed everyday objects and figures to suggest an alternate reality.

Surrealistic imagery often drew on deeply personal and intense emotions, dwelling on the strange and bizarre, and distorting and transcending time and space. Surrealists created an irrational dream world by using the techniques of strange perspectives, harsh lighting and shadows, and double exposure. In addition, they modified and enhanced or blurred visual details, using distortion, primitive content, and intense and unusual colors.

Man Ray was a prominent photographer and painter in the Surrealist movement, who was influenced by the collages of Marcel Duchamp. Man Ray combined classical techniques with unorthodox photographic processes, such as solarization, photomontage, and photograms. The photogram—a method of placing objects directly on light-sensitive paper, exposing it to create an image of shadows and silhouettes—allowed him to create images of everyday objects transformed into something strange and mysterious.

A Post-Surrealist photographer making use photograms is Adam Fuss. Fuss' technical celebration of the print and his use of the photogram process simultaneously allows him to explore nature and investigate the photographic process. Much of his work has involved placing objects on Cibachrome paper—a high gloss color paper with great color fastness—and exposing it to a light source. His exploration in color and light involves the use of primitive content such as dead birds, animal parts, and human babies.

Fuss' *Babies* series was created by placing the babies in a tray of water on top of a sheet of Cibachrome

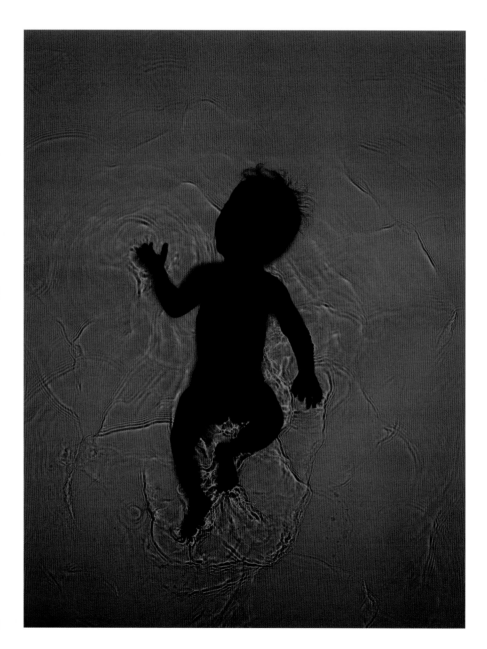

paper. The ripples that surround the baby's movements are reminiscent of the womb in which they remain suspended. The image is intensified by the contrast between the warm orange glow of the background and the near-black silhouette. While the orange suggests the warmth of the sun, it also creates a feeling of discomfort—the use of the complement or "alter ego" of blue (which stands for tranquility and calmness), creates a jarring contrast to the silhouette of the innocent baby.[4]

As is the case of the *Babies* series, color can be adjusted and accentuated to express emotion, and that emotion can be used as symbolic inference to reflect a personal subjective reality. When comparing Fuss' *Babies* series to the *Motherland Chronicles* by surrealist photographer Zhang Jingna, it is clear that their approach to the figure-ground relationship is widely divergent. While both create dreamlike scenarios that are frozen in time and enhanced with color, Fuss uses one symbolic color devoid of textural elements, while Jingna creates highly textured backgrounds.

In *Motherland Chronicles*, Jingna makes direct reference to her inner childhood fantasies, dreams, and aspirations, creating environments in which the figure is encapsulated by— and contrasted to—the highly focused or blurred backgrounds. The style of the work has a quality of dark fantasy, with Jingna creating a surreal environment, where a singularly colored light gives some of the figures in the images an eerie glow.

In the Secret Garden sees Jingna use a complementary scheme of highly intense oranges and blues, surrounding a monochromatic figure with bleached white hair. A superimposed white sheer fabric glazes over the intense color of the flowers, enhancing the contrast. As with the work of Fuss, the dreamlike quality suggests the capture of an intimate introspective moment suspended in time.

Photography: Zhang Jingna

Opposite: *Untitled*, 2011. Adam Fuss' *Babies* series was created using a sheet of Cibachrome paper in a tray of water. The baby was placed on top of the paper and then it was exposed to a light source.

Above: *Motherland Chronicles—In the Secret Garden*, 2013, by Zhang Jingna. In the foreground figure, cool colors have greater dominance by the use of intensity and clarity as opposed to softer colors in the background, which are muted by transparent grays. This creates a dream-like ambience.

03.02 color in photography / conceptual photography

CONCEPTUAL PHOTOGRAPHY Lucas Samaras' surrealistic images were created by hand manipulating Polaroid film emulsions to create color-saturated images. In his series Photo Transformations (1973–1976), he uses his face and body as subject, distorting and manipulating hundreds of poses. Alone and naked in his apartment, Samaras made unnatural images of himself using intrusive compositions under brightly colored light. These often frightening images reflect a dreamlike vision of self-obsession.

Samaras discovered that the wet dyes of Polaroid prints were highly malleable; pushing on the photos, moving and shifting the chemicals, allowed him to make and remake his own image, allowing the colors to run, turning his image into a series of beautiful stains, creating intense areas of jolting color. Unsurprisingly, the computer and the digital camera further extended his ability to imprint his image upon the world. In his 1978–1980 series of photographic portraits, *Sittings*, Samaras asked his subjects to strip and present themselves as they wished, then jumped into the frame—fully clothed—to create an awkwardness and tension.[5]

Using the associative powers of color to enhance meaning, contemporary artist-photographers no longer have to limit their color application. One such artist, Sandy Skoglund, relies heavily on color in her elaborate installation pieces, with contrasting colors or monochromatic color palettes typifying her work. In her piece, *The Cocktail Party*, Skoglund created an installation in which mannequins/guests interact with each other and move in response to motion detectors. The set, entirely covered with resin-coated Cheese Doodles (a snack food), is reminiscent of a childhood pleasure within the context of a consumer-driven adult society.

The photograph of the installation is altered so that people replace some of the mannequins, bringing a more personal and grounded reality to the image. In both instances—installation and photograph—the yellow/orange color of the Cheese Doodles dominates the scene, exciting the viewer with its intensity and accentuating the notion of childhood delight and vulnerability.

In the work of Mariah Robertson, the photograph becomes the installation. Robertson places complete emphasis on the process and the physicality of a photograph, with studio practice seen as both subject and environment. Her photographs are created using traditional darkroom techniques, and can be as long as 100 feet (30m), often being draped from ceilings and over walls in a ribbon-like fashion that goes beyond the pictorial framed image. These pieces are comprised of recognizable figurative images, interspersed with expressionistic splatters drips and streaks—Robertson is able to create a plethora of color using various chemicals, including developer and bleach at various temperatures and consistencies.

Robertson's photo paintings and photograms are both colorful and have the immediacy of abstract expression. In her piece entitled *88* (2010), she uses an entire roll of glossy archival paper, covering it with bright colors and randomly placed faded figures. A series of black-and-white tiles are placed throughout the piece to enhance movement, whiles blues and greens complement the intense oranges that float along the rim.[6]

Opposite: **Lucas Samaras'** *Photo-Transformations*, 1974. It appears that Samaras creates areas of intense color coming from different filtered lights. Some mixing appears—cyan, magenta, and yellow—at the point at which the chair meets his body.

Below: **Sandy Skoglund's** *The Cocktail Party*. The readily identifiable Cheese Doodles have a calming effect on the viewer due to the association with comfort food. However, the viewer is also struck by the disproportionate amount of yellow in this piece.

The Cocktail Party © 1992 **Sandy Skoglund**

CHAPTER THREE

COLOR AND THE WRITTEN WORD:
ROOTS AND ORIGINS

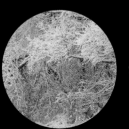

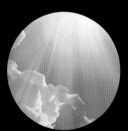

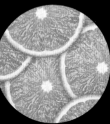

EXPERT: **KIM TRIEDMAN**

Kim Triedman is both an award-winning poet and a novelist. Her debut novel, *The Other Room*, was released in 2013 following the publication of three poetry collections: *Hadestown, Plum(b),* and *Bathe in it or Sleep.*

Can you tell me a little about your writing background

I'm both a poet and a novelist. I was a bit of a late bloomer: I didn't start writing creatively until my late 30s. Since then I have been very productive, and the desire to write has felt all-consuming at times. My first novel, *The Other Room*, and two full-length poetry collections, *Plum(b)* and *Hadestown*, were published in 2013, and all three were recognized in major national competitions. Another collection, *Bathe in It or Sleep*, was released prior to this in 2008. I also developed and edited an anthology in response to the 2010 Haitian earthquake—*Poets for Haiti: An Anthology of Poetry and Art*—which benefited Paul Farmer's Organization Partners in Health.

What is the importance of color in your writing?

I write in color. I always have. For me, sensitivity to color is a kind of sixth sense—strong enough and central enough to demand its own particular category. I don't know why this is so, though it is not surprising to me that many of my fellow poets are also visual artists. Perhaps what joins us is a heightened sensitivity to the physical and sensory characteristics of the world around us, and a drive to make connections based on these sensitivities. For all of us—artists and poets—the imperative is to translate these sensitivities and impressions into our own work.

Do you think that color words can make an emotive statement? And if so, in what way?

My own writing tends to be extremely sensual, often deeply rooted in nature. Color is evocative in the way that all beauty can be evocative: it demands my attention; it requires me to stand up and take notice. This can also hold true for light, texture, and design—qualities that contribute to and elaborate on an overall experience. However, for me, color has its own particular clarion call. It offers so much more than just its own state of being. It imparts mood and tone and a universe of associations. It is urgent and sustaining, like oxygen for the heart and soul.

COLOR, LANGUAGE, AND CREATIVITY The relationship between color and words has been reflected in cultural development throughout history. Color is intrinsically tied to verbal expression, describing what we see, feel, and even hear. Neurologists have studied individuals who experience synesthesia seeing color when they read words. Psychologists have studied the relationship between emotive expressions and color, while social scientists, such as anthropologists and linguists have studied color terms to understand the development of language within a community and the relationship those words have to community evolution, including their roots and associations with slang. Over the following pages, writer Kim Triedman discusses the connection between color and language in her poetry.

The most creative and intuitive artists and writers utilize the color-word relationship in their poetry and art. While both poetry and color can elicit feelings or thoughts individually, together these forces combine to create a synesthetic experience that greatly enhances emotive response. Many famous poets have incorporated color phrases in their work to enhance the visual image. Color words are utilized as metaphors in creative writing and poetry to conjure up visual images or emotive feelings, or as a symbolic representation of socio-political or cultural association. The following poem, "Provisions," attempts to convey just how powerful a force color can be to those receptive to it.

Consider first the name of the poem: "Provisions." Not everyone would include color on a list of life's essentials. Note that the daughter in the poem can only assume the pomegranate is for eating; the husband, who rolls it down the hallway for the dog, sees it as a form of recreation. But to the narrator, as to anyone trafficking in visual/sensual experience, color is a kind of *sine qua non* of existence. It is a necessary thing; a provision for the journey. And as the narrator of the poem muses in the final stanza, "I am not sure why it matters so much/but it does."

The use of color can also reach beyond what is required, to what is desired. In the poem, "Momentum," I pay a kind of homage to color as something not just necessary, but seductive and urgent.

PROVISIONS

I bought one pomegranate this morning just
  to admire it.
They were two for five dollars, but I was only
  purchasing color.

Can we eat it? my daughter asked that evening.
  She was limping through her chemistry
  homework,

Not until I'm finished, I answered vaguely,
  wondering what exactly that meant.

It sat on the counter, defining red. Even the
  tomatoes knew not to argue.

When my husband came home, he palmed
  it absently then rolled it down the hallway
  for the dog.

It's in my office, now, catching the afternoon sun.
I'm not sure why it matters so much but it does.
I know that the seeds inside are waiting,
  jewel-like, encrusted in their pulpy womb.
But for the moment I'm content just to see it
  there when I turn my head.
Sitting quietly on the sill.
Concentrating all that color in one place.[1]

MOMENTUM

On the fifth day of the snow
  the daughter leaves, saying,
I may be back.
The sky does not exist.
In the kitchen: soup, simmering
  until the end of time.

The mother.
It is the long hour before dinner,
  and dark. She walks,
  from the kitchen to the hallway
  and turns, looks back
  to the beginning.

On the fifth day of the snow
  the daughter leaves, saying
I have no choice.

The sky exists, but elsewhere
  and oh so many colors. There is
  a pulse, like drums, there is
  the suckling red.

No, she says, gathering her
  things about her, I don't care
  for any soup.[2]

Pomegranate

Sunset

Pay special attention to the second to last stanza, in which the grown child is pulled powerfully into her own adulthood. The sky is "elsewhere/and oh so many colors. There is/a pulse, like drums, there is/the suckling red." The daughter has no choice: the many colors of the future, the scarlet of passion and adulthood. These are the inevitable seduction. Colors may also be used in more explicit ways based on the specific associations they call forth. Either directly or indirectly, the poet can play on such associations: the green of envy, the blues of depression, or the pure white of innocence. In my final two poems, which bracket the front and back ends of my collection *Plum(b)*, I riff on the color yellow. Interestingly, though, the two poems conjure entirely different associations: in the first, "Witch Hazel," yellow is the color of life emerging. In the latter, "Accoutrements," it is the color of guile.

In "Witch Hazel," yellow is the color of rebirth, of possibility, of spring flowers, of new growth; it is the pastel yellow of baby chicks and sunlight. In the second poem, "Accoutrements," the yellows represent a different thing entirely. Note, in particular, the fourth stanza, in which specific associations are actually spelled out: power, cowardice, anger. Overall, however, the use of yellow in this poem suggests a kind of guile—a willful manipulation underscored by the narrative itself. The deception is complete when we arrive at the final line of the poem, in which the narrator chooses the "blood-orange" of a new settee as a kind of a cynical rejoinder to the earlier request for discretion. For the most part, color enters my poems obliquely, without my conscious awareness. As is true of my process as a whole, it insists itself, it knows why it needs to end up on the page. It's only later, when I go back, that I see why it is there, what it has added, how it has underscored the message implicit in the whole. In poetry, every word matters, and it is never an accident that a "light hisses blue, blue" or that an invasive evening primrose, duplicitous to the end, spreads her "carpet of chromium goodwill."

Witch Hazel

Evening Primrose

Blood Orange

WITCH HAZEL

Winters lie long up here—lead-bellied
  and mean.
Evergreens grow even darker in the cold.

Outside, the witch hazel prostrates herself
  to an unruly wind.

Two people at a small wooden table.
Imagine them taking their morning coffee,
  their blue china mugs.
A dog curls beneath them by a cast-iron grate.

Say one of them looks up and gazes at the
  sky—absently, perhaps, wondering about
  this or that.

An eye could come to rest upon a small yellow
  flower – spindly, unkempt in its way – yellow
  nonetheless.
It is late February—not even the beginning
  of the end of winter.
New souls have yet to stir within the tireless
  womb.

It is not impossible. Imagine the flowers came.

Say they even existed.[3]

ACCOUTREMENTS

I have learned.
This winter when I re-painted the living room
I checked in with the others first.
Yellow was the consensus—not a color
  I would have chosen.

Pale, they said, like straw, they said.
Muted, discreet.

Thus recognized, they went back to things
  unrelated to color.

But I smiled on my way to the paint store.
I knew that there was still
  a universe out there—
  the yellows of emperors and cowards;
  the yellow of bile.

When the room was finished, everyone
  was delighted. Yes, of course,
  they cooed, it was the perfect choice
  of color. No one seemed even
  to notice the lesser of my domestic
  gambits—

A trompe l'oeil hearth.
Sheer lace for the windows.
The blood-orange of the new settee.[4]

COLOR WORDS: THEIR POWER AND MEANING

As with much etymology, color words have their derivations based in Proto-Indo-European languages (4000–3000 BCE) from Europe, India, Iran, and Anatolia Proto-Germanic languages; ancestors of the Saxon, English, German Norse, Norwegian, Dutch, Danish, Icelandic, Faroese, Swedish, Gothic, and Vandalic languages (2000–500 BCE); and in Old English (400 CE–1100 CE), an early form of English that is also sometimes called Anglo-Saxon, as used in England and Scotland.[5]

In terms of perception, we understand that lightwaves emitted from a source travel to an object where they are reflected, absorbed, or transmitted with respect to the color and surface quality of the objectin question. The energy then stimulates the receptors in the eye that send messages to the brain that then interprets it. In her book, *Color Terms in the Old Testament*, Athalya Brenner, reviews how color language has evolved. She talks about how the experience of seeing an object and its color becomes internalized into personal experience, and about the fact that color sensation initially is received as non-verbal images independent of language. This

early impression becomes engaged in the brain and becomes representative of the color/image and then helps with future recognition. She suggests that these color experiences, which she believes are exaggerated with the increasing intensity of the color, begin to work as a reference point from which to explore related color experiences. Prior to language development, infants can differentiate and respond to color.[6] As children develop language skills they develop the capacity to define and identify colors with greater specificity and can convey those words to others.

Below & opposite: **The results of Marcel R. Zentner's study into whether young children can detect a relationship between color and emotional expression, suggested that children as young as three and four tended to associate bright colors with the word "happy" and more subdued colors with the word "sad."**

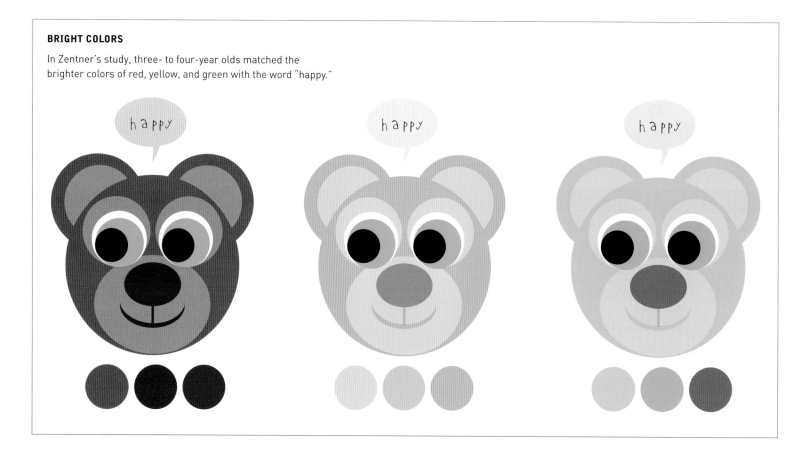

BRIGHT COLORS

In Zentner's study, three- to four-year olds matched the brighter colors of red, yellow, and green with the word "happy."

Working under these premises, Brenner studied early biblical color terms in Aramaic to understand language evolution and development. She describes how words for colors were affiliated with life needs, and therefore color in words were dependent upon associations with an object. As a result, many colors end up having more than one meaning. Yellow, for example, was affiliated with both a sickly pallor and with the gleaming of gems. Brenner is one of many who have studied color terms in different cultures to understand the culture itself.

The analysis of color terms has become standard in studying language development. Basic color terms are studied across many different cultures. Linguists Brent Berlin and Paul Kay did a multilingual study of color terms and determined that there was a set of 11 universal color terms: white, black, red, green, yellow, blue, brown, purple, pink, orange, and gray.[7] A world color survey was developed to test the existence of cross-language color naming and the relationship to cultural development of a community with respect to these terms.[8] In 2009 research was extended to include 110 basic color terms.

While the same colors may be identified by many cultures, that does not mean they carry the same weight and meaning in each one. We have seen that even in one language several meanings can be assigned to the same color. Marcel R. Zentner carried out a study reported in *Preferences for color and color-emotion combinations in early childhood* in which Zentner tried to determine whether young children can "detect consistent relationships between colors and facial expressions of emotion."[9] Zentner suggests that at the age of three or four, children might begin to create abstract relationships. In the study Zentner found that children aged three to four tended to match bright colors (yellow, red, and green) with the word "happy," and dark colors (blue, brown, or black) with the word "sad." Preferences also varied by gender. Boys matched red with happy faces twice as often as did girls, and brown with sad faces four times as often. Zentner found that boys and girls reacted similarly to yellow and blue, and green and black had little emotional connotation. Even at this young age it would appear that certain colors have differing degrees of attractiveness and emotional meaning.[10]

DARK COLORS

In Zentner's study, three- to four-year olds matched the darker colors of blue, brown, and black with the word "sad."

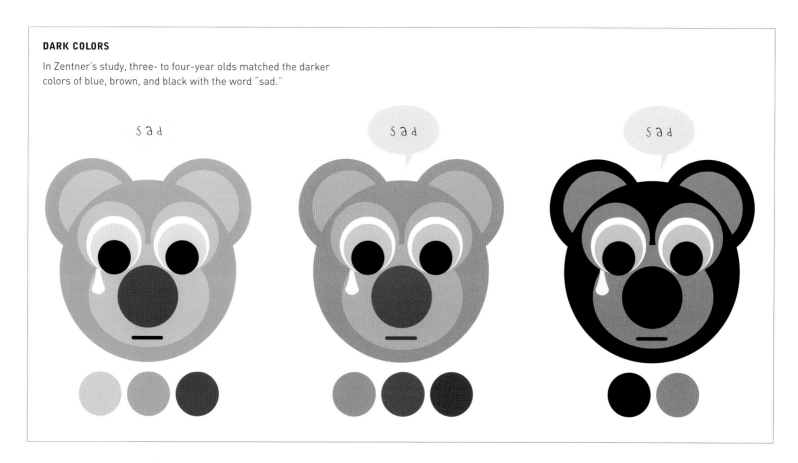

COLOR DEFINITIONS AND PHRASES While colors may have some universality in cultural useage and response, slang color phrases may not. There is often some sort of geographic socio-politico or historic incident or experience from which the phrase stems.

In *A Dictionary of Word Origins: A History of the Words, Expressions, and Clichés We Use*, author Jordan Almond explores the evolution of certain slang phrases. He asks, "Why do we call despondency the blues?" and answers his own question, "because blue devils were a common form of apparition experienced by those suffering delirium."[11] James Rogers in his book, *The Dictionary of Clichés*, talks about the etymology of "red herring" as meaning a diversionary tactic. He says it stems from "A herring that is cured by smoking turns red. It also has a strong odor."[12]

BLACK

ROOTS
From the Proto-Indo-European *bhleg*. This was changed to *blakkaz* in Proto-Germanic, to *blaken* in Dutch, *blach* in Old High German, and *blaec* in Old English. *Blaec* also meant "ink," as did *blak* (Old Saxon) and *black* (Swedish). "Dark" (also *blaec* in Old English) derived from the Old Norse *blakkr*.

SYMBOLIC MEANING
Burning, blazing, glowing, shining, power, elegance, formality, death, evil, mystery, gloom, grief, strength, formality, dignity.

SLANG PHRASES
Black sheep: "an outcast or disreputable member of a group, especially with respect to family. Stems from a defect that causes a sheep to have black fur that was not dyeable and therefore undesirable—the mark of the devil in eighteenth- and nineteenth-century England—originally a mark of integrity in biblical times."[13]

Pot calling the kettle black: "criticism given by someone of something they themselves possess or are guilty of—as generally understood, the person accusing (the 'pot') is understood to share some quality with the target of their accusation (the 'kettle')."[14]

Little black book: a book of contacts, particularly for past or potential dating partners. "The term more often refers to address books that can reveal information about people's past boyfriends or girlfriends, as well as potential dates for the future."[15]

WHITE

ROOTS
From the Proto-Indo-European *kwintos* meaning simply white or bright. *khwitz* in Proto-Germanic, *hvitr* (Old Norse), *hwit* (Old Saxon) and *wit* (Dutch). Old English *kwit*.

SYMBOLIC MEANING
Peace, purity, innocence, delicacy, refinement, sophistication, cleanliness. It is considered to be the color of perfection.

SLANG PHRASES
Whitewash: "to mask or cover up crimes, scandals, or other negative acts." Whitewash is literally a cheap white paint or coating of chalked lime. The word was used in a political context when, in 1800, a Philadelphia *Aurora* editorial said that "if you do not whitewash President Adams speedily, the Democrats, like swarms of flies, will bespatter him all over, and make you both as speckled as a dirty wall, and as black as the devil."[16]

White elephant: "a useless or costly item." A white elephant is something that is costly to maintain or is incredibly hideous to the owner. It is both the name of the albino variety of the mammal that was worshipped in some southeast Asian countries and a gift exchange game often played during the Christmas season in the United States."[17]

White Christmas: the appearance of snow on Christmas day.

He suggests an alternative interpretation, "people who were opposed to fox hunting sometimes drew a red herring across the path ... the dogs would give up on the fox and follow the scent." As we have seen, many idioms in our language today are varied and may have several origins. Color colloquialisms have many possible derivations, symbolic meanings, and associations. The development of slang phrases is dependent on experiences in the political and social interactions throughout the history of a community.

PURPLE

ROOTS
Ninth century CE Old English has *purpul*. This is borrowed from the Latin word *purpura*—the Latin name of a particular kind of shellfish which, when ground up, produces a bright purple dye, which in turn was taken from the older Greek word *porphura* to describe the same sea creature. The word *purpura* later began to refer to the dye, and eventually the color of this dye. This dye was very expensive, and purple was considered a color of royalty throughout Europe. When this dye was exported to England, the word *purple* was imported into English as well. Today "purpura" is used by doctors to describe purplish discolorations of the skin.

SYMBOLIC MEANING
Associated with royalty, power, nobility, luxury, ambition, wealth, extravagance, wisdom, dignity, independence, creativity, mystery, and magic.

SLANG PHRASES
Purple prose: flowery and excessively extravagant writing style. This phrase originated and was derived from the phrase "purple patches," which was first seen in a poem by the Roman poet Horace.[18] Purple patches are also sometimes called "purple passages" or "purple prose." "They were originally a figurative reference to florid literary passages, added to a text for dramatic effect. They were the literary equivalent of adding a patch of purple material to an otherwise undecorated garment. Purple was the color reserved for emperors and other distinguished statesmen in imperial Rome."[19]

BLUE

ROOTS
Often confused with yellow. From the Proto-Indo-European *bhle-was* meaning "light-colored, blue, blond yellow" and had its root in *bhel*, which meant to shine. In Proto-Germanic the word was *blaewaz*, and in Old English it was *blaw*.

SYMBOLIC MEANING
Trust, loyalty, wisdom, confidence, intelligence, faith, truth, and heaven.

SLANG PHRASES
Blue in the face: "lost patience, exhausted speechless from excessive anger, exact origin unknown—when someone gets worked up attempting to convince someone of something, they lose so much oxygen from trying to talk too much and their face starts to turn slightly blue from all the de-oxygenated blood."[20]

Out of the blue: "something that occurs suddenly or unexpectedly. 'A bolt out of the blue' or 'a bolt from the blue,' which refers to a completely unexpected and surprising act, like a thunderbolt from a clear blue sky." First cited in Thomas Carlyle's *The French Revolution* in 1837. It meant literally a bolt of lightning coming from a sky without storm clouds. [21]

GREEN

ROOTS
From the Proto-Indo-European "to grow," *ghre*, *grene* (Old Frisian), *graenn* (Old Norse), *grown* (Dutch). In Old English it was *grene*.

SYMBOLIC MEANING
Growth, harmony, freshness, and fertility. Green has strong emotional correspondence with safety. Dark green is also commonly associated with money. Green has great healing power. It is the most restful color for the human eye; it can improve vision. Green suggests stability and endurance.

SLANG PHRASES
Greenhorn: inexperienced or naive person. "Greenhorn" first appeared back in the fifteenth century meaning a young ox with new, or "green," horns. ("Green" has been used as a metaphor for "young" or "inexperienced," by analogy to a young plant, for hundreds of years.) By about 1650, "greenhorn" was being applied to newly-enlisted army recruits, and shortly thereafter "greenhorn" came to mean any inexperienced person."[22]

Another possibility, from the seventeenth century, relates the phrase to the jewelry manufacturing industry. "This jewelry, which looked like a cameo, was made of horn, heated, pressed into a mold, and placed in a silver frame. 8If the horn got overheated, it would turn green. Mistakes are most often made by those who are new to the craft, so new apprentices would be called greenhorns because they mistakenly turned the horn green."[23]

The grass is always greener on the other side. "Circumstances, situations, lifestyles seem better than one's own, even though that isn't necessarily the case."[24]

"Optical and perceptual laws alone will make the grass at a distance look greener to the human eye than the blades of grass perpendicular to the ground. The 'truth' of this metaphorical proverb can, of course, also be observed often enough in the countryside when a cow or a horse is trying to get at that juicy green grass just on the other side of the fence. And since people are equally dissatisfied with their lot in life, it should not surprise anyone that a modern psychologist has spoken of the 'greener grass' phenomenon by which modern individuals continually evaluate supposedly better alternatives for themselves."[25]

YELLOW

ROOTS
Thousands of years ago, yellow was considered to be closely related to green, and in Proto-Indo-European it was *ghel* and meant both yellow and green. In Proto-Germanic, the word was *gelwaz*. Subsequent incarnations of German had the word as *gulr* (Old Norse), *gel* (Middle High German), and *gelo* (Old High German). As late as Old English, yellow was written *geolu* and *geolwe*.

SYMBOLIC MEANING
Sunshine. It's associated with joy, happiness, intellect, and energy. Yellow produces a warming effect, arouses cheerfulness, stimulates mental activity, and generates muscle energy.

SLANG PHRASES
Yellow-bellied: cowardly.

"Yellow-belly" is also a term used to describe people born in the Fens of Lincolnshire in England.[26] The first known use of the term expressing the cowardly meaning, comes from an account of a military skirmish in Texas, reported in The Wisconsin Enquirer, April 1842:

"We learn from Capt. Wright, of the N. York, that it is the intention of the Texans to 'keep dark' until the Mexicans cross the Colorado, and then give them a San Jacinto fight, with an army from 5000 to 7000 men. God send that they may bayonet every 'yellow belly' in the Mexican army. The US usage initially applied specifically to Mexicans, who were soon to be at war with the USA. Whether the 'yellow' reference was a racist allusion to skin color, ill-health, or to a likening to snakes, lizards etc. isn't clear."[27]

Yellow journalism: disreputable or not legitimately researched journalism.

"At first, yellow journalism had nothing to do with reporting, but derived from a popular cartoon strip about life in New York's slums called Hogan's Alley, drawn by Richard F. Outcault. Published in color by Pulitzer's New York World, the comic's most well-known character came to be known as the Yellow Kid, and his popularity accounted in no small part for a tremendous increase in sales of the World. In 1896, in an effort to boost sales of his New York Journal, Hearst hired Outcault away from Pulitze. Hearst ultimately won this battle, but Pulitzer refused to give in and hired a new cartoonist to continue drawing the cartoon for his paper. This battle over the Yellow Kid and a greater market share gave rise to the term yellow journalism."[28]

RED

ROOTS

In Proto-Indo-European, red was *reudh* and meant red and ruddy. In Proto-Germanic, red was *rauthaz*, and in its derivative languages *raudr* (Old Norse), *rod* (Old Saxon) and *rØd* (Danish). In Old English, it was written *read*. The Proto-Indo-European word for red, *reudh*, remained largely unchanged for thousands of years, showing up in English *red*, Spanish *rojo*, French *rouge*, German *rot*, Icelandic *rauðr*, and Welsh *rhudd*. Not only did it lead to these words for the color itself, it also led to red-related English words like "ruby," "rust," and "rubeola" (the measles).

SYMBOLIC MEANING

Fire and blood, so it is associated with energy, war, danger, strength, power, determination as well as passion, desire, and love. Red is a very emotionally intense color.

SLANG PHRASES

Red-letter day: a very important or special day. The phrase "red letter day" dates back to at least 1385, when members of ancient monasteries and convents were responsible for producing calendars. They would use black ink for writing most of the calendar, but used red ink to mark important dates such as the days of Saints or other religious occasions, or holidays. The red ink was easy to see at a glance.[29]

Caught red-handed: to be caught in the act of a crime or misdemeanor. "The expression 'caught red handed' has its origins in Scotland around the fifteenth century. Given how it was used in the earliest references, the phrase 'red hand' or 'redhand' probably referred to people caught with blood on their hands from murder or poaching."[30]

Paint the town red: to dine, dance, and have fun in town. "The allusion is to the kind of unruly behavior that results in much blood being spilt. There are several suggestions as to the origin of the phrase. The one most often repeated, especially within the walls of the Melton Mowbray Tourist Office, is a tale dating from 1837. It is said that year is when the Marquis of Waterford and a group of friends ran riot in the Leicestershire town of Melton Mowbray, painting the town's toll-bar and several buildings red."[31]

ORANGE

ROOTS

This color's name derives from the Sanskrit word for the fruit, "naranga." This transformed into the Arabic and Persian *naranj*, and by the time of Old French to pomme *d'orenge*. It was originally recorded in English as the name of the color in 1512. Before then, the English speaking world referred to the orange color as *geoluhread*, which literally translates to "yellow-red." When oranges (the fruit) were exported from India, the word for them was exported too. Sanskrit *narangah*, or "orange tree," was borrowed into Persian as *narang*, "orange (fruit)," which was borrowed into Arabic as *naranj*, into Italian as *arancia*, into French as *orange*, and eventually into English also as *orange*. The color of the fruit was so striking that after importing the word with the crop, English speakers eventually began referring to the color by this word as well.

SYMBOLIC MEANING

With joy, sunshine, and the tropics. Orange represents enthusiasm, fascination, happiness, creativity, determination, attraction, success, encouragement, and stimulation.

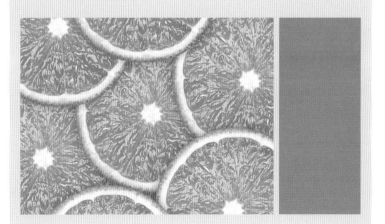

PART FOUR

COLOR AS A DYNAMIC FORCE IN DESIGN

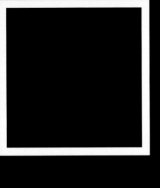

CHAPTER ONE

DESIGN ELEMENTS AND PRINCIPLES

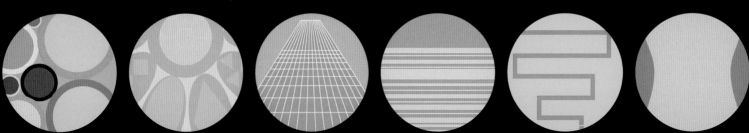

EXPERT: **ADRIAN BURKE**
BS, Studio Art: Textile Design and Photography, Skidmore College; AAS, Apparel Design and Service, Seattle
Central Community College; MFA, Design and Technology, Parsons School of Design. Adrian specializes in
quality surface design development and digital design technology for the apparel and textile industries. She
serves as a digital textile print broker, assisting clients with design and production for digital textile printing.

Could you talk about what you do and the type of training and experience it took to get there?

I became interested in textile design because my mom had a silk-screen cottage industry in the Caribbean when I was growing up. I specialized in textile design for Apparel with a focused masters degree in design technology. I worked as a Textile CAD designer for TJX. I focused on print design work, embroidery design, and woven design. The fabrics are manufactured globally and made into apparel products.

Can you describe briefly the process of making a surface design?

So it starts with collecting inspiration material, creating sketches for an original design. We start by creating a number of motifs and elements, and we usually use at least two or three different key elements to make a good design. Once the elements are drawn, cleaned up, and refined, we go on to the next step of developing the pattern and creating the layout. There are lots of different types of patterns. There are patterns that use individual or a combination of several motifs; there are textural patterns, and continuous all-over patterns.

How do you know that a singular image is going to work color- and design-wise when you put it into repeat?

The best way to know that the design repeat is working is by printing out a large area of it. You check a repeat by making sure that it's nice and effective, attractive and consistent, and there are no other flaws. When you see it over a large area, that's when you can determine whether it is successful or not. You can see if any elements are lining up or there are open spaces in the design that need to be fixed. It's usually a process of doing two or three printouts to be satisfied that your design is correct.

How do you choose the colors for the design?

From inspiration material you pick out the colors and develop a palette. Another option is to get color information from design services that specialize in predicting color trends. When the print design is finalized it is put into fashion colors. Sometimes we have to use a specific number of colors, while other times we are able to choose. There can be a maximum of eight colors in a print to meet a price point for the apparel product.

Once you have created the design, how do you know where to use each color in order to enhance the design?

Generally, with two-dimensional pattern design, we employ two-dimensional design principles, and apply a color hierarchy. We might have one main color, referred to as a key color. The rest of the colors may support that main color in the design. Once in a while there are two key colors and the other three colors are neutral, or less dominant.

The colors consist of key colors being dominant, with other color values and intensities being subordinate. This contrast makes the design look stronger. From a design perspective, you also want certain colors to recede, and some colors to come forward so you actually create visual depth. You have to choose which elements you wish to be a focal point—for example, flowers in a floral print; you may want the flowers to come forward and the leaves and vines to recede back. The warm colors would be on the flowers because they read hot and come forward. The cool, more subdued colors placed on the vines will recede back, and as a result we get depth of field. If we don't apply these principles, then the designs can look flat, which is not effective.

DESIGN ELEMENTS Design is a process based on a need to communicate information, express a point of view, sell a product or a service, or enhance or create a product or environment. Designers know that color choices are very important in conveying meaning and appealing to the senses, so it is important that color is used to enhance the intended statement. As we have seen, color is a vast and complicated subject with scientific, historical, and socio-political influences.

Color works best in conjunction with design elements, so prior to a discussion of design, it is important to look at these basic design principles, which can be considered the building blocks of a design. These elements include point, line, plane, shape, volume, scale, texture, space, weight, and form, and work together to create a design structure that allows us to get our message across with conciseness and strength. The structure created by these elements is guided by the design principles of balance and symmetry; scale, proportion, and space; movement and flow; and emphasis and focus.

THE ELEMENTS OF DESIGN

Point: A position at the beginning or end of a line.

Line: A series of points moving the eye in a direction. At its straightest it defines an edge of a plane. A curved line can enclose an organic shape. It can be thin like a pencil mark, or thick like an Expressionist brush stroke. Lines outline shapes.

Movement: Lines can also be used to add dynamism to a design and help concentrate the viewer's attention in one area.

Plane: A surface that has length and width, but no depth. It is defined by lines.

Shape: Refers to the linear form of an object. A shape can be either geometric or organic—geometric shapes include circles, squares, rectangles, and triangles, while organic shapes stem from nature, with curved lines rather than hard edges.

Volume: The amount of space that is occupied by a three-dimensional object mass (length × width × height). Volume is illusory in a two-dimensional artwork.

Scale: The size of a shape or object. Scale is a measurable quantity that can be judged by contrasting two objects—objects further away tend to be smaller in scale.

Texture: The surface quality of a shape. Texture can be created visually, by imitating actual textures that appeal to the sense of touch. Pattern is an ornamental texture that provides visual excitement to the viewer.

Space: The place in which a shape (in two dimensions) or a solid (in three dimensions) exists. It is called "positive" space if it is the space of the object, and "negative" space if it's the space around the object.

Visual weight: Depending on the combination of scale, texture, color, and shape, an object can appear to be "heavy" or "light." Some colors are proportionately heavier than others.

Form: A defined shape.

Structure: The place in which forms exist.

Left: Because of our personal experience there is a subconscious relationship between colors and design elements. This is especially the case with driving directives. The octagonal shape combined with the color red forms a symbol that is understood to anyone who drives. Because they are so closely affiliated most drivers would respond to shape and color alone.

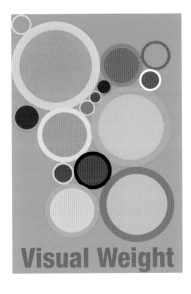

Visual Weight

Movement

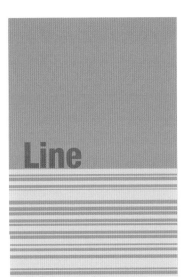

Line

Volume

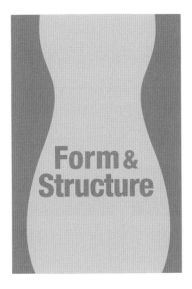

Form & Structure

Shape

Scale

Point

Plane

Texture

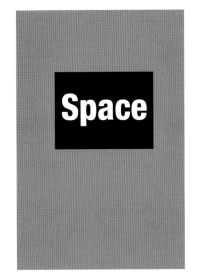

Space

This page: **The elements of design are the fundamental building blocks on which design is constructed. These elements are illustrated here and include, space, texture, plane, point, scale, shape, form and structure, volume, line, movement, and weight.**

DESIGN PRINCIPLES An image is created by combining different design elements. The relationship between the various design elements and the tools used to create that relationship are based on the principles of design. Being well versed in these principles will enable you to create sophisticated designs that maintain overall unity while creating visual excitement and variety.

Balance and Symmetry

Just as a musician uses chords and rhythm to create auditory harmony in music, so a designer uses design elements to create visual balance and harmony. Balance refers to a state of equilibrium—an equal distribution of visual weight through the combining and positioning of design elements.

One way to create visual balance is through pictorial symmetry. In order for a piece to be symmetrical, two halves of the picture plane have to have equal weight. Elements that are seemingly the same size, shape, and relative position can create symmetry, but they will give a "static" quality to an image. Asymmetrical balance uses dissimilar objects in different positions that have equal weight. This can be achieved through texture, scale, and complexity of form—for example, an object with a smooth surface can create balance with a smaller object with a highly textured surface.

Balance

Unbalanced
The color balance relationship is one third white to two thirds orange. In order to create balance the black rectangles have to decrease in intensity or value and the white square has to increase in intensity.

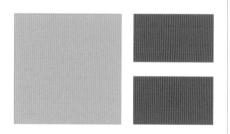

Balanced
There are many ways to create balance with color and design. In order to create visual harmony the attributes of color—hue, intensity and value can be shifted. Design elements are used in conjunction with the color to enhance balance. Because the orange is saturated, the proportional relationship between orange to light blue is slightly altered. To create color balance, the orange rectangles must be proportionately smaller than the white square.

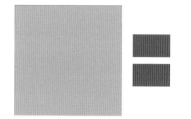

Symmetry

Symmetrical
The elements of the design are repeated on either side of the design. If you fold it in half in either direction they will be exactly the same. The design elements can be complex or simple just as long as they are identical.

Vertical axis

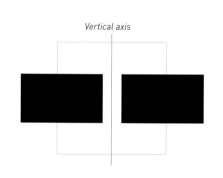

Asymmetrical
Asymmetrical design uses different objects in different positions that have equal weight. The diagram shows a square offset by two rectangles. Even though the two elements are different in shape they balance each other in weight just as a kilogram of carrots would balance a kilogram of apples.

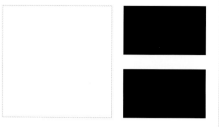

Scale, Proportion, and Space

When discussing the relationship between two different forms, we can contrast them by their scale, proportion, and their space. When comparing two forms, the greater the scale difference, the greater the contrast. However, the size differential between forms is often not enough to distinguish them—the properties of these forms can enhance contrast.

Placement, texture, pattern, and color can all alter the spatial relationship, and enhance the visual difference between objects. Placing an object at the bottom of the picture plane will enhance its visual strength by bringing it forward in space, for example. Texture, pattern, and color can also enhance the object. If one takes two identical forms and places them next to each other, the one with greater texture, greater pattern, or stronger color will stand out most. Positioning the less textured, patterned, or colored form at the top of the picture space will make it stand out even less.

In accordance with Joseph Albers' color theory, a larger square that is lighter in value can be balanced by a smaller square that is darker in value; a larger square with lower intensity can balance a smaller square with greater intensity. Meanwhile, Goethe suggests that balance can be created with varying amounts of complementary color—that ⅓ orange space is balanced out by ⅔ blue space. Accordingly, a picture plane can be balanced by using forms scaled and colored in these ⅓ to ⅔ proportions.

Movement and Flow

Another important design principle is visual flow. When looking at a design it is important for the viewer's eye to move around the page. If there is an area of focal importance, design elements can be used to direct movement to this point. Black-and-white or colored lines can set a path directing the viewer to the focal image, or lines can be used to form a pattern variation that moves in a specific direction. Color can also be used as part of the pattern, or can be utilized separately by creating a gradation leading the eye to the most intense color.

Emphasis and Focus

The focal point sometimes needs to stop movement and stand with great prominence in the foreground. It must be contrasted in some way so as to draw the viewer's eye toward it and stop it when it arrives. An active surface with a calm area can create flow and rest, while background color and simplified forms can create contrast to an active focal point. In the same fashion, quiet, low-intensity color can enhance flow to the bright spot on the canvas, and the use of complementary color may also enhance the form.

Above left: **If you study** *The Birth of Venus* by Botticelli, you see that there is a central figure with two figurative images one on either side. While not identical, the visual weight is balanced. The dominance of a primary triadic color palette enhances the harmonic flow of the painting.

Above: **In Degas'** *The Green Dancer*, c. 1880, asymmetrical balance creates greater movement and flow throughout the picture plane. The value of the dancers' clothing helps with flow, as does the diagonal line of the composition of the dancers in the foreground. In addition, Degas uses more blue-green in the foreground figures and orange in the background figures. This creates color balance proportionately.

CHAPTER TWO

COLOR IN PRINT

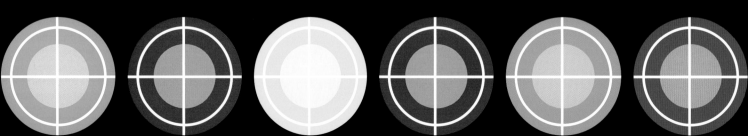

EXPERT: **MICHAEL OSBORNE**
Michael Osborne of Michael Osborne Design, President and Creative Director
of the San Francisco-based graphic design firm, MOD/Michael Osborne Design, Inc.

I wondered if you could tell me a little bit about you and your firm's background?

I went to college after I got back from Vietnam. Afterward, I came up to Palo Alto and got a job. A few years later I got offered a big freelance job and left my real job, not realizing that when I got the freelance job done I wouldn't have a job anymore. It was when the Atari games first came out. I did all the sales and promotional materials for Atari and then pretty soon I had a client, then another client. If you think about everything it takes to start a business you might not start one. For me, it just happened. Little by little we became more focused on packaging, which had been a favorite of mine at school. The problem when you have a small firm is that it is hard to get good packaging projects. For example, I really wanted to do some packaging for Dreyers ice cream. I hadn't done any ice cream packaging before, and once you break through somewhere, you have to be really careful at what you get good at because that is what you are going to get more of. Fortunately, somewhere along the line I got introduced to Sebastiani Winery. My first wine label was for them. Then one thing led to another, and I ended up doing wine label packaging. Next I got Shasta Cola. They have around 16 different flavors. I ended up coming up with a color flavor system for that. It was quite a challenge. It takes time, but you have to work up to the projects that you really want to work on. About 90% of what we do is for food and beverage and consumer goods. We make private labels and beverage packaging, with an emphasis on wine and spirits.

Could you tell me the process that is involved once you get the client? How you might go about it and what role color plays in the process?

After we get a project, our first task is to study until we know almost as much about our client's business as they do. Sometimes our biggest design problem is understanding what the problem is. A well-defined problem is half solved. I get asked questions all the time, for instance about where I get my inspiration and ideas. The answer to any question is inside the question. Our first priority is listening to the client and absorbing the brief. We do research to see what's happening in the marketplace and with competitors, what the demographics are, and what's not connecting in the marketplace. We do a lot of work before pencil hits paper. Then I sit with my sketchbooks and work out some possible designs. I go over my designs with my staff and with the creative director. If you take all the goals and the objectives, everything that is in the design brief, everything that the client wants accomplished, and put it in piece mode its got everything in there, everything. This will work for almost anything, not just packaging. We will have several solutions that are all correct, but all weigh out differently. Figuring out which one is the most correct is what creates a more interesting conversation for me. If you show up at a meeting with four versions of the same answer, you don't have a lot to talk about. My job is to make sure that what we are doing is part of a great design; is it evolutionary, is it revolutionary, or is it somewhere in between? If it is a new product launch, we have to make sure that the design is going to work for their target consumer.

COVER STORY Color is one of the strongest design tools in the box, and a savvy designer can integrate it and utilize its powers to create a great design. It is one thing to appreciate and understand the theory, the associations, and the emotional impact of color, but it is another to be able to apply that information as a designer. It is the ability to utilize it to communicate a message or to enhance the context of an image that puts graphic designers to the test each and every day.

A designer who understands the theoretical, psychological, and contextual aspects of color—its moods, meanings, and associations—is able to use the communicative qualities of color to define and enhance their message. From a design perspective, color acts as an attention grabber, a statement maker, a perspective changer, a persuader, and an associator. The questions then revolve around the idea of defining design goals and choosing colors and schemes that support the concept both visually and contextually.

The use of color has many benefits when it comes to design: it can improve visibility and convey structure, enhance and clarify the message, establish identity, create a symbol, convey a mood, stir up an association, and express a metaphor.

How color is utilized starts at a conceptual level when the designer defines his goals. The goals vary not only with the purpose of the message that they are conveying, but also by the type of materials they are creating. The development of a brand identity might require a flexible and complex color scheme for use in different contexts, while a magazine cover that uses a design singularly just needs to draw attention at a newsstand. However, in both instances a good cover design must carry some punch, using type, image, layout, and color to make a cohesive statement.

Once the purpose behind the design has been discerned and an approach has been formulated, a decision has to be made as to what design principles should be used. At this point, design elements are chosen that support the principles and enhance the concept. For our purposes, color is the chosen element, and it can be utilized in a variety of ways dependent on the type, style, and message of material designed.

A design area in which color is especially relevant is the area of figure-ground—the color of the background versus the figurative focus of the design. On the cover of *The Optimism Bias: A Tour of the Irrationally Positive Brain*—designed by Peter Mendelsund—the color pink is used in the focal image. While quantitatively small, its addition to the single

frame of the eyeglasses portrays "rose-colored glass" and associated connotations of optimism. However, only one lens is pink—the other remains the gray of the background—creating a "half empty/half full" scenario.

The power of the rose color against a totally achromatic background simply and effectively suggests the content of the book, which discusses how the brain generates hope and compares the ideology of optimism versus pessimism. The image portrays the major role that optimism has on our behavior, even to the point of strengthening our ability to recollect. The glasses are placed centrally above the symmetrical, soft, and elegant type. One is forced to view the type through the frame in both gray and pink, suggesting the need to understand pessimism and to gain an increased awareness of the importance of optimism.

This can also be seen in two different cover designs for the novel *After Dark*, by Haruki Murakami—one designed by Chip Kidd and the other by John Gall. Both use a similar palette and subject matter, but with differing visual impact. *After Dark* is a novel set in Tokyo over the course of a single night, and both Kidd and Gall play on the interchange and ambiguity of the slightly surreal tale. A successful designer at Knopf Doubleday Publishing Group, Kidd created the cover for the hardcover version of the novel, published in 2007. He uses a photographic image of a neon-lit Tokyo "pachinko parlor," broken down with a series of vertical lines that make it resemble a soft pattern of interwoven color. The bright yellows, reds, and violets combine with the broken edges to enhance the surrealistic vagaries of the characters in the novel.

Gall, the former art director at Vintage and Anchor, also uses geometric forms in his cover design, employing small dots that resemble Morse code. Using a cropped portrait of a face bathed in soft light, Gall focuses on the beautiful sister who spends most of the novel lying alone in a dream state. He portrays her cropped face, with the single visible eye closed, light against the dark background. The dots trying to

Right: In addition to the visual transparency and hue of the rose-colored lens, the obvious placement of the glasses establishes a human association by being essentially eye level. This point of view gives us perceptual understanding and visual identification.

The
Optimism Bias

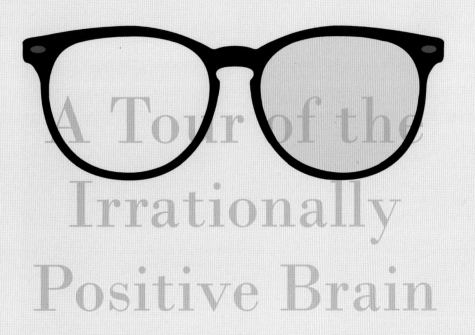

A Tour of the
Irrationally
Positive Brain

Tali Sharot

"Fascinating. . . . Even if you're a dedicated cynic, you might be
surprised to learn that your brain is wearing rose-colored
glasses, whether you like it or not."
—NPR

communicate, but merely glancing the surface, float on top, creating a sense of distance in a similar fashion to Kidd's distortion of the characteristics of the space and the girl within, reinforcing the alienation that is present in both images. While the color of Kidd's design draws the viewer in, they are blocked by the geometric designs.

Peter Mendelsund, associate art director at Alfred A. Knopf, used a simplified color palette in conjunction with texture and pattern for two book covers designed for novels by Ben Marcus, creating a visual link between the two titles. For *The Flame Alphabet*, Mendelsund created a geometric design that employed a series of cutout, collaged flames in discordant color. The intensity of reds and oranges and the disproportionate

use of yellow create a feeling of disquieting color, while the jagged shapes reflect the angst of the tale. The type—slim blue lettering on top of white, rectangular, cutout squares—looks like it has been slipped into place, representing a disconnected calm within a storm.

In his second cover for Marcus—for a series of short stories entitled *Leaving the Sea Stories*—Mendelsund again uses a cutout design, but here the shapes form a more analogous color scheme that is representative of the sea. The blue-green harmonic color palette moves with rhythmic flow across the page, while the type—again still in the form of small rectangles with slim lettering—is placed in an angular, random fashion throughout the cutout sea.

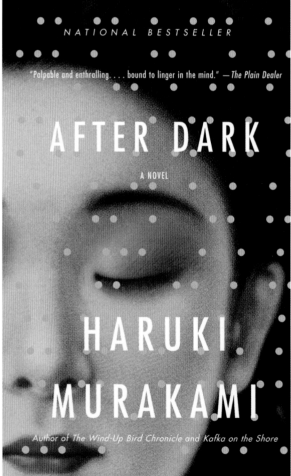

Left: It is interesting that both covers use simple geometric shapes as a dominant overall element on the page. The color in Kidd's design (left) is a stronger component of the design than in Gall's (right). The use of rectangles combined with intensity of color gives the cover a sense of movement into a dreamlike ambiguous space making the connection between the reality and dream state visual. Gall presents a more straightforward rendition by focusing on a figure with her eyes closed. Geometric elements seem to add a visual and emotional protective layer.

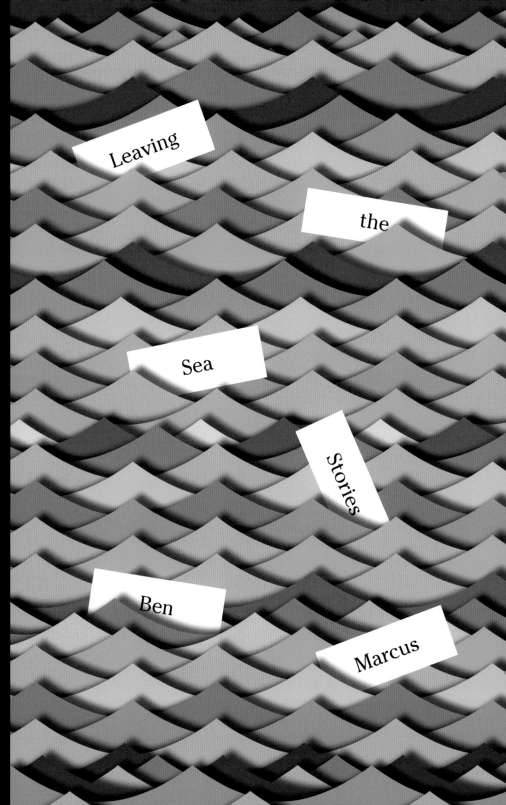

Above & right: **Both covers done by Peter Mendelsund are distinctively identifiable as books by Ben Marcus.** In both covers, shape, color, and pattern dominate the design. In *The Flame Alphabet* (above) the scale of the triangles combined with color and placement determine the mood. While the pattern is constant with the exception of type placement, the shifting of colored elements and the disproportionate use of yellow gives the cover a discordant feeling. While the *Leaving the Sea Stories* (right) cover features an analogous color scheme, the texture of the cut-out design elements suggest activity rather than the calmness associated with the colors. The positioning and color of the type adds another element to the design.

COLOR AND TYPE Another area in which color can play a significant role is typography. Colored type can be used to create a focal point for emphasis, to enhance what is being said, and to complement overall design. When talking about typography, the elements that concern the designer are letterforms—serif or non-serif, spacing, size, style. Concerns revolve around legibility, how clear the words are and readability, how easily they are read. We choose type in order to communicate an idea or concept and we judge it from a design standpoint by detail, size, and style. When we talk about color and typography we are concerned with how color will enhance these concerns.

In an article entitled, "Typography, Color, and Information Structure," Keyes talks about the relationship between color and typography. Although the study is based on technical documents, several interesting color/type observations are discussed. Keyes talks about how color focuses the reader's attention to organizational patterns. Color is seen by the reader prior to processing the type. Headings and subheadings in red, for example, would help organize the reader's understanding of the topic. Keyes also comments on color saturation, value, and proportion. She states that contrast is key. Black and white might be the best choice for documents, but color can be used as long as compensatory measures such as scale, boldness and thicker typefaces are used. She also comments on the fact that deep values create more contrast and are therefore better for type. Yellows, reds, and oranges are harder to read than greens, blues, and violets. As we have learned about color relativity, the color and the strength of the type is dependent upon the background color and the contrast implied.[1] A wonderful example of this is the graphic book *Conundrums*, designed by Harry Pearce of Pentagram. Designed with simplicity and focus, the book is a collection of graphically designed word games constructed in a similar typeface and a monochromatic palette. The design is enhanced by the relationship between intense orange, black, and white, and their continual interchange within and around graphically placed words.

For the cover, Pearce chose to split the word "conundrum" into six rows of letters that alternate black and orange (on a white background), set down the right edge. The subtitle—Typographic Conundrums—and author name appear in much smaller type, again in black and orange. The back cover places the word "Back" in black, underneath which the word "Front" appears twice in orange. Beyond the words and their cryptic meanings, it is the complex relationships between the foreground letters and their negative space (background) that enhances these carefully chosen variables.[2]

The constant interplay throughout the pages of the book are so distinctive, so readily identifiable and stylistic, that Pearce was asked to provide a spread of conundrums in the recipe book *Hungry? The Innocent Recipe Book for Filling Your Family with Good Stuff*, as well as creating conundrums for the Saks Fifth Avenue holiday catalog.

COLOR AND TYPE

Type is quintessential in periodical design, and color is an excellent way to enhance the relationship between type and image. Whether it is *Oprah*, *Vogue*, *Dwell*, or any other magazine, type color is often adapted from the central image. Flexibility of design is made possible by the way in that color is utilized. Once the colors of the image have been identified there are still numerous options available to the designer as to how to use the chosen color in a color palette, as well as its placement on or around type.

In terms of color palette, we can employ various color combinations depending on the message we are trying to communicate. Whether it's an identical color creating a monochromatic relationship between image and type or a complementary relationship to create contrast, if designed correctly it will help bring unity to the design.

Dwell magazine has employed many different colors for its masthead. While the color appears to stem from the image, the schemes vary—sometimes it will come directly from an architectural or interior element and sometimes it will contrast it.[3]

Below: **The contrast between chromatic color of the type and achromatic dominance in the image create a contrast between them. Notice the woman's blue outfit and the red on a few selected books and the corner of the painting. The triadic palette that the images and type form together unites the cover.**

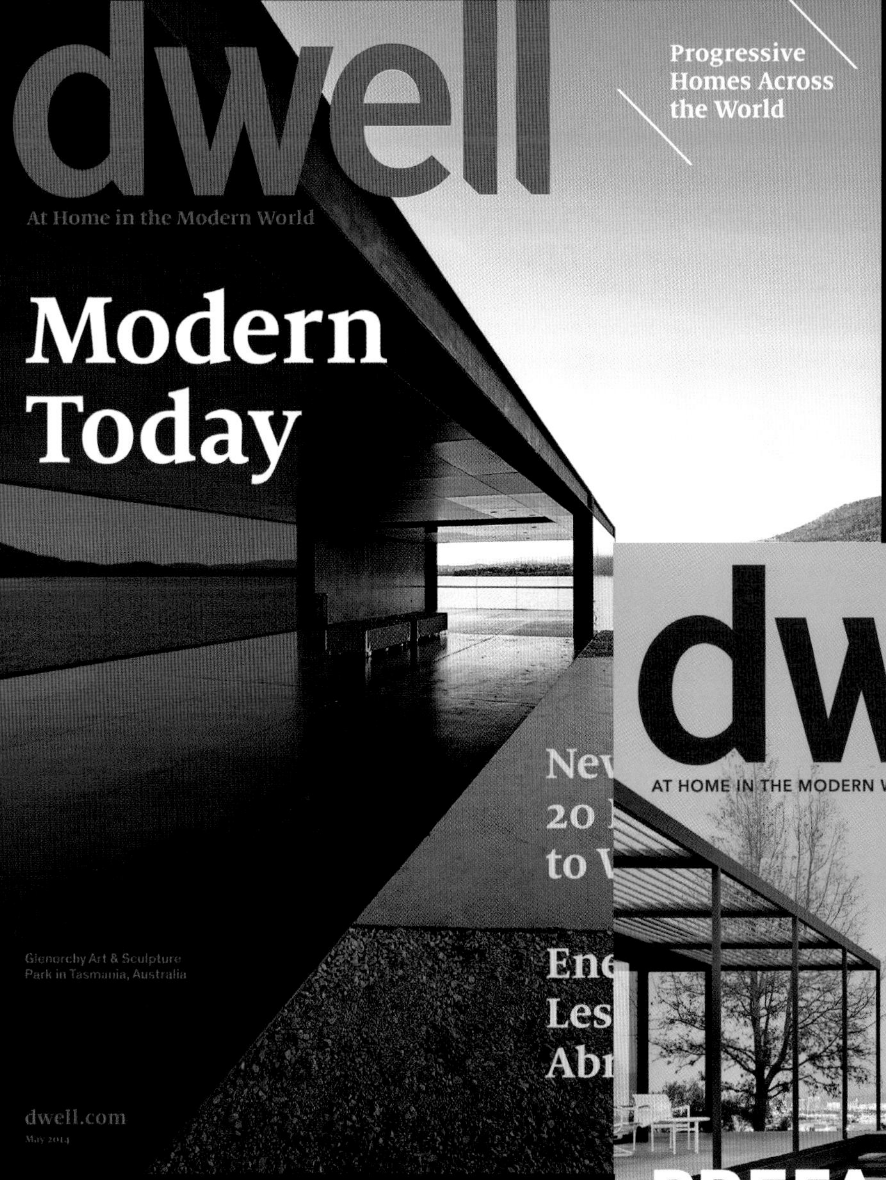

dwell

At Home in the Modern World

Modern Today

Left: The type color stems directly from the image, but the increase in value and intensity enhance the statement in this monochromatic palette. Consistent with the scheme, all typefaces are different values of the same hue.

Glenorchy Art & Sculpture Park in Tasmania, Australia

dwell.com
May 2014

New
20
to V

Ene
Les
Abr

Right: The dominant color is blue, but the scheme can almost be considered analogous because the background is blue-green while the foreground type is blue-violet. This creates contrast while establishing unity of image.

dwell

AT HOME IN THE MODERN WORLD

Is Prefab Right For You?
9 Essential Questions

Design Icon
Q & A with Shigeru Ban

PREFAB NOW

11 Modern Residences From Around the World That Defy Expectations

A MARVEL IN VENICE
The Latest Dwell Home
by Sebastian Mariscal

dwell.com
Dec / Jan 2014

Marmol Radziner's
Desert Creation
Outside Las Vegas

COLOR AND IMAGE An important aspect of color publications is a focal image on the cover. Whether it is a photograph, a graphic, or an illustration, it must make a statement that relates to the style and the story of the publication—this statement is supported by the color tone of the image.

There are a variety of color application methods that can be used, depending on the type of publication and the message it is conveying. The color palette can be established through the choice of the image itself and by controlling the time of day that it is taken. The image can be modified or retouched. If we are dealing with graphics or illustration, we can focus our energy on developing a color palette that is consistent with the tone and of the publication. Color combinations can also be created in an imaginative way so they convey a particular mood.

You can manage the color of a cover image by using a photograph with the color palette that creates the mood you are looking for. For example you could take a picture of a tree with colorful leaves for a fall issue of a nature magazine, or have a model wearing the color of choice for a fashion magazine.

In the creation of the cover for *Boston* magazine after the marathon bombings in April 2013, shape, color, and texture were arranged to make the cover especially poignant. Editor Wolf Johnson talked about the background to the cover: "Design director, Brian Struble, and deputy design director, Liz Noftle, took shoes from marathon participants and arranged them in the shape of a heart."[4]

The heart-shaped rendition made out of sneakers from runners to honor the bombing victims had a gradation of color going from dark grays and blacks at the corners, through white, green, and blue, to red at the center. The concept was described as follows: "By itself, each shoe in the photograph is tiny, battered, and ordinary. Together, though, they create something beautiful, powerful, and inspirational. Remove just one shoe and you begin to diminish, in some small way, the overall effect. Collectively, they are the perfect symbol for Boston, and for our response to the bombings." Within the magazine there were stories of the runners, and on the back cover, the same shoes, but placed soles up.

Beautifully colored photographs can be taken with a knowledge of the color of light. Photographers must understand how color appears at different times of day. Jad Davenport, a naturalist photojournalist with

National Geographic talks about his process: "I use Nikon digital camera equipment—a D800 and various lenses. My process includes researching the subject I'll be shooting, making a pleasing composition in the field and then waiting for a moment, for something interesting to happen. I photograph in only natural light. Natural light tends to be warmer in the evenings and mornings, and cooler in bright sun in the middle of the day. You can manipulate the color the camera sees by changing the white balance in your camera."[5] As discussed earlier, the color of light is measured in degrees Kelvin (K), with lower temperatures being reds and yellows and higher temperatures being the blues and violets at the opposite end of the visible spectrum.

Color shifts throughout the day, and photographers can take advantage of this. Before sunrise, for example, the color temperature can be as high as 10,000K, when the only illumination comes indirectly

COLOR TEMPERATURE CHART

Light Sources	Color Temperature in K
Clear Blue Sky	10,000–5,000
Overcast Sky	6,000–8,000
Noon Sun and Clear Sky	6,500
Sunlight Average	5,400–6,000
Electronic Flash	5,400–6,000
Household Lighting	2,500–3,000
200-watt Bulb	2,980
100-watt Bulb	2,900
75-watt Bulb	2,820
60-watt Bulb	2,800
40-watt Bulb	2,650
Candle Flame	1,200–1,500

Opposite: When you study this powerful image you can see the color variations within each pair of individual sneakers. It is interesting to see that parts of the color palette are shared with neighboring sneakers to create an overlapping of colors.

Boston

We Will
Finish The Race
The stories behind these shoes
begin on page 70

10,000K, when the only illumination comes indirectly from the blue sky, producing a strong blue-colored light. However, at dawn the light measured can be as low as 2500K—warm and red as the sun rises. As the morning progresses, the color temperature rises—early morning is about 3000–4000K, while midday is closer to the "neutral" color temperature of 5500K. Of course, this also depends on the weather—a photograph taken on a cloudy day will appear cooler, at around 7500K, while shady areas on a sunny day may have a color temperature as high as 10,000k. The color temperature of the sun in the afternoon will decrease to 3000–4000K, once again reaching 2000–2500K as the sun sets and reds dominate. After sunset, the light again becomes blue at 10,000K.

A perfect example of a form for which lighting is of utmost importance is wildlife photography. This is one of the most difficult and time-consuming forms of photography. In addition to deciding on subject matter, location, and design of the background, wildlife photographers must compensate for the variability of the animal's position, direction, and proximity to the camera. "As the photographer cannot control any of his lighting conditions, and the use of flash photography on night-time creatures is a one-time shot, so distance from the subject, angle from the sun or moon, time of day, weather conditions, lens size and flash diffusers are all factors that come into play for the lighting of a single shot and single series of shots."[6]

Digital cameras can automatically balance the color temperature by setting the white balance. If the camera's white balance is set to Auto, the camera will read a scene's color temperature and try to set a "neutral" result. Most cameras also have a range of preset options (Daylight, Cloudy, Incandescent, etc.) that allow you to manually adjust the white balance according to the light source. You can also alter color at the post-production stage—adding or subtracting color; intensifying or reducing its impact; or superimposing images.

Color can also enhance meaning when used in an illustrative capacity, and magazines have often asked great artists to illustrate their covers using their personal style and color. From the mid-twentieth-century onward, various prominent artists have been asked to create paintings on topics in order to add personality to the issues—Pop Artists such as Warhol, Rauschenberg, and Lichtenstein all contributed to *Time* magazine, for example.

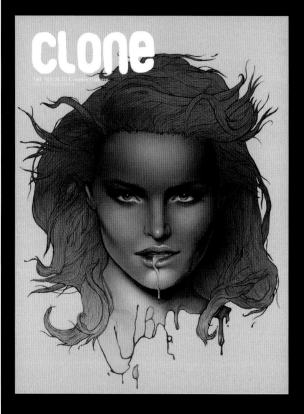

Above: *Clone* is a Spanish art and music pop magazine that uses intense color for its cover image. Grzegorz Domaradzki, illustrator, talks about the illustration: "I was asked to design a cover and opening illustration for *Clone*. The topic was pleasure, so I wanted something eye catching and "sexy" to begin with. I also very much wanted to go with ultra vivid colors. It's no secret that both yellow and violet work together well as they are complementary colors, so I knew and expected, that when used on the artwork they would make it stand out among other titles."[7]

Right: *The Ride* is a journal of personal stories about bicycle riding. Several illustrations done for issues explore exquisite detail and a wonderfully expressive color palette. With a goal of personal expression in mind, the editors approached their favorite artists, illustrators and photographers. Because it is done as an expression of love, there are no advertisements and the staff donates its earnings to various charities. The contrast between nature and architectural elements is emphasized by color and technique. Harmonious color washes on natural elements contrast to increase intensity and black linear outlines of architectural elements.

CATALOGS AND ANNUAL REPORTS Creating a design for a catalog or annual report is similar to designing a book or periodical cover, in that the cover must convey a message and attract the reader. However, it must also carry the design throughout the entire volume, so it is important to ensure consistency. At the same time, different design decisions are needed for different intents.

The content of a catalog or an annual report will vary with the size and type of organization and its underlying purpose. When it comes to design—whether online or in print—the job of a designer is to create an interesting design that attracts the reader initially, and organizes the information in such a way as to promote clarity and conceptual understanding throughout the piece.

There are various options available to a designer, including the use of interesting fonts and infographics, and also printing techniques or animations (online). An understanding of color palettes and color families might give the variety and unity that a catalog or annual report might need to attract attention and maintain interest. Color can also be used to carry the concept from cover to cover, guiding the reader through large quantities of material while creating focal interest points. While there are limitless color choices open to graphic designers, there is quite a limited use of color design when it comes to annual reports. In the paper, "Color in Graphic Design: An analysis of meaning and trends," researchers Barbara E. Martinson and Carol Waldron of the University of Minnesota review a study that they did on color usage in annual reports from 1993 to 2000. They tried to identify patterns of color usage focusing on color choices and scheme development, and the use of achromatic color from data ascertained from two prominent graphic design publications, *Print* and *Communication Arts*. What they found described in their overall analysis was that: "One third of the annual reports used a palette that included black, white, and one color from the quadrants one and three (red to yellow). Nearly one fifth of the designs used black, white and one color from the quadrants one and three (cyan to blue) [on the color wheel]." The largest samplings taken were from technology, financial, and health sciences and these industries predominantly used option one. 40% of natural resource companies also used this combination. Over 34% used complementary colors for balance and contrast. The most frequent combination was black, white, and red or brown, which follows historically early printing where red was used for emphasis."[8]

Often, the color palette has to be taken from an existing brand identity, but it can be applied in various ways to establish company sentiment. This was the case with the 2011 annual report for Osum Oil Sands Corporation, which was created by Joe Hospodarec (creative director), Hans Thiessen (designer), and Max Maythe (copywriter) of the WAX design agency in Calgary, Canada. Simplicity and stability were key to the design, conveyed by the use of simple infographics, concise content, and a cover with little more than a few abstract forms and an unobtrusive title. The simple, analogous color scheme consisted predominantly of a subtle blue-gray color with blue-green vertical rectangles, suggesting not only calmness and corporate stability, but also trust, loyalty, and wisdom. The color enlivens the design, while the interior graphics appear as horizontal color blocks with limited type to enhance the idea of strength and balance. Color and design remain constant on the company website.

While color enhanced the design and content of the Osum Oil Sands Corporation annual report, it was integral to the essence of lighting company Zumtobel Group. To create its 2011–2012 annual report, Zumtobel Group turned to Brighten The Corners studio of London, who worked in collaboration with artist Anish Kapoor. Because color and light are so intrinsic to the workings of a lighting company, they created sister volumes for the annual report: a highly conceptual color piece, and a black-and-white volume focusing on annual facts and figures in 8 pt. type. The volume of pure color, based on the film by Kapoor named *Wounds and Absent Objects*[9], was a video projection done in 1998 involving a loop of color energy that evolved and morphed into different palettes. While the volumes are different, they make contrasting complements—one in black and white representing the "nuts and bolts" (the financial and factual material) of the business, and the other an emotional visual expression of color and light that is devoid of words. Together they express the complete picture of the company: one representing a grounded, well-organized, practical business, and the other suggesting creativity and enormous possibility.

Right: **This is an example of a fictional annual report. It is very important for colors used on the cover of a report to flow through to the internal pages and infographics creating a unified design concept.**

Lorem ipsum dolor sit amet,
consectetuer adipiscing elit

Lorem ipsum dolor sit amet

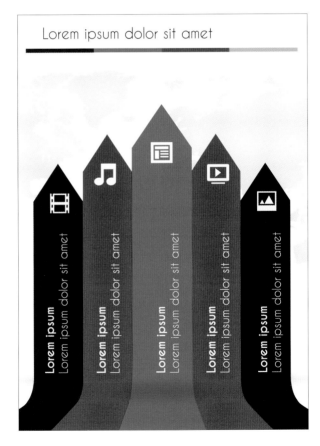

Lorem ipsum
Lorem ipsum dolor sit amet

Lorem ipsum
Lorem ipsum dolor sit amet

Lorem ipsum
Lorem ipsum dolor sit amet

Lorem ipsum
Lorem ipsum dolor sit amet

Lorem ipsum
Lorem ipsum dolor sit amet

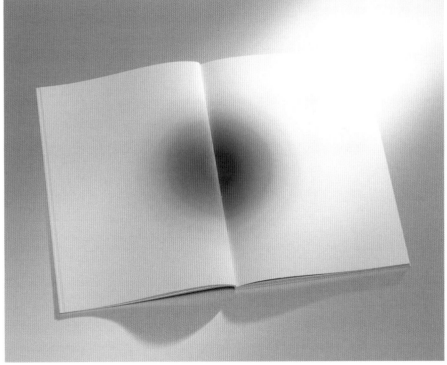

Above: When you look at these pure images the intensity of color is greatest at the center mimicking a light source or lamp. It is not only indicative of a light, but also the center of an idea. This work, which features a series of ten neon colors based on Anish Kapoor's video, contrasts with the more technical pages that contain all the information relevant to the client, but which are approached with the same circular design.

The color approach for catalog design has slightly different goals to an annual report. The secret is to create a catalog that appeals to an individual's desired lifestyle, with the purpose of promoting sales of the products within. Catalogs must create a need and desire for the individual buyer within their target market. The goal is to attract the viewer by place, lifestyle, and design while focusing on the product.

Blu Dot—a contemporary furniture company founded by John Christakos, Maurice Blanks, and Charles Lazor—hired Stuart Flake of the What Agency to create their catalog, Blu Dot 15. Flake used the furniture to create 43 pages of furnishings placed together in interesting combinations, all seen from different perspectives. He succeeded in creating an artistic type catalog for a furniture line, complete with oddly placed furniture seen from the sides, front, and top, unlimited by the scope of the page.

The colors used stem from the furnishings and accessories—sometimes just one element appears on a page, and sometimes the entire page is filled with color. With the exception of these pages, the backgrounds are mostly achromatic but for the presence of randomly placed colored smoke. Shadows and textured items play a role in some images. The color adds visual interest with its often intense presentation, and moves the reader through the catalog. The design is successful because the vignettes become larger than life, making the reader focus on the furniture and its characteristics.

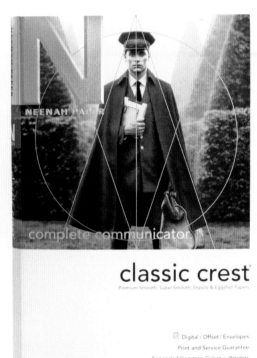

Opposite: The color and design elements in Stuart Flake's Blu Dot 15 catalog work together to create an unusual cubist-influenced multi-perspective style design. Primary colors enforce the intensity of purpose and simplicity of design.

Above: For a company like Neenah Papers, using colored paper and design is consistent to their brand statement and useful for their product merchandising. Design Army has used surrealistic imagery and color palette to realize its design concept.

Color is also central to the merchandise of paper manufacturer, Neenah Paper. Using colored materials, Design Army—a Washington-based design company—redesigned Neenah Paper's promotional material and swatch books for its Classic papers. Working on the idea of the "perfect 10," Design Army chose the 10 most commonly used colors. The redesign included these 10 colors across six finishes in four classic brands with the purpose being to "present the brands as a family's unique individualism as well as to bring them to life in a compelling way." Using a slightly oversized scale they created images of things imaginarily perfect, presenting the idealistic in new and different ways. In trying to give a "classic" product a new look, Design Army created surreal images such as a woman with three hands holding a book, mirror, and lipstick, and a postman in a topiary garden. To attract a younger design crowd, a promotional video was also created, entitled *What Moves You?* Starting in black and white, the video proceeds to add various colors and geometric patterns that act as a background to dancers dressed in black and white.[10]

CHAPTER THREE

COLOR IN BRANDING AND IDENTITY

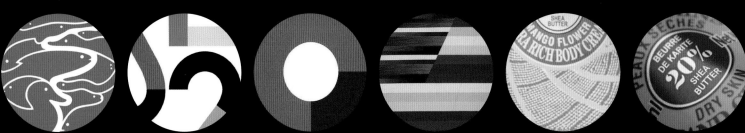

EXPERT: **DAVID KUNITZ**
David Kunitz, Innovative Design & Development Consultant at D-Kid group and Former Vice President of Design at Hasbro Corporation.

Could you talk about your background?
I decided that industrial design was where I needed to be and it's been great since. I went to Purdue University in Indiana. I am more of a technical as opposed to a fine-art designer. Mechanics and machinery—those are the things that I am interested in. My intention on graduation was to be designing computers and I was working through a head hunter who said I needed practice with my interviewing skills, so would I mind going to a toy company and doing an interview there. I had so much fun at the interview (it was with Hasbro) but I didn't hear from them and I got two other offers. With the encouragement of my father, I called and I talked to the designer that had interviewed me. He said that he couldn't believe that HR hadn't told me that there is a hiring freeze. My father then suggested I call HR saying "what's the worst that could happen!" So I called up and they said that the hiring freeze had just ended two days ago and that the design department had some openings. They started the paperwork there and then, and that is how I got my job and the beginnings of a career in toy design.

When you were designing toys did you utilize color palettes as part of that system? When would color choices come in, and how were they made?
The first thing that I worked on was Transformers—a series of robots coming in from Japan all mismatched, very bright colors, with no storyline. There were no good Transformers or bad Transformers at that point, and what Hasbro did was pretty incredible. I participated in creating a design language, a color palette, and a storyline. In doing that, we created the good and the bad—it determined what Transformers really is, with Decepticons and Autobots battling each other and battling for a reason. We used the color palette to define roles. Originally it was purples and the blacks for the Decepticons, and bight red and blue—some of the brighter colors in the palette—for the good guys. When the product came out, kids could just look at the thing and say that is a good guy or that's a bad guy.

How do people know what was a bad guy color? How did you decide on that?
In G.I. Joe, for the most part, military colors were for the good guys with lots of greens. It could be a brighter green even though the military wouldn't use it. Greens, browns, and black were allowed to crossover between the good and the bad, and for the bad guys lots of reds and purples, and variations of those, such as maroon.

Are there certain colors that are seen as child-friendly?
That's a great question. There are a lot of theories on that, and many opinions. I had an experience where I came across a preconceived notion about color for boys' toys. I had just started working at Tyco Toys, and I was asked to direct the re-coloration of some existing products. The product I presented to the head of marketing had a tiger motif with a lot of orange in it. He proclaimed that orange doesn't sell to kids. I had to explain to him that I was aware of a toy boat that was mostly orange and sold at record volumes and was hugely profitable. The room erupted in laughter because, I found out later, this marketing person, first of all he doesn't like orange; second thing, he said boats don't sell. I think any color can sell, it just has to be appropriate for the toy. For example, in the 1980s highlight pink was used on some vehicle labels and it sold very well.

Would you like to talk about something you are working on currently in terms of design and color?
Wonder Blox is a product that works with an iPad or a mobile device that has a front-facing camera. The camera looks up to see a mirror that looks back down to see what is on or around the device. I am involved in just the design end of it. One of the things that we really had to concentrate on was making sure that the color palette, from the logo to the blocks to the game, shared the same design language. The visual language of a product has to be cohesive and I like to have a common language when I am working on a product. Color has to be at the forefront of your mind basically right from the beginning.

LOGOS Every company uses color in its identity and branding. While there can be some slight variation, everything from the company logo to its annual report to a trade show booth must have a consistent visual look. A strong logo design often includes a strong brand color—Coca Cola red and UPS brown, for example—meaning that color can play an important role in a company's marketability.

A logo must have the flexibility to be produced not only in different scales and on different materials, but also it must have clear color design that makes it a recognizable emblem. In a study, "Exciting Red and Competent Blue: The Importance of Color in Marketing," Lauren Labrecque and George Milne try to establish the importance of color in brand management. They created four studies in which they collected empirical data from both psychology and marketing literature and studied the effect of color and design properties on branding. They researched and studied over a hundred brands of different types, comparing grayscale logos and brand names to colored designs. The research supported the idea that there was a relationship between color and "brand personality" with respect to hue, saturation, and value. Making changes to hue and intensity will affect consumer reaction. One of the things they found was that intensity has a positive association with ruggedness and a negative association with sophistication. They also suggest that it can affect the desire to purchase the product.[1]

Color palettes can be specific to an industry, but associations may vary across different cultures. In the article "Logo Color and Differentiation: A New Application of Environmental Color Mapping," Zena O'Connor suggests that color mapping might be a sophisticated way of determining cultural colors with respect to logos and graphic design. Already used in architecture, this process "identifies color characteristics within a given environment," creating a database of color characteristics within a specific environment.[2] When designing regional color palettes, a tool such as this might provide interesting and relevant information.

While most companies utilize primary and secondary colors for their brand identity, leaning heavily on the primary triad red/yellow/blue, a creative leap could enhance brand recognition as it did with Apple's use of rainbow colors. Even the use of more than one color could make the difference. Primary color can be used in a unique fashion, as it has been in the logo for Grey, a New York advertising division

of the Grey Group. Originally founded as Grey Studios named after the color on the walls, Grey Advertising asked design firm Chermayeff & Geismar & Haviv. The logo for the firm was the word "grey." Instead of using the obvious choice of color, red was chosen. According to Tom Geismar, "our design concept was simple: we took the blandness that 'grey' represents and turned it on its head by making it as bright and vibrant as possible, using a bold vermilion red. It's the discrepancy between the company name and the color it's depicted in that makes it interesting."[3] Resembling the Stroop test—which uses different colors to the actual word name to derive brain flexibility—this approach forces individuals to stop and consider whether it is red or gray.

Another identity created by Chermayeff & Geismar & Haviv was for the Tennessee Aquarium. The focus of the aquarium is the freshwater fish and wildlife that inhabit the Tennessee River and so the design of the logo and other graphics needed to reflect this habitat. With the globe-shaped logo the design suggests a world, teaming with activity and wildlife. Tom Geismar elaborates: "The focus of the aquarium is on the wide variety of fish and wildlife that inhabit the Tennessee River and all the tributaries that feed into it. Those winding waters are represented by the white lines."[4]

GREY
FAMOUSLY EFFECTIVE SINCE 1917

Once it has been designed, the way in which a logo is tied into the company's corporate identity is what matters. Even if it has a strong design, a logo cannot stand alone, and it is that complete visual statement that—if designed well—can make a company stand out. For example, Michael Osborne Design used the color and pattern from the logo design of the San Francisco Museum of Modern Art to create products for the museum store, including hats, bookmarks, tote bags, umbrellas, notebooks, mugs, and lunch boxes. In turn, the products reinforce the identity of the museum. In addition, the bright colors and graphics used on shopping bags, promotional products, and packaging was a resounding success.[5] By taking design elements from the logo and utilizing them to create products, Michael Osborne enhanced the museum brand and reinforced its identity.

IDENTITY The importance of color in creating identities is portrayed in the work of Snøhetta Design, the company that was hired to create a visual identity and feasibility study for Oslo's bid for the 2022 Olympic Games. Using "playful graphics and strict geometry" based on the "simplicity and openness of the Nordic culture," the Norwegian design company adopted the color and circular motif of the original Olympic rings designed by Pierre de Coubertin in 1913. Both the logo and colorful photographic images in collateral materials were contained within a circular form, and the identity combined both cultural and historic elements within the design. While the color palette started out with Nordic references, later versions utilized the original colors of the Olympic rings. Snøhetta's design/presentation included interior architectural elements and signage, collateral printed material, and digital design for the new website.[6]

Color also has geographical and cultural meaning for American Airlines, who tasked FutureBrand with rebranding the airline. On the designer's website, FutureBrand talks about how it "helped American tell a story big enough to inspire the kind of change needed to reconnect American with its customers and reconnect American's people with the company." The goal was to be clear and confident yet welcoming and engaging, creating feelings of optimism and progress that are uniquely American. The airline wanted to present itself as participators in the passenger's experience, offering a world full of possibilities.[7]

While it could be a difficult transition, FutureBrand chose to redesign the iconic logo conceived by Massimo A. Vignelli in 1967. The logo that had been in use for almost 45 years—Helvetica type with a blue eagle graphic—was replaced with a contemporary, abstracted version of this symbol of the American spirit. The color shifted subtly away from navy blue and red, with the flat, stagnant color replaced by a value gradation that enhances the idea of flowing movement. In this way, the new design replaced an outdated version, but still maintained the associations and symbol of the original.

American Airlines' identity had always made reference to the symbol of the American flag, so the rebranding included not only the logo, but also an abstracted flag to feature on the wing of every plane. It is also used on terminal kiosks and plane interiors, and the color palette is carried through all collateral material and digital media. In the case of American Airlines, the color palette and design directly relates to the brand mission: to reflect the exploratory nature and positive outlook that permeates American culture.

Below left & right: **The bolder use of type without decorative striped elements on the side of the plane enhance the importance of the word American. The replacement of the logo for a strong recognizable graphic flag element not only adds visual interest, but implies the feeling of strength and power represented by America.**

Above & left: The use of achromatic elements in the numbers and letters featured in the design for Oslo's bid for the 2022 Olympic Games creates an intensity of color and complex forms. The suggestion that multiple parts within in each form create a whole, which then is part of a greater whole, is significant in that it suggests the unity involved in an Olympic event.

COLOR THAT PERSUADES: PACKAGING Typography, images, and color are all important elements of design, but color is critical to package design because the product being packaged must compete with other products on the shelf in order to persuade an individual to approach and purchase it. Since people sense color prior to any other element, that fast glance over a supermarket shelf makes color a primary lure, so the packaging must balance brand identity with product purpose. When you think a about a product, color associations become readily apparent—Coca Cola red is an obvious global example.

Shuo-Ting Wei, Li-Chen Ou, M. Ronnier Luo, and John B. Hutchings in their article, "Package Design: Colour Harmony and Consumer Expectations," discuss a study in which they use fruit juice packaging to study the relationship between color and psychological response. Assuming that the idea behind packaging is to create a harmonious pleasing effect, the study aimed at examining the relationship between the color harmony and the likeability of the product with specific respect to the consumer response due to color choices. Wei had previously done research with orange juice packaging which suggested that package design and product information influenced expectations. Although they did believe that their study was contextual, research indicated that if light or dark colors rather than mid-tones were used in the package, then the product was seen to be of high quality. They found that color harmony on the packaging resulted in high expectations for the product, and that intensity correlated with freshness and, as with the orange juice study, freshness was affiliated with bright colors.[8]

Today, sustainable, environmentally friendly products are in demand, and this extends to their packaging—it is not only a matter of creating a strong color palette and design, but also about the packaging itself. Companies such as Whole Foods have a reputation to uphold and want to keep shoppers coming back for their organic and local foods and green practices. Green is a lifestyle, and many product lines are based solely on this concept.

When designing with eco-friendly materials, a pop of rich color or other design elements can be superimposed on them. Many packaging manufacturers offer several environmentally friendly options, so you can have pattern and color with sustainability. Cosmetics company, L'Occitane en Provence, considers the weight of its packaging, the amount of waste, and the environmental impact of its products, specifically designing its packaging so that it comes in components that can be broken down. It also has a preference for recycled materials and on its website states that: "the essential functions of packaging are not necessarily compatible with environmental concerns. L'Occitane has decided to follow precise guidelines, with the goal of constantly and gradually reducing the environmental impact of its packaging. We have therefore chosen an eco-design approach, selecting materials that are the least polluting or already recycled, using resources that are renewable or that come from sustainably managed forests, and designing easily recyclable packaging."[9]

Color on the package can also relate to content. While a label can profess regional or brand identity, it

can also be used to differentiate between products in a line. A good example of this is a series of packages for Linksys wireless routers designed by Landor associates, a global brand consulting firm. Because of the complex nature of the product, a clear and simple way to distinguish between the products was necessary. A color-based capacity chart was designed to allow customers to make the correct choice.

To add to the complexity of color and packaging, color choice may vary due to technical and cultural environments or events. This is true from a material perspective because packaging can entail multiple material substrates and a variety of formats and printing methods, which can change the way in which the color is translated onto the packaging. In addition, color has different meanings in different regions, so it is hard to strike a balance between local identity and world assimilation. In any resort town around the world merchandise is created and packaged with specific reference to the community. A beach resort might have packaging with fish or shells on it along with the name of the resort imprinted. Local

colors would be used to enhance the memory of the experience that the purchaser might have when he or she returns home from the vacation. Standard everyday items such as cups and T-shirts become branded elements themselves. Corporate colors may be minimized or substituted in favor of the local color. Nestlé's packaging for its chocolate gift products for the Diwali Festival mimicked the local color. Fitch, an international branding design company, was asked by Nestlé to create packaging and displays.

Fitch recognized that, "Firstly, we needed to create a strong and ownable brand language that would ensure that Nestlé's range stood out at the point of purchase. Secondly, we wanted to build a sense of anticipation and excitement."[10] Consequently, iconography and design were taken from the festival of lights, with blocks of intense regional color used to make the product stand out.

Above: **During the Diwali festival of lights, Rangoli— Indian folk art—filled with diametric patterns and vibrant colors is drawn on floors. The full-spectrum palette and white linear design associated with Rangoli has been referenced by Nestlé in its packaging.**

PART FIVE
THE COLOR EXPERIENCE

CHAPTER ONE

COLOR IN THREE-DIMENSIONAL DESIGN

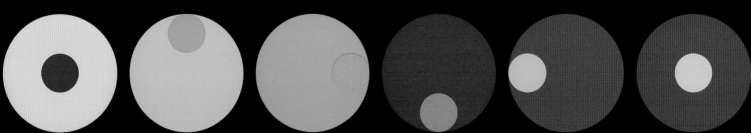

EXPERT: FRANK MAHNKE
Author of *Color, Environment, and Human Response, Color and Light in Man-made Environments,* and co-author of *Color: Communication in Architectural Space.* President of the IACC (International Association of Color Consultants/Designers) since 1988, and the Director of the IACC Education/ Accreditation Programs conducted worldwide.

Could you talk a little bit about your career path, how you became interested in color and how you ended up where you are, including the IACC and how it evolved?
My interest in color started at the age of 12 through my art training. Art is the background to learning to see, and to analyzing and broadening the horizons of impression and expression. This led me to my career path as a color consultant/environmental designer, lecturer, and author. I became the IACC Vice President for the USA in the mid-1980s and then took over as IACC President International after Dr. Heinrich Frieling retirement from this post after 30 years. Since then, in addition to the original IACC Salzburg Academy, we have added eight more educational facilities worldwide. A second academy is in the planning for North America.

As a firm believer in the physiological/psychological approach to color, how much credence do you put into cultural response that include the socio-political, historical, and geographical aspects of color perception?
To quote Dr. Küller: "One of the most striking features of the results concerning preferences, connotations, and color-mood associations is the consistency from one individual to another, from group to group, and cross-culturally." We are therefore working with what is called the "Universal Psychological Reactions". This does not preclude the existence of cultural and group-specific associations and symbols based on their traditions, religion, and philosophy, but the universal psychological reactions are global. I have conducted research on this question since 1991 with various countries, geographical, and cultural groups with the IACC Seminar students. After all these years, since 1993–2014 the findings of the color association study have remained amazingly consistent.

Do you believe that synesthetic approach to design where color and sound might be combined is a broader way to enhance the environment?
Whether or not synesthetic effects can be used to enhance the environment depends on the task of the environment. In the architectural environment it is recommended especially to counteract specific environmental problems. For example, heat is supported by red through orange and compensated for by light blue, blue-green, light green, and white.

Do you think that it is important to use theoretically harmonic color schemes and harmonies of contrast in creating a psychologically balanced environment?
Yes, I strongly believe in harmonic color schemes and contrast in creating a balanced environment. However, the key word is contrast. A monochromatic harmony based on one hue varied in lightness and saturation results in monotony. The same holds true for analogous harmonies. The key is complementary color: an environment that is predominantly warm in its visual expression warm must have accents of cool and vice-versa, for example.

What is the role of color designer in today?
The main task of a color consultant/designer is to understand color in all of its facets and interdisciplinary aspects. A professional color consultant/designer needs to understand the design considerations in architectural environments, which includes the psychological effects, neuropsychological aspects, visual ergonomics and emotional aspects. A color consultant must also learn to "see" and therefore experience the man-made environment; to regain or fine-tune sensitivity.

DESIGN ELEMENTS AND PRINCIPLES As we have seen, color is a fundamental aspect of design. On a two-dimensional surface it allows the viewer, whether looking at a painting or a book cover, to determine how a piece is viewed and the context that is derived from it. It can be used to create focus, movement, and balance, and to experience an emotional response dependent upon color choices, placement, and proportions that are used.

In the three-dimensional world, color is just as powerful if not more because the extent of the color effect in the physical environment can be more readily experienced. So in order to talk about three-dimensional objects, there are additional design elements that must be discussed:

- **Vertex:** The point at which all planes come to a point, often a corner
- **Edge:** The point at which two planes intersect and the outside limit of an object. An edge defines the boundaries of the mass.
- **Mass:** How much substance or matter there is within an object, often measured by weight.
- **Face:** An individual surface of a solid object.

What distinguishes the two-dimensional from the three-dimensional is depth. While a three-dimensional object can be represented on a two-dimensional surface, it is an illusion, whereas objects that exist in three-dimensional space are concrete realities.

One can understand the differences by studying the square versus the cube on a two-dimensional surface and in a three-dimensional space. For the purpose of this discussion, let us assume that the square has the same dimensions as the cube. The square has one plane, while the cube has six identical planes that comprise its top and bottom, both sides, and back and front. The illusion of a cube can be created on a two-dimensional surface with visual manipulations of perspective, space, pattern, placement, and color, but it is just that—an illusion. These qualities may vary dependent upon how the designer frames the illusion, but in the three-dimensional object, these elements are constant no matter where you place the cube. While the appearance may change depending on the perspective from which the cube is viewed, they maintain their structural integrity and elemental characteristics.

Design elements and relationships that exist in two-dimensional space also exist in three-dimensional design, but because of the increased complexity of the form, the elements have a more complicated context. If a cube is built in three-dimensional space it must have actual weight, color, texture, and shape—it is a composite of these characteristics that create the complete appearance of the object from all angles.

These factors will also influence the environment in which it is placed. While a three-dimensional form can stand alone and be moved to different locations, it still has a relationship with its environment, and that relationship can vary. For example, if the cube was wedged in a corner it would have a different presence than if it was placed in the center of a room or hung from the ceiling. Its presence would also change depending on whether it was seen in a small room with low ceilings or in a vast warehouse. The color of an object may look different outside, under natural light, as compared with an interior space under fluorescent light. The color of the object might look different in a red room or a green room. The same factors of relativity that we experience in two dimensions can be experienced in three dimensions. An intense red cube in a small space placed at the center of the room will probably appear larger than a muted pastel pink cube in the corner of the same room. In addition to these design properties, principles that have been discussed previously in the context of two-dimensional design—balance and symmetry, scale, proportion and space, movement and flow, emphasis and focus—all occur in three-dimensional space too.

CIRCLE / SPHERE

While a solid object can be described in terms of three characteristics—plane or face, edge, and vertex—a sphere is a circular form with a curved surface that has none of these qualities. It can, however, be defined as a form whose center point lies equidistant from every point on its surface.

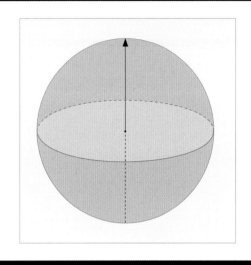

SQUARE / CUBE

A cube has six identical square faces or sides. Where two faces meet there is a common edge, and where three faces meet at a corner there is a vertex.

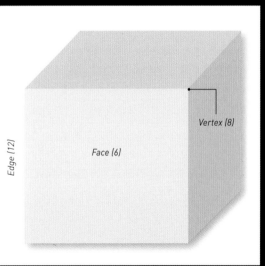

Vertex (8)

Edge (12)

Face (6)

TRIANGLE / PYRAMID

Although this pyramid has a triangular base with three sides that join at a vertex, pyramids also include solids with a multisided base, (polyhedron) as long as the triangular faces meet in a vertex.

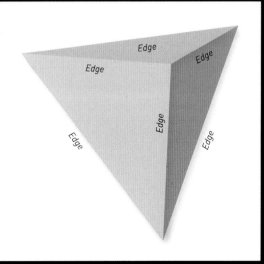

Edge

Edge

Edge

Edge

Edge

Edge

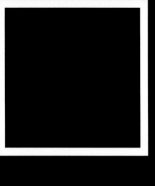

CHAPTER TWO

EXPERIENTIAL DESIGN

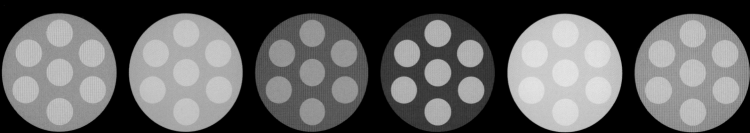

EXPERT: JONATHAN WEINERT
Senior marketing and technical writer at Philips Color Kinetics from 2008–2013. Currently he is
Strategic Content Development, B2B Marketing Communications, Philips Lighting.

Could you tell me a little about your background, and your role at Philips Color Kinetics?

I wrote most of the technical and marketing publications for Philips Color Kinetics from 2008 through 2013. Philips has enjoyed a thought leadership position in lighting for many years—partly as a result of our policy of accuracy and transparency where technical specifications are concerned. It can be a challenge to explain the differences between LED and conventional lighting, and how to make valid comparisons between them. In 2009, I wrote *LED Lighting Explained*, a brief overview of the then-current state of the LED lighting industry. The book, which explains important concepts in LED technology, specification, and color performance for non-technical audiences, became the company's de facto position statement on LED lighting technology.

Could you explain what LED lighting is and how it works with respect to colored light?

LED lighting is fundamentally different from conventional incandescent and fluorescent lighting. It's solid-state and digital, so it stands in the same relation to conventional lighting as the computer stands to the typewriter, the digital camera to the film camera, the DVD to the video cassette, etc. LED light sources are microchips that typically sit on a circuit board, like any computer chip. LED stands for ''light-emitting diode.'' All diodes produce electromagnetic energy in the form of heat and other kinds of energy waves. LEDs are engineered to produce electromagnetic energy within the visible spectrum. By varying the materials of which they're constructed, LEDs can be manufactured to produce colors across the entire rainbow of visible light. Often, LED light sources produce a single color and then are combined to produce a range of colors. If you combine red, green, and blue LED sources in a single lamp or fixture and then vary the relative intensities of each color, you can produce millions of colors within a color gamut (range) defined by the individual color points.

Could you talk about how you utilize lighting systems to establish color palettes and mix colors?

Lighting control consists of switching (on/off) and dimming. Conventional lamps produce only one color so all you can do is turn the fixture on and off, and vary its intensity when on. Lighting control for color-changing LED lighting is also only switching and dimming, but dimming can be used to vary the intensities of individual LED sources in relation to each other, producing millions of colors.

Color-changing LED fixtures require a digital controller to mix colors. Controllers vary in complexity and capability. With simple wall-mounted controllers, you can manually adjust the color of color-changing LED fixtures in an installation, create simple effects—colors slowly shifting through the spectrum, for instance—and switch and dim all fixtures in unison. More sophisticated digital controllers let you create and display light shows. Light shows can combine and layer many individual effects to create intricate, dynamic displays. Software programs for light show authoring give show designers the ability to map and group fixtures, and assign effects to them on a timeline. Color-changing LED lighting fixtures or light points can be individually controlled to create the illusion of movement, or even to render large-scale video.

Are there different kinds of equipment suited to different color ranges or intensities?

LED lighting fixtures are available in just about every configuration you can think of—from single-color or single-white to color-changing and tunable white. Philips recently introduced IntelliHue advanced color mixing technology. IntelliHue uses a special combination of white and colored LED light sources to create a much fuller spectrum of light than was achievable before, even with multi-channel LED light sources. IntelliHue can produce both intensely saturated color-changing light and high-quality tunable white light from the same fixture.

DISPLAYING WITH COLOR Once the packaging process has been completed and the product has been manufactured, there is a matter of positioning the product. Whether it is on the shelf, tabletop, or a freestanding display, the idea is to set the merchandise apart and enhance the brand. The design of the display, the signage, and merchandise placement are all very important considerations when attempting to make products stand out.

The concept development, design, and implementation of a successful display comes under the realm of visual merchandising and exhibit design. The role of the visual merchandising manager is to create a plan that will draw the buyer to the merchandise and instigate a purchase, while remaining true to the brand. This is done through a combination of elements including lighting, signage, graphics, fixtures, mannequins, and props and decorations. Design elements that are heavily relied upon are color, texture, line, and composition, while the creation of movement and flow through unity, variety, and emphasis, along with the creation of contrast and excitement is also important. These principles can apply to various retail locations within a store, such as windows, interior displays on platforms or counters, and display cases. Merchandise can also be displayed against a wall or as part of a shelf display unit.

The application of color will differ according to conceptual development, location, scale, and design of the merchandise, and lighting. If the merchandise is large and brightly colored, then the color of the fixtures or shelves might be more muted; if the lighting is bright and the merchandise is muted, the surface quality of materials chosen might be reflective. The idea behind both scenarios is to create contrast and visual excitement, without overshadowing the brand.

Traffic flow is of utmost importance, and color can be used in visual merchandising to promote movement through a space. A mannequin placed at the back of a store dressed in three or four layers of colorful clothing will undoubtedly draw customers to it, but the scale and balance of the color used is of great importance —there is a fine line between attraction and repulsion, and harmony and discord.

Below & opposite: **In this retail establishment the palette and its positioning enhance the traffic flow and highlight the merchandise. Focal points are created by proportionate use of triadic color (red, yellow, and blue). Their intensity acts as an attention-grabbing device, which is balanced by contrasting achromatic color.**

STORE WINDOWS When it comes to retail, the major reason for creating an exhibitor display is to either convey information or attract attention to a line of products or a brand. Displays usually accomplish this by using the retail space to make a thematic statement about the product, lifestyle, art, or design, often basing this on topical events or seasonal change. Color can be added to a display through signage, graphics, fixture materials, props and decorations, and merchandise choices. Once the conceptual choices are made, elements of design are considered that support the overall plan.

For the purposes of window design a statement or point of view is imperative. In order to make a statement, both design and concept are crucial. Whether the window is based on a conceptual idea or an event, the visual balance or imbalance that is created between the merchandise and its surroundings is what attracts the attention of the passer-by. It is the relationship between the color palette, the design, and the merchandise that is crucial to the success of the presentation. It is the choice of color properties of hue, intensity, and saturation combined with surface texture, proportion, and placement that can be used to entice an individual into a selling space. We have seen how color can influence the consumer in terms of marketing and product preferences. Displays that work use color combinations that enhance mood. Whether it's a bright hat, paint or colored light, a preplanned color palette is imperative. Colorful merchandise can be put to good use, especially along an otherwise empty wall.

Choice of merchandise revolves around a statement about the style of the store. The color chosen for a window display can come from the merchandise itself or a color scheme that clashes with or complements it. If we wanted to create a

Below: **In this Saks Fifth Avenue Christmas window (2013), a monochromatic color scheme in blue creates visual contrast in the thematic presentation of the story of Yeti, a wanderlust flake artist.**

He climbed Saks and made snow that was brilliantly pretty.
And to this day, the Yeti crafts flakes for the city.
The moral? Don't give up! Be artful! Be ready!
And set your sights high—you just might see a Yeti.

YOU AIN'T SEEN NOTHING YETI.
Come inside to get the Yeti Story, take a Yeti home, or visit the

Above: Color and type can be used creatively when creating store windows. In the "Travel to Tahiti" window for Kate Spade, the typeface combines with an intense pink to suggest a calm, flowing reference that supports both Tahitian color and the clothing on the mannequin.

Above: The use of angular, overlapped type and a variety of intense colors adds to the intentional chaos and energy of the Punk window.

05.02 experiential design / store windows

dramatic window, we could employ a complementary or a split-complementary palette. If the merchandise is orange-based, then the background elements, wall color, props, decoratives, and signage could be blue-based. Dependent upon the price point and the store target market, the intensity of the value of the scheme would vary. For example, a teenage store might employ neon-based complements, while a high-end home furnishings store might employ pastels.

In Kate Spade's "Travel to Tahiti" window, parts of the tropically colored Tahitian print dresses and blouses are graphically painted on the window. In addition to store graphics, props in tropical colors were also used, with the oversized words "Travel to Tahiti" picked out in hot pink.[1]

For New York Fashion Week, 2011, Bergdorf Goodman asked artist Jason Hackenwerth to create balloon installations to complement the Yves Saint Laurent windows. The richly colored balloon pieces came together to express and complement the spring tribute to the bold and full colors of the YSL display. Another colorful set of windows was created by Bergdorf Goodman in honor of a show at the "Mimicking the Metropolitans" design show about the influence of the punk movement on design. The Bergdorf Goodman design team dressed mannequins in bright clothing and placed them within a neon color graffiti cocoon. The overall color and movement were so strong that foreground and background stand in unison just as the design of the design of past and present. Background color is important but it must be conceived with respect to the window concept.[2]

Symbolic color can enhance a thematic display. In 2011, Selfridges began a campaign to engage the public in the idea of ocean conservation, and every year it creates a *Project Ocean* exhibit that it refers to as "retail activism."[3] As an attention-grabbing device, LED lighting was used to transform the façade of the historic London store into a shimmering blue ocean of color. Since then, Selfridges has created various *Project Ocean* displays, dominated by the color blue, creating an association with water, tying together all aspects of the exhibit and its associated merchandise.

Below: **Selfridges'** *Project Ocean* campaign happens on a yearly basis to engage the public in the idea of ocean conservation. LED lighting was used in 2011 to transform the historic London storefront.

ENVIRONMENTAL GRAPHICS When creating a brand, signage is an important element. Not only must the signage be attractive, but it must also include information that needs to be conveyed about the product or the subject of the exhibit. Signage must be designed to be concise, readable, and convey brand identity.

In order for a sign to be readable there should be contrast between the letters and the background color. While the greatest contrast is created by complementary colors at their highest intensity, a sign made in that way would be blinding because the color would reverberate strongly. However, if the principles of relativity are applied, color combinations can be created that will enhance readability.

One possible design direction could employ the use of value contrast, using darker letters on a lighter background. It is known from research that lime green is the most readily viewable color, so dark letters on a lime green background will catch people's attention. The reason for using a bright background color is that there is proportionately more of it than type, and this makes the signage viewable from a greater distance. Although lime green is better, yellow is also an easily seen color and this is why we often see yellow as a signage color.

It is important to take brand colors into account when creating signage, and it must also be sensitive to the design and color of the environment in which it is placed. Bruce Mau Design was asked to design the graphics for the Regent Park School of Music in Toronto, Canada. As part of a redevelopment project, the school was given a space within the Daniels Spectrum, a community center devoted to arts and culture, with the purpose of bringing dance, music, theater, and visual arts together. The school worked with faculty staff volunteers and Bruce Mau Design to create a new identity that communicates the idea of "seriously fun." The lively graphics—based on musical instruments and boldly colored doorways—is carried through on marketing brochures, merchandise, and the website.[4]

Right: **Musical shapes and blocks of primary and secondary color are combined with black-and-white elements and patterns that create a playful unity inspiring and energizing students as they pass through the lengthy corridor of the Regent Park School of Music.**

WAY-FINDING Signage comes in many forms, but it is especially important when it comes to creating way-finding systems. The goal of a way-finding system is to convey information that leads participants from one place to another. Placed at intersection points it not only gives direction, but also provides choices as to which way to go. A successful way-finding system must make it clear to the onlooker how to move through a space, so it must have clarity, definition, and contrast. Signage must also be sensitive to the design and color of the environment in which it is placed.

Signage doesn't have to be bold in order to make a strong statement, but it must have consistent visual traits, including color design and materials. Anything from vinyl to wood, metal, or neon can be used, just as long as there is a visual tie to the brand. The play on materials is what makes the identity for Ravensbourne in London so interesting.[5] When Ravensbourne (formerly Ravensbourne College of Design and Communication) moved to a new open-concept facility it wanted to create a new identity that was consistent with the creative thinking that takes place in the building.

To start with, Foreign Office Architects (since dissolved) used 28,000 anodized aluminum tiles in three different shapes and colors to surround the building with a tessellating pattern based on Penrose tilings a nd influenced by the floral motifs and complex patterns of the Arts and Crafts movement. Design company Johnson Banks took the tiling motif and used it as the basis for a signage system within the building. They blew individual tile shapes up to a large scale and painted them onto the interior walls, wrapping them around the corners of walls and ceilings and stenciling important information onto them on each floor. Concrete columns in the classrooms were also labeled. While the palette for the signage was muted and monochromatic, it echoed the building's exterior, with intense color brought in by the interior furnishings to complement the structure.[6]

Right: **Combinations of three equally small geometric shapes placed in patterns to produce a vibrant surface works with a muted palette to create a vibrant ever-changing surface façade for Ravensbourne. The low-intensity color allows the surface activity to be quiet, but remain interesting.**

Color can be the central focus in a way-finding system with the use of color coding. Color-coding is a design tool that improves user experience. Different colors can be used to define areas on a screen, in a textbook, or in an interior space. When used in an interior space, color coding can separate and define specific spaces while in turn guiding individuals around an environment. Color-coding makes complex organizations of space accessible to the user. It can act as a shorthand. From determining what floor you are on, to finding a way around an airport, hospital, or subway system, etc., color-coding can bring comfort to what may be a stressful experience. It serves as a solution for explaining directions in a multicultural, multi-linguistic environment. Town planners often adopt this design tool to define different urban areas within a city.

Above left: The three façade shapes taken from the exterior of Ravensbourne, adapted and enlarged to create the school logo combined with the graphic breakdown of the name in strong achromatic letters creates a sense of energy characteristic of a school steeped in the design process.

Left: Stencilled white numbers used for clarity and way-finding on each floor, combined with oversized shapes in muted colors, derivative of the façade, were used to define direction and enhance the brand continuity and identity. The scale of the colored areas increases their visual presence even though the color remained muted.

COLORED LIGHT: THE POWER OF ATTRACTION Creating a retail environment that allows customers to understand and become comfortable with a theme or process can be most useful in the sale of goods. According to Martin Pegler in his book, *Visual Merchandising and Display*, ways of using light efficiently include avoiding the use of bright white lights on mannequins, and light across the display rather than down. He also suggests using colored lights to create color environments for the merchandise. Rather than the merchandise itself, instead focus the color on props and backgrounds. If there is a need to increase the intensity of the merchandise, he suggests the use of pastel filters. In addition, Pegler warns that colored lighting at night will appear different.[7]

Colored lights are a powerful tool in creating a mood. Because we understand that color evokes mood, we can employ color in its purest form as colored light to create a design unity over a space or provide an interesting focal area within a larger space. This works extraordinarily well with respect to the design of an exhibit or display. The use of color can draw attention to an object within a space and enhance the desired response.

Using colored light was a great way to create an environment for a very large exhibit that formed part of a centennial renovation of the Los Angeles Natural History Museum. Designed by CO Architects, the renovation included "a redesigned front façade, terraces, and communal areas, and a series of glass pavilions housing a live butterfly collection."[1] The space was designed to resemble an aquarium to fit a 63ft (19m) fin whale skeleton suspended in mid-air in the Otis Booth Pavilion. The design team at KGM Lighting, led by partner Dan Weinreber and designer Patrick McCollough, used blue LED lights to create a low-resolution video screen behind the whale, which was designed to resemble an aquarium. When entering the exhibit, the lighting creates the feeling of swimming with the enormous mammal and staring up at the sky from its perspective.[8]

Colored lights can be used on the outside of the building to stimulate and attract individuals to a location. The intensity of the light and the pattern in which it is used can reinforce directives and encourage flow into and throughout a space. This was the case at the Poznan City Center, Poland, an area that includes the main railway station and a shopping mall. In 2010, TriGanit Development worked in conjunction with Philips and the city to revitalize the area. Part of this revitalization process included the creation of three colored light installations for the shopping mall,

which used LED lighting and control systems for both interior and exterior lights.

To illuminate the north face of the mall, which is covered with diamond-shaped glass panels, 14 columns were constructed at a distance of roughly 50 feet (15m), containing lighting fixtures that projected light onto the building's façade.

Meanwhile, the east façade had color-changing lights built into its overhang to create stripes of color and wall washes around the mall entrance. Color fixtures were also placed in the interior.[9]

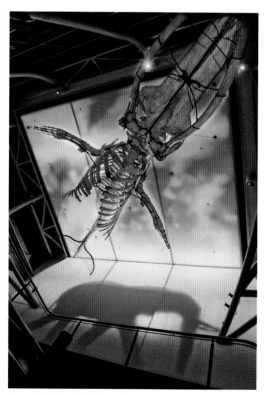

Photograph by Anthony Masters
LIGHTING DESIGN: **Kaplan Gehring McCarroll Architectural Lighting**
Dan Weinreber, Design Partner & Patrick McCollough, Project Designer
ELECTRICAL CONTRACTOR: Morrow Meadows Philips Color Kinetics

Below left & top right: **Colored lights and animal silhouettes are used to create an inviting surreal habitat for the 63-foot fin whale specimen in the Otis Booth Pavilion, which can be seen both from within and outside the museum. While blue is associated with the ocean, pinks and oranges suggest the warmth of refracted light from the sun.**

Below right: **Colored lights are used to draw visitors toward this downtown revitalization project in Poznan, Poland. Notice how warm colors highlight the entrance.**

Photograph by Anthony Masters
LIGHTING DESIGN: **Kaplan Gehring McCarroll Architectural Lighting**
Dan Weinreber, Design Partner & Patrick McCollough, Project Designer
ELECTRICAL CONTRACTOR: Morrow Meadows Philips Color Kinetics

Photograph by Jacek Bakutis
PROJECT MANAGEMENT: TriGranit Development Philips Color Kinetics

05.02 experiential design / colored light: the power of attraction

CHAPTER THREE

COLOR CONSULTING: THE PROCESS

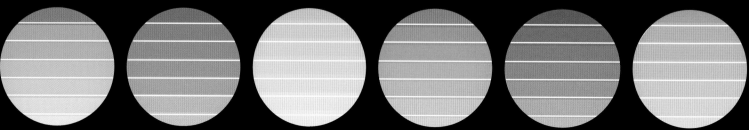

EXPERT: **HARRY ADLER**
Founding member of C2 paint company and owner of Adler's Hardware

Could you tell me about yourself and your background, and how you got into the paint store and into C2?

I started working at my family's store when I was ten, in 1964. Paint was a small component of our hardware store but that evolved with the advent of the box store—Home Depot and Lowes, specifically. Data showed that many hardware stores had gone out of business that were close to a Home Depot. There weren't any Home Depots in Rhode Island at the time, but it occurred to me that we would be vulnerable to them. It made sense to change our product mix and become more focused the things Home Depot was not good at, which was selling home decorating to females. We researched what home decorating products meant and we came up with paint, fabric, window treatment, wall covering, and ultimately decorative hardware. We started selling Pratt and Lambert paint in 1988 and that is when we becoming a serious paint retailer. They were a good supplier and remained that way until 2005 when I heard that Pratt and Lambert had been sold to Sherwin Williams. A group of us independent retailers joined together to create our own paint company, which is called C2 paint. We chose to cater to those who work with color, feeling that if we could satisfy the most discerning then we could satisfy anyone. If you take a high-quality product that is affordable and has great application properties and durability, and have the top designers in a marketplace endorse the brand it, gains credibility.

Could you talk about how your use of pigments differs from that of other companies?

That is really the key to creating better color and it's not at all unlike going to the art supply store and finding artists' acrylics and oils. Paint pigments come in a variety of qualities. The difference in the pigments C2 uses is finding pigments that are well ground—that's the critical element. The grind of the pigment defines the resolution of the color. It's like a finely pixilated screen which comprise of many and small dots versus fewer and larger dots, which create a fuzzier and low resolution image. There is also an element of durability that can now be incorporated into pigment by including a resin in the pigments that gives the color additional hardness. Mixing dark colors diminishes the durability, but by using a resin containing pigment it keeps the paint quality stable. Then you need to think about how you blend those pigments. If you are making a blue, do you mix a blue and black, or do you create what are commonly referred to as "full-spectrum colors," which do not contain black and have more than four different pigments and often include complements. If you mix red and green, blue and orange or violet and yellow all grouped together so you create a more dynamic color. C2 has incorporated a full spectrum approach to all of its colors.

Could you talk about your marketing approach?

One of the major differences with C2 is our approach to marketing. When we dealt with need around paint color with design professionals, the two things that I heard designers express were that they wished that color could be edited in terms of numbers, and thoughtfully presented so you didn't have to wade through the "ugly colors" to get to the ones you loved. The other universal desire was to have accurate sampling material. Better accuracy means larger samples. We use the paint that goes on your walls in the manufacturer of the paint chips, modified slightly to get harder quicker so that samples don't stick to each other. We have 496 not 4,960, some with the same number, which creates confusion and wastes a lot of time wading through less loved colors to get to the ones that you want. In addition one of painters' primary concerns of the is coverage—that is opaqueness that doesn't require multiple coats. If we can't produce a color that covers in two coats, we don't have it as part of our color palette.

COLOR CONSULTING Although color is used widely, some people want or need an expert to help them create a palette for their personal requirements. This is the role of a color consultant, who combines a theoretical and subjective understanding of color to work with clients, develop a product line, improve personal appearance, and improve the appearance and functionality of their living and working environments.

A color consultant for products works as part of a design team to create the color palette and materials specification for a product line. Theoretical information concerning color harmonies and relativity are combined with trends research and marketing to create suitable color specifications. The consultant must understand not only what colors are in fashion, but must also be aware of palettes appropriate to the specific industry and the geographical orientation of the target market. They must also understand the psychological implications of color choice—in other words, how the target market will react to their color choices. Two prime examples of this type of color consultant are Leslie Harrington of the Color Association of the United States, and Leatrice Eiseman, of the Pantone Institute. Another important area of color consultancy is in design spaces. Color consulting in this area includes creating color palettes for industrial, corporate, retail, educational, healthcare, and residential spaces. It can vary from one specific site to a chain of stores or a multifunctional real-estate development. In terms of function, the job can entail choosing the paint color for a kitchen through to colorizing equipment or machinery. A great deal of accumulated knowledge is necessary for this process.

Within the field it is also possible to focus on exteriors. You can work with historic properties to try to bring back historic color through research and investigation. Another option would be to work with a developer to create a plan for a variety of newly planned houses. This form of consultancy might involve site investigation, as well as research as to who might be buying these homes. In addition to creating several interchangeable palettes (depending on the home style) the job might also entail product specification including trim siding, roofing materials, shutters, and doors. Another option is a paint and materials specifier for an educational institution or healthcare facility. There is also a need for color in terms of safety with respect to manufacturing.

Below: **There are a variety of ways that paint can be specified. Here, a range of colors is presented in linear format on paper strips arranged by value.**

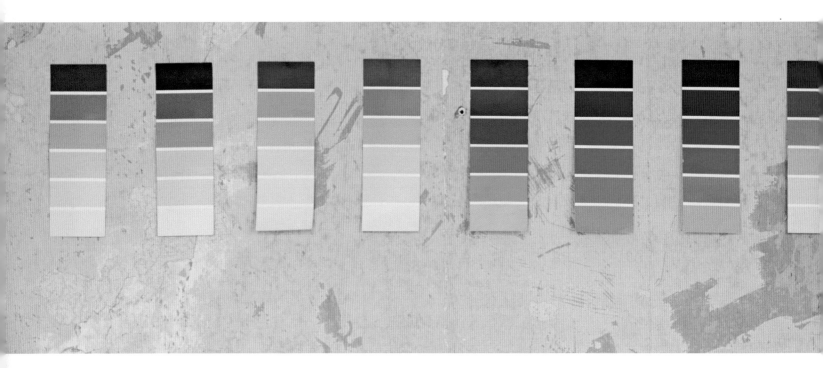

It is important for color consultants to use research and assessment skills so that they can base their palette creations or alterations on environmental and theoretical information. Assessment might include everything from talking to the individuals who inhabit the space to a study of materials that already are part of the design. This should include both the interior—such as surface and flooring materials—and the exterior observations—such as landscaping and neighborhood. If the room or site already has furnishings, a palette should be presented that shows both the colors and the proportions that are used. By doing this, the consultant can determine what kind of harmony exists already. If the palette is not harmonious then the problem can be altered with judicious use of color. If the space has not as yet been finished then mood boards that capture the feeling of the space, and its palette can be used to plan the final outcome. A review of the light sources is also important to take into consideration. Natural light and the way the space is arranged will determine color intensities and values. The type of lighting, the color of the bulbs, and the intensity of that light will influence color. Colored floorplans and elevations combined with a materials board would follow.

Fundamentally, knowledge of basic color palettes and theoretical harmonic color schemes is vital as a jumping-off point for their palette development. Theoretical color schemes are also very important if you are trying to resolve a color issue.

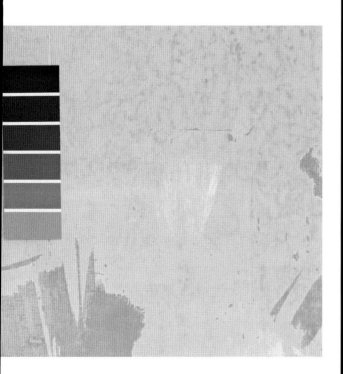

Top & center left: **Color consultants utilize their knowledge of color palette development to bring together fabrics, and floor and wall coverings into a harmonious scheme. In addition, they must consider their proportionate quantities—in other words, dominant versus accent color —with respect to the material's visual strength and texture.**

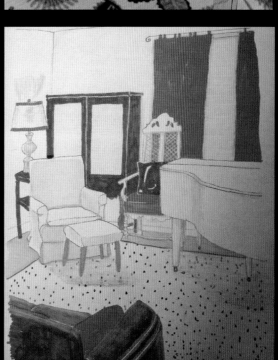

Left: **In this student drawing by M. Kagan, the intensity shifts to create a room within the parameters of a monochromatic color scheme. Reds are presented in high-intensity fabrics next to muted wooden furnishings.**

RESIDENTIAL INTERIOR COLOR CONSULTING A great deal of environmental color consulting is done in the area of interior residential work, but what a color consultant does will vary greatly from individual to individual and from project to project. A consultant may focus on a type of space, such as healthcare or education, for example, but even within a single area there are a variety of tasks. An interior color consultant may be asked simply to paint a room, or commissioned to create an entire house plan, complete with material specifications and interior furnishings. While most projects lie somewhere in between, the process—from conceptualization to installation—remains constant.

Let's start with the initial assessment, which involves defining what the problems are and what work needs to be done to resolve them. The assessment begins with a series of questions about the site and the client's tastes. Questions about a client's likes and dislikes and personal taste should be combined with questions regarding their behavioral patterns. Ask questions about their daily routines, for example, do they sit in the den or kitchen to watch TV. Make sure to ask about color preferences too—what colors are they most comfortable with, and which rooms do they like best in their house and why.

This should be followed by a site evaluation for both interior and exterior. It should include landscaping, neighborhood terrain, community (suburban/urban), and style of house. Is the property in a new or established neighborhood, and what colors of materials already exist? This includes landscape colors, structural materials such as granite countertops and floor stain color, paint colors (both interior and exterior), and furnishings. It is also useful to identify light sources—both natural and artificial—and to take photographs for reference, if allowed.

The next part of the process is analysis, This involves trying to get a complete understanding of the project from the collected information and identifying the problem. In terms of color this can be done with a proportional color chart. After you match all the colors in a space, set them up vertically from floor to ceiling in a proportional fashion based on how much of each color is in the space. Even if it is harmonic, consider patterned fabrics as one color, using either a mixture or the dominant. In this way you can determine whether the palette is harmonic and is in proportional balance. It is also important look at the palette to see if it is appropriate to the task that takes place in the room.

Opposite: Structural elements such as this fireplace may be painted out to enhance color balance within a space. The gray was a strong decision with respect to the intense color used in the rest of the space.

Below: The intensity of the green fabric on the chair gives a focal point to the room while balancing the complex pattern on the fabric of the window shade.

If there is an active color in a space where quiet is needed, it might detract from the environment.

Do not forget furnishings and accessories, but note that an established room has less freedom of choice—options here might include modifying the palette through a change of paint color or the removal of a fabric or a rug. If you have a room with a color imbalance, accessories such as pillows or cushions in complementary colors may help.

Once the analysis is completed a presentation can be developed from color scheme concepts and ideas. For a blank space, a palette could be created from building materials or an inspirational piece such as an artwork. A mood board can be created that expresses the color palette and lifestyle that you think your customer client might enjoy. I was once designing a client's home from top to bottom, and started by creating a palette based on her life, her desires, and what was already there. This gave me about 20–25 colors. Arranging them spectrally, I made sure that they formed a cohesive palette, so that no matter what was chosen, flow and harmony would result. In this instance, I realized that she had a particular liking for blues, so I decided to work with a complementary palette for the whole home.

Once the color palette is determined, the next step involves creating a plan for placement and emphasis that is harmonically balanced. Color schemes for each space must be selected, followed by choosing a dominant color and placement. Modification of color in terms of intensity and value must also be considered, and at this time the consultant must be conscious of both the immediate space and the surrounding areas—don't forget to consider the architecture of the room and the color of the adjacent spaces or hallways. Once approved, elevations and floor plans can be colored, and a color materials board can be completed.

COLOR CONSULTING—PRIMARY CONCERNS There is an infinite variety of approaches to design and an equal number of potential issues to be handled. Three primary areas of importance are color and space, color and light, and color and proportion. A perfect example of color changing the space it is in can be seen through the use of dark blue. Dark blue in a small room may feel very tight and cave-like, but if you use a lighter value it will expand the space. If you use dark blue on the bottom 8ft (2.4m) of a wall, and a lighter color on top in a large space with high ceilings, the color will humanize the space and make the room more comfortable.

The intensity of color can alter spatial perception. If you use an intense color on the walls of a room with a tiered ceiling and gradually change the value/intensity as you go up each tier, for example, it will unify the room and give it a feeling of height.

Color can enhance movement and flow within a space by creating a focal point within a space. The placement of color will also alter the space. A prime example of color placement is a hallway in the Napa Valley showcase home at Charles Krug Winery created by designer Emily Mughannam. Her description of the home as "a whimsical chinoiserie" sets the tone for a green surface on the ceiling of this elegant hallway.[1] While the ceiling color brightens, the circular light fixture creates patterns on the surfaces, enhancing the warmth and whimsy of the space. Muted doors, carpet, and walls balance this bold color, while maintaining its playful spirit. Accent color was used in a modern kitchen created by J. C. Schmeil of Merzbau Design Collective for a lake house in Austin. Here, the orange-blue palette was used with a great intensity of color. Achromatic color support came from the reflective turquoise blue surface of the cabinets, with the clear water association. Warm wood and an intense burnt orange chair complement the scheme.[2]

Color is so mutable relative to other colors and lighting conditions that it can be necessary to actually alter a color on a wall to make it appear to be the same color as the rest of the room. This is often due to the way in which light affects the space, as lighting can change the appearance of a room entirely. If one color palette is used throughout a room employing different light sources, the color will appear different. If you look at a series of images of one interior with different light sources, you can see a complete alteration of color. As with Monet's *Haystacks*, we understand that even under natural light, color shifts according to the time of day.

Another major concern is the amount of color that is used in a room. Many of us have had the experience of picking up a swatch at a paint store, bringing it home, painting it on the wall, and saying "what was I thinking?!" The larger the space the color covers, the more of a statement it makes. Especially intense colors can be unbearable in a spacious room, so it's probably best to think of a balanced scheme prior to choosing your paint. If you want to use a bold color in strong space, go ahead, but make sure that it is balanced with materials or furnishings.

Opposite: The green trim painted on the doorway to the room at the end of the hallway works in tandem with the green ceiling to bring a tranquil balance to the space.

Below left, right & bottom: The oxidized exterior steel panels are a sumptuous red-orange color that perfectly complements the lacquered turquoise kitchen inside this stunning lake house.

OTHER COLOR DESIGN SPACES In his book, *Color, Environment, and Human Response*, Frank Mahnke talks about color in relation to healthcare design. He proposes that the color palette must be responsive to the patients and staff that live and work in the space, attending to both their psychological and physiological needs to ensure health and well-being.[3] Palettes of great intensity and contrast might not be useful in a healthcare environment. Even a children's hospital may not do well with overly bright and stimulating colors. On the other hand, while Alzheimers' patients have to be in an environment that will not agitate them, because of problems with depth perception, some sort of contrast is necessary to aid visual problems. Color choices and placement must enhance good medical diagnostics and procedures. A new MRI machine has been devised that allows changes in lighting in the space in the testing room to enhance patient comfort. Color can also aid patients and visitors in an informative way as a wayfinding system helping them navigate from one area to another. Some areas of a hospital should provide color interest. A lobby area sets the tone of the hospital while trying to make patients feel at ease.

Most types of commercial office spaces and manufacturing plants require that color be task-based. John Pile in his book *Color in Interior Design* suggests that office spaces that are occupied for long periods of time should be varied dependent upon available light.[4] Offices with windows favor cool colors, and those that have a south- or west-facing exposure should have warmer colors than those that face north. Those that rely on fluorescent lights should use warmer colors. While the literature on interior office design is not all in agreement in terms of color design, there have certainly been some useful observations. Nancy Kwallek, in *Color in Office Environments*, reveals some interesting results. In her studies on productivity and color, she tried to determine the effects of interior office color on productivity and the mood of workers. She studied the effects with respect to the complexity of the environment, the time spent in the room, their genders, and their personal responses to stimuli. The workers were tested under different conditions with different variables. An important conclusion drawn from the studies suggests that interior color does have impact on cognitive functions of workers, but is variable due to personal color response.[5]

Manufacturing space differs because of key established colors that engender specific responses. Red is used for fire safety equipment and hazardous containers, while blue is used for electrical controls, and yellow that stands for caution is often the color of moving equipment. In manufacturing, product color is very important. If the product line is colorful the machinery should be low intensity. Some contrast is needed, however, to determine where one task ends and another starts.

On the whole there seems to be a greater need to study the effects of color on interior space. Anat Lechner, Ph.D, and Leslie Harrington, in a review of literature presented at the Design & Emotion Conference in Sweden, 2006, suggest more research has to be done that integrates other fields such as psychology, social psychology and sociology, and business management, to understand fully the implications of color in spaces. Response to color is the result of complex relationships between individuals and their environments, and should be studied with a holistic, inclusive approach.[6]

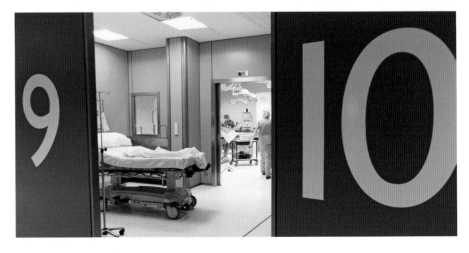

Below: The blue-green color of the operating room is helpful to surgeons and patients alike. Blue is an extremely calming color, so can help a patient to relax and a surgeon to focus. Oversized room numbers are great for navigational purposes.

Left: **Color can be added onto the structure of a manufacturing space to detract from monotony and create a visually comfortable environment in which to work. Yellow is also a color used to denote moving equipment.**

Below left: **Colored machinery can enhance awareness of the machine's physical space thus avoiding unnecessary injury. This is a useful concept as long as it does not compete with the product and add to visual confusion.**

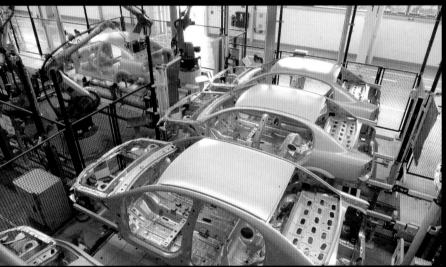

Left: **The balance between the primarily achromatic desk area and the warm and colorful common areas defines the workspace as a more serious environment. The splashes of color soften it and link it to the more relaxed area.**

Above: **The red on the conveyor belt enhances the continuity and flow of the space while highlighting the edge of a moving machine.**

PART SIX

COLOR ON THE MOVE

CHAPTER ONE

COLOR IN FILM AND ANIMATION

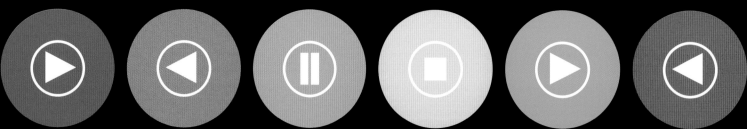

EXPERT: **BETSY CONNORS**
Holographic artist and designer.

Could you tell me a little bit about your background?
I studied traditional art at college in the U.S. and in France. While in Paris, I was inspired by other artists and filmmakers to use newer technological mediums. There was often an argument that we should be using film, video, computers, and whatever the latest technology was to express ourselves, reflecting the times and technology of the day/culture. When I came back to the U.S., I studied film and photography, and then worked successfully in video, producing artworks for Museums and public television, and eventually I received a fellowship at the Center for Advanced Visual Studies at MIT. I became interested in holography there, and enrolled in a Master's program in Spatial Imaging at the MIT Media Lab. I built my own holography lab, and taught at the Media Lab for sixteen years.

Could you talk about your artworks and how color is used in them.
My work in holography is concerned with nature as a primary subject. I use landscapes as a subject to explore my interest in juxtaposing technology with nature, and bringing attention to the concerns many artists have about environmental issues, and the creation of art works to heighten an awareness of the man-made changes damaging our planet.

One of the first installations I did, called *Future Gardens*, combined holograms of Western and Eastern landscape imagery to create a holographic landscape 17ft long. There were 40 holograms, and each hologram had a dedicated light. Each light was controlled by a computer program and could be turned on and off and dimmed. A contemporary music score, created specially for the work, controlled the lighting program. The type of holograms used in the work are called "white light transmission holograms," and they act like prisms with white light illuminating them from behind the film. When the light is on you not only see 3D the image, but, when two or more holograms were lit, one behind the other, the projected color would mix producing whites and purples—colors not typically seen in holography.

Holograms are the technology where you can see 3D without the need for glasses. They are recorded using single wavelengths of light from a laser, typically red (632nm) or green (55550nm) frequency, but are played back using ordinary white light for either a full spectrum or single color display.

I recently did a work called *Light Leaves* where shadows of leaves blocked the light to the displayed holograms, using a simple robotic micro-controller for motion. It gives the work an ambient feeling of the way that wind moves light through trees. We are always trying to get the newest mediums to do what the previous mediums have attained technologically. So with holograms, we not only want 3D, but full color, motion, sound, and instant transmission to our computers.

What color tools might you use in a hologram?
Holograms are made using a different single frequency/color laser. In most cases a master hologram is created and from that a white light illuminated copy is made so that the hologram can be seen using ordinary white light.

There are two main types of copy holograms: the transmission hologram, which acts like a prism and splits the color into a spectrum, red projected out at the top of the hologram, green in the middle, and blue at the bottom; and the reflection hologram, where a single color output is controlled by the changes in the thickness of the emulsion when exposing the film. Full pseudo color transmission holograms are created by changing the angle of the setup and making three exposures to change the color output. Full pseudo color reflection holograms are made by swelling the emulsion three times to create three-color images. There are also real full-color holograms made using three different color lasers (RGB) and panchromatic film. When combined with LED lights to match the wavelengths of the lasers, the real color holograms are so realistic there is only a slight difference between the real and actual subject of the hologram. Holograms are virtual images of colored light projected behind or in front of a film and artists are in a way painting with colored light in space.

HORROR Similar to experiential design, film and animation both utilize a combination of beautiful lighting, wonderfully designed sets, and elegantly created costumes to create the ambiance and support the characters. Digital color in media can enhance the underlying story and visually enrich the viewer's experience in a variety of directions. It is the cinematographer's role to capture that visual experience on film. Software and technology allow for secondary color and design decisions to be made in post-production where almost anything can be edited or altered by a combination of color correction and color grading. In addition, a colorist can isolate objects and color ranges and manipulate them individually. It is possible to affect color change individually shot by shot or collectively in its entirety. Corrections can be made so that shots taken at different angles at different times can be color-matched through the use of levels and other tools. Color can be enhanced, creating a mood or a feeling appropriate to the type of movie and its intended impact.

There are a variety of artistic and visual reasons for working with color, but in horror and fantasy movies it is most often manipulated to express or heighten a mood or feeling. The tradition of horror movies can be traced back to film pioneer Georges Méliès' 1896 short, *Le Manoir du diable* (*The Haunted Castle*), but the Gothic horror tradition was not popularized until the 1930s and 1940s. Most horror movies of that time were based on popular novels, such as *Dracula, Frankenstein, The Hunchback of Notre Dame*, and *Dr. Jekyll and Mr. Hyde*. They reflected the cultural anxieties of the era, and were seen as a way to escape the daily woes of the Great Depression.

As black-and-white film used a simple photographic emulsion, it was much easier to produce than color, so many filmmakers in the 1940s, including

Below left: **Filmmakers used tonal variety to create drama prior to the advent of color films. This is exemplified by the bright lights that are cast on the cross and Frankenstein's face.**

studios such as RKO Radio Pictures Inc., relied on tonal contrast in place of color. Dark shadows created a nightmare world that left a lot to the imagination, while dark makeup was used to enhance facial features, making heroes beautiful and villains more sunken, twisted, and inhuman. In addition, scenery was created with bold lines and jagged shapes to create a heightened emotional response.

The first horror movie to be shot in color was *Doctor X*, directed by Michael Curtiz in 1932. It used the original two-strip Technicolor process, and was shot by cinematographer Ray Rennahan, a pioneer of color cinematography. Although the darkness of black was still commonly used to evoke terror and suspense, other dark colors, such as blood reds, eerie greens, and menacing yellows, also became standard evokers of terror, disgust, and fear. As the horror genre evolved, color became the main avenue of evoking emotion.

In the 1999 movie, *Sleepy Hollow*, director Tim Burton—well known for his color palette in *Edward Scissorhands* (1990)—employed a limited color palette to create and enhance contrast. The film is a fictional story of a New York Police Constable, Ichabod Crane (played by Johnny Depp) who is sent to the village of Sleepy Hollow in 1799 to investigate a series of murders by decapitation. Ignoring the belief of the townspeople that a headless horseman in search of his missing head committed the deaths, Crane searches for the cause of the victims' beheading. His thoughts change when he himself encounters the ghost. Burton uses color to create contrast between a realistic period piece and fantastic dreamlike scenarios. The color in Burton's film is thus tied both to the narrative and to his own personal vision. While the film is set in dark grays, blacks, and blues especially outdoors, situational pops of color, appear during significant moments. This contrasts the warm browns and yellow highlights of interior scenes, and soft lighting combined with smoke complements the eerie tones. The majority of color—especially with respect to the scenes in which deaths occur—is low in intensity, except for the blood. In contrast to this usually dark, dull world, the dreams that the main protagonist, Ichabod Crane, has of his mother are filled with color, as are scenes with Katrina (Christina Ricci). Indeed, Katrina is the only character to wear light pastel-colored costumes, making her stand out and allowing her to be viewed as the epitome of goodness in a town that is full of lies and deceit.

Below left: While the image of the Headless Horseman appears to be gray, on closer inspection there is a complex mixture of muted color that enhances the image and gives it a greater depth and richness of feeling than the achromatic image opposite.

Below: A contrast in color between Ichabod Crane and Katrina reveals aspects of their personality. The fact that Crane is portrayed mostly achromatic, with black clothes and a pale complexion, enhances his austere character and the fact that he refuses to believe in the supernatural. Katrina is characterized by warm colors and bright flesh tones.

FANTASY AND REALITY Fantasy films were pioneered in the early 1900s by Georges Méliès, using an early form of special effects called "trick film." With their special effects and animations, along with their intense lighting, elaborate sets, and dark or tragic undertones in the plot, Méliès' movies can also be seen as early examples of the horror genre. The introduction of Technicolor, which allowed fantasy to evolve into a more distinct genre, with early works such as *The Wizard of Oz*, *Tarzan the Ape Man*, and *Snow White and the Seven Dwarfs* coming to fruition.

This distinct genre has been developed with developments in CGI animation, a process that uses computer graphics to create animated 2D and 3D images, allowing filmmakers to create fantastical elements, scenery, and characters with greater ease. Rather than having to make hundreds of scale models, constantly adjust lighting schemes, and build expansive (and expensive) sets, it is possible for directors to use computer animation to create breathtaking effects.

As a result of CGI post-production editing, movies could balance the real world with a fictional one, with imaginary characters appearing in real or fictitious settings. However, such processes have major color ramifications, and the more CGI is used, the greater the control over the color of scenery and characters needs to be: complete CGI usage results in total color control being necessary.

The extent to which CGI is used depends on what is trying to be achieved. One film series that relied heavily on live shots, scale models, and post-production editing was *The Lord of the Rings* trilogy. Director Peter Jackson used every advanced tool available at the time to bring his vision to the big screen. Peter Doyle, an accomplished colorist and creative director, did the color grading work, which involved taking the Super 35 format film and scanning it in order to transfer it into a digital format. Once on the computer, a huge variety of tools were available to make color changes. Highlights and shadows could also be isolated and manipulated, before the digital file was recorded back onto film.[1]

Left: *The Wizard of Oz* (1939) juxtaposes the sepia-toned colors of the scarecrow and Dorothy's home in the heartlands of Kansas with intensity of colors that represents Oz. This suggests a visual connection between the scarecrow and the land that Dorothy so desperately wants to return to.

In filming *The Two Towers* (the second installment in the trilogy), less controlled light was used on the actors throughout. Instead of applying a color scale, a simple black-and-white-based scale was used to evoke the feeling of separation of the fellowship, both literally and metaphorically. In an article for *American Cinematographer* magazine entitled "A Fellowship in Peril," Andrew Lesnie, the movie's director of photography, contrasts the visual effects in the first two films of the trilogy: "I was able to follow the travails of each group and decide what was appropriate for the mood at any particular moment. Middle-earth is descending into a very dark time, and the characters are battling to find light at the end of the tunnel, so the film needed to be more realistic and aggressive than *The Fellowship of the Ring*. The overall feel is less magical, and the story has become fractured and splintered."[2]

Lesnie worked with Doyle, enhancing the feeling of "creeping menace" by creating distinct detail to promote anger and fear. Because the theme involved the elves leaving middle earth, the color palette revolved around autumnal colors. The characters' skin tone was given a fairytale quality. In post-production, colors were modified in unusual ways. For example, in order to warm an outdoor scene, green was removed, allowing for an increase in magenta, which was moved toward gold, allowing for greater definition in the grasses. Doyle also color graded *Harry Potter and the Deathly Hallows, Part 2*. In *The Deathly Hallows*, darker colors were used to express a more mature theme. There was a lot of digital exploration to determine how mood would be altered by the lighting effects, and how much would be graded. While it is the job of lighting designers to create the extent of light, the final degree of darkness was accomplished with the grading. Software and technology allow for secondary color and design decisions to be made in post-production.

Above: **With The Lord of the Rings trilogy: "The idea was to present a more realistic and aggressive coloration to enhance detail and thereby increase tension. Using a Hue Luminance Saturation color space as opposed to cmyk, [Peter] Doyle was able to reduce color. This allows for variation in color intensity, and the resulting contrast between the detailed and less defined areas."[3]**

FANTASY AND FICTION While some fantasy films use very realistic backgrounds, the environment in James Cameron's 2009 blockbuster, *Avatar*, was completely imaginary. Using a combination of existing techniques and state-of-the-art new technology, the creation and production of *Avatar* was a highly sophisticated and extended form of CGI. At the heart of its creation were photorealistic computer-generated characters, created using a technique known as "motion-capture animation," which was developed to capture the precise movements of a person and transfer them onto a computer-generated character. As a result, more than 70% of the movie was made digitally without the use of real sets.

Set in the mid-twenty-second century, *Avatar* tells the story of an indigenous culture on the fictional planet Pandora, which is threatened the expansion of a mining colony. Although Cameron wanted to keep the indigenous population human enough to understand their emotions, the color of their skin intentionally bears no resemblance. Cameron's passion for blue was apparent in an interview with Marshall Crook of the *Wall Street Journal*: "I guess I just like the color blue. I mean it's the color of night, it's the color of the ocean, and as a scuba diver I've spent a lot of time looking into the deep blue, the pelagic blue. It's just a gorgeous color and it's a great accent color for the human face."[4] While blue was an unusual color choice, Cameron's skill made its usage believable. The use of the color blue allows the viewer to interpret the actions of the avatar and their environment without associations with a particular race or group of individuals. They can in that sense be more readily associated as part and parcel of the environment in which they live. Cameron's interest in biology is evident in the extent to which he organizes the Pandoran biosphere. By using blues and bio-luminescent pinks, the sense of environmental harmony of the film is enhanced. Cameron worked with experts to make the flora and fauna as scientifically feasible as possible.

Below: The fanciful orange-pink patterned plant life in *Avatar* complements the blues of the figures. Their swirling shape and towering scale adds movement, energy, and life to the vision of Pandora.

Right: What makes a blue skin color believable is that there are facial references and human emotions that are expressed by these characters.

THE COLORS OF ANIME While horror and fantasy movies often take from reality, animation relies entirely on the writers, directors, and colorists for its palette. Coloring animated movies the traditional way (by hand) was limited in flexibility because recurring characters or scenery could not be changed or continuity would be lost, but creations on the computer can easily be changed or altered. Even with the advent of CGI, the use of color is still an artistic rather than technical decision, with color choice often depending on context—for example, green hair may be out of place in a movie based on a historic event, but it might be believable in a fantasy animation.

The earliest commercial animations made on film were produced at the start of the twentieth century, but it wasn't until 1915 that the first feature-length animated film appeared, with Pinto Colvig's *Creation*. By the 1930s, animators were creating movies by drawing each frame or by making cut-outs that were moved around and shot separately. Although this type of animation was prohibitive in terms of time and cost, the Japanese government subsidized a number of animators, including Kenz Masaokae, who produced *Chikara to Onna no Yo no Naka* (1933), the first anime to use both celluloid

animation and recorded sound. During this time, Western influence, particularly from America, had a big impact on Japanese animation. Especially with respect to Walt Disney's animations, such as *Snow White and the Seven Dwarves* (1937).

However, the adveny of the characteristic anime style we know today came in the 1960s. Realizing there was high demand for animated fantasy, but no establishment to fill that demand, Osamu Tezuka—now known as the "godfather of anime" and "the father of manga"—put his manga career on hold and created

Below: It is interesting to note the complementary contrast between the red-orange tonalities of the figure colors and the blue-violet tonalities of the waves. Ponyo acts as a visual focal point and is painted with very little tonality, while the ocean surrounding her is replete with active tonal layering.

Mushi Productions, Japan's first television animation studio. Mushi Productions released Tezuka's first big series *Tetsuwan Atomu* (*Astro Boy*) in 1963, based on the popular manga series of the same name. *Astro Boy* was a huge success, not only in Japan, but in America as well.

Today, an arguably bigger name in anime is Studio Ghibli, which was founded in 1985 by animator and manga artist Hayao Miyazaki, along with Isao Takahata, and Toshio Suzuki. The majority of Miyazaki's films are created by hand on paper, with much of his art done in watercolor. Unlike American animation, scripts and storyboards are created simultaneously, so work starts on the animation before the story and storyboards are finished.

Skin tone and hair color are important in anime, and two great examples of the color and technique of Studio Ghibli are evident in *Ponyo* (2008) and *The Wind Rises* (2013). The animations target two diverse markets—children (*Ponyo*) and adults (*The Wind Rises*)—and use two different approaches by the same colorist, Michiyo Yasuda.

Ponyo was produced using traditional, hand-drawn animation to tell the story of a goldfish that falls in love with a boy and wishes to be become a girl. Yasuda, who has spent most of her career as a

color designer for Isao Takahata and Hayao Miyazaki and is considered an expert in the realm of ink and paint, chose and mixed the colors for *Ponyo*, but did not physically paint it. Instead she used Toonz software to digitally create the color. Yasuda started the process with storyboards. With respect to the palette she says: "When I saw Mr. Miyazaki's storyboards, I was shocked and knew that I had to drop the old ideas of coloration… I wanted to specifically translate the storyboards' color into film color. I tried to create colors that were sometimes raging and other times really gentle."[5] While Yasuda believes that color enhances the meaning and the emotion of the film, she does not feel that color has specific meaning. She did, however, associate each character with a color: Ponyo was pink or red because she was based on a red goldfish, for example. To Yasuda the colors were as important as the words in story-telling, and she therefore wanted to create a very colorful story.

Above: The color palette of *The Wind Rises* differs from Miyazaki's other work in that it is more subdued and realistic. Perhaps it represents the conflicting feelings he had about planes, expressed in the plot of the film, with respect to their beauty and destructive capabilities. Meanwhile, the watercolor approach and the use of pastel colors adds softness to the imagery.

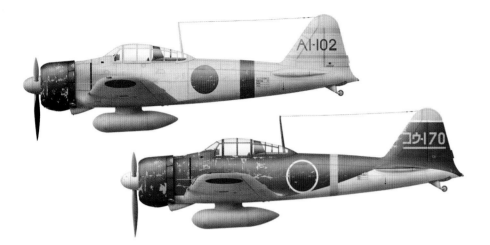

Left & below: While the colors of the original Mitsubishi planes served as a starting point for the design and coloration of the planes in *The Wind Rises*, the colors were eventually knocked back to conform to the muted pastel palette of the film.

Right: The red dot was representative of Japan's flag and was the military aircraft insignia for Japan during WW2. Today it is incorporated into the logo for Japan's ground and maritime forces..

Yasuda created the color design for Miyazaki's final film, *The Wind Rises*, realised in 2013. Directed and written by Miyazaki, and produced by Toshio Suzuki, it tells the story of an aeronautical engineer, Jiro Horikoshi, whose love of planes causes him to design the Mitsubishi A5M and A6M Zero fighter planes used by Japan during World War II. This piece of historical fiction is based on real people, including the famous Italian aeronautical designer Giovanni Battista Caproni, who tells Horikoshi in a dream that "the world is better for the beauty of planes, even if humankind uses them unwisely."[6]

Pictorially detailed, and with beautiful coloring, the film depicts the events of early twentieth-century Japan. For the most part, the film was hand-drawn in exquisite detail. Discussing the film, Richard Corliss of *Time* magazine describes the color: "Rural vistas rendered in the most delicate pastels, like the watercolors Nahoko paints as Jiro courts her."[7] In a land heading to war, Miyazaki makes sure the colors are apparent but subtle. The low-intensity landscapes were considered quiet for Miyazaki films with the use of sober browns and grays to reflect the destructive events of the time.

Yasuda allows the depicted object, character, or scene to guide her color choices based on the pigments and dyes that were available at the time in which the film takes place. Her choice of palettes is based on the mood she is trying to create. She believes that color has meaning and meaning enhances the film.

DISNEY COLOR CULTURE Founded in 1923 by brothers Walt and Roy Disney, Disney Studios was responsible for producing *Flowers and Trees* in 1932, which was the first commercially released color animation to use the three-strip Technicolor process. Disney animation held on to hand-coloring until they began using digital ink in 1989. Prior to the move to digital creation, creating an animated film for Disney was a step-by-step process that started with the creation of a storyboard showing different characters and plots; then progressed to the recording of the dialog by voice actors; and then planning the musical score.

At that point, sketches for the final animation would start with individual images of moving characters drawn on layers of clear tracing paper on a lightbox, with the image changing slightly with each frame. Once these sketched images were approved, they would be traced using ink onto sheets of transparent celluloid, and painted using colors that were mixed and refined in-house. *Snow White and the Seven Dwarfs* (1937) used around 250,000 celluloids (or "cels") created in this way. The stages for the scenes, or backgrounds, were painted in watercolor, and then the cels were placed over them and photographed in Technicolor.

Today, Disney uses CGI and Stereoscopic 3D in collaboration with hand-drawn art, and the progression from hand-colored cels to digital color has allowed color to become richer and more complex. Along with advances in the creation of three-dimensional depth, a more "believable" cartoon can be realized.

Frozen (2013) is one of Disney's most popular animated movies, based on the Hans Christian Anderson story, *The Snow Queen*. It is a heartwarming story of the relationship between two sisters. Elsa, the older sister and princess of Arendelle, has supernatural powers to create snow and ice, that get out of hand while playing, accidentally hurting her younger sister, Anna. Afraid of her powers, she decides that she must stay away. When their parents are lost at sea, both girls are forced to live insular, lonely lives, only to be brought together at Elsa's coronation. However, Anna's desire to impulsively marry causes Elsa to reveal the wrath of her powers. Horrified, she flees, leaving Anna behind and her kingdom frozen. With the help of ice harvester and mountain man Kristoff, his reindeer, and a living snowman, Anna finds her sister. Elsa, upon hearing what her powers have done to her kingdom, becomes so distraught that her powers burst out of control and freeze Anna's heart, which causes Anna's whole body to slowly turn to ice. Dragged back down to the kingdom and sentenced to death, Elsa is shocked to find Anna

using the last of her strength to save her life. This act of love for her sister unfreezes Anna. Realizing that love is the key to thawing the ice, Elsa returns warmth to the kingdom.

Complex technical software was utilized to create effects including software to generate snow, create both sisters' hair, and to create the texture, movement, and stretch of the fabrics they wear. While most of the film was computer generated and employed motion-capture technology, many hand-drawn images were also used. The film, directed by Jennifer Lee, with

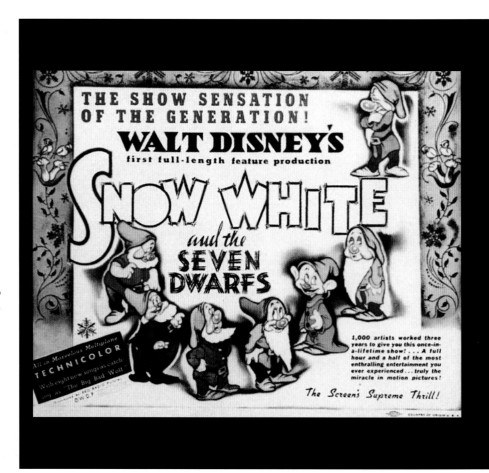

co director/animator Chris Buck, and visual development artist Michael Giamo, takes a lot of its visual language from the Norwegian Fjords. A team was sent to Norway to study the physical and cultural environment, especially with respect to clothing, interior design, and material culture. This included the patterns of the decorative painting known as rosemaling, and other folk art and decor. The directors wanted to create a film in which the characters and the environment worked in unison, placing emphasis on the scale and depth of the Fjords juxtaposed to the characters. The Fjords themselves contributed verticality and scale to the environment.

The color design was very complex and saturated, especially with respect to the ice palace, and the use of transparency, translucency, and reflection. Lewis Siegel, of Walt Disney animation studios, in his article "Frozen on Ice: rendering frost and ice on *Frozen*," talks about the need to render realistic and aesthetically pleasing ice. When creating the ice, he describes the need to control the rate of light refraction in order to render the beautiful color and portray hue shifts due to internal reflection. A technique called chromatic attenuation was used to create a realistic feeling. Rather than shifting to black, objects were shifted toward a chosen color when the ice got thicker.[8] In the article, "Immersed in Movies: First Look: Designing the Winter Wonderland of 'Frozen'," writer Bill Desowitz talked with the lighting designer and visual development artist, Lisa Keene, about creating a natural look while layering color onto the ice using "natural glacier-like colors." Lisa spoke about the relationship between Elsa's emotions and the lighting, where inner illumination was used. For example, blues and violets were used when Elsa was at peace in her castle, while yellow and oranges were used when she was challenged by the knights. Michael Giamo said: "I think more reductively in terms of palette. Mostly on the cool side, but when [Elsa] battles the guards we used a bolder palette of yellow used to symbolize caution."[9] The lighting designers were very careful to re-enforce the idea of emotion. They also did not want the snow to look white or grey. When the mood was dark, grays tended towards blue violet.[10]

Below: *Snow White and the Seven Dwarfs* was Walt Disney's first full-length cel-animated feature film. The detail and careful drawing of each cel, while simplistic, had beautiful color, whereas the newer digital versions focus on linear detail.

Costumes are another area of design that can be used to reinforce the overall environment. Jean Gilmore was brought on to create costumes that would be consistent with the Norwegian feel that visual development artist Michael Giamo wanted, creating costumes with a high level of detail including trim and stitching. She created costumes that related not only to the characters, but also had cultural associations. While Giamo did not want to replicate the actual style, he wanted the costumes to contribute to the environment as a whole. Not everything had to be strictly Norwegian. Elsa's costume incorporated reflective surfaces to suggest ice crystals and snowflakes, while Kristoff's clothes are more primitive and are a direct translation of the Sami people's usual attire. The purple cloaks worn by both girls—Elsa at the coronation and Anna as she tries to track down her sister—seem to acknowledge responsibility and growth.[11]

In the conception and creation of *Frozen* we see a perfect example of how color and culture are interlaced. The relationship between color, light, and reflection is intrinsic to Elsa's powers and the storyline itself. We see how the value and intensity of a color shifts when it is touched by light. We experience the sophistication of the design and the meaning of the colors; purple symbolizing power, nobility, ambition, and dignity, which are characteristics of the sisters as they mature. Blue is used to represent the natural world and symbolize the trust and loyalty that Elsa has for her sister. There is also historical reference to royalty reflected in the Tyrian purple, an expensive dyestuff accessible to royalty and piety. With the violet color from the film (Radiant Orchid) chosen by Leatrice Eiseman as the Pantone Color of the Year, 2014, we see the development of new designs and products. We see color as a continuing appreciation of the past, incorporated into the present and with great possibilities for the future.

Right: **What is so interesting about this image is that both reflection and transparency are evident. The colors of Anna's face in the reflection on the ice and the torch remain true, but decrease in intensity while the highlights on her face increase in intensity.**

PART SEVEN

APPENDIX

GLOSSARY OF COLOR TERMS

Abstraction: An image that has been changed so much that only the intrinsic form remains.
Absolute white: The achromatic color seen when all light is reflected back to the eye. It can be used as a reference point for the measure of absolute reflectance.
Absorption: The ability of a material to absorb all colors of light with the exception of the color of the object that is reflected back from the surface. It refers to the energy released as a result of interaction with the material.
Achromatic color: A "color" that is either black, white or grey, without any hue being observed. It refers to having no discernible color.
Acrylic: A water-soluble polymer that acts as a medium or binder with pigments that allows paint to dry both tough and flexible.
Additive Mixing: The process of mixing of color from multiple light sources. Mixing the light primaries red, green, and blue light in equal proportions results in the creation of white light. When these three are combined at varying intensities, a gamut of different colors is produced. Secondary light colors include: Cyan (blue and green), yellow (green and red), and magenta (red and blue).
Analogous Color Scheme: A type of harmonic color scheme that includes three to six adjacent colors on the color wheel. It is always good to use a complementary accent color to enhance the scheme.
Aniline: An oil-based solvent used in the preparation process of dyes and inks.
Art Deco: A design style that occurred in the 1920's and thirties that was characterized by responded to the machine age with the use of sleek simplified forms
Art Nouveau: A design style that had its roots in the arts and crafts movement and emphasized decorative characteristics of curving lines.
Attribute: A distinguishing characteristic of a sensation or perception. Colors are often described by their attributes of hue, saturation and lightness.
Balance: A visual state of equilibrium, with respect to art and design. This can be accomplished with all design elements, including color, with the modification of attributes, placement and proportion.
Bioluminescence: Light emitted from a living organism as a result of the released energy from a chemical reaction.
Biometric color: Color that is common in a respective biome.
Black: While there are many colors that are deemed black even though Chroma is present, pure black is considered an achromatic color. In theory, black can be referred to as the complete absence of reflected light, in other words a very low saturation and luminance. This occurs when all visible wavelengths are absorbed.
Brightness: The degree to which a color sample appears to emit or reflect more or less light. This attribute of color is used in the HSB (Hue, Saturation, Brightness) color model. Its colorimetric equivalent is luminance.
Casein: A water-soluble protein present in milk that can be used as a binder in an emulsion to create paint.
Chroma: The purity or saturation of a hue. The highest intensity of a color free from black white or any other color. This attribute of color is used in the LCH (Lightness, Chroma, Hue) color model.
Chromatic: All colors with the exception of pure black pure white or a mixture there of can be said to have color and are therefore chromatic.
CMYK: Cyan, magenta, and yellow correspond roughly to the primary colors RGB of additive mixing, but are used for subtractive mixing in printing. Theoretically CMY should produce black, but technical limitations make it necessary to use black to enhance the greys and shadows and create a true black (K).
Cognitive Color: The cognitive aspects of color can include behavioral, psychological, and physiological aspects of color. It can include color categorization, color-coding, color naming, the Stroop Effect, spatial organization of colored visual objects, and color memory. It is a way to understand the human color response with respect to the cognitive tasks such as thinking, remembering, and problem solving.
Color: A certain wavelength that exists on the visible spectrum. It can also be seen as the result of a perceptual response in which photoreceptors in the eye are identified, dependent upon spectral wavelengths or a combination of wavelengths that are reflected from material object. Each color has attributes of hue, intensity, and value, and are seen in accordance with an object's reflectance and translucency that are transmitted through or emitted from it.
Color Correction: A photographic or electronic process that is used to compensate for the unwanted absorptions of process inks and also the deficiencies of the color separation process. Color correction can also refer to any color change done on the part of the photographer, designer, or videographer.
Color Depth: The richness and complexity of a color.
Color Dominance: A color that is the strongest or used the most in a design.
Color Temperature: The temperature of a light source, whether it be warm, neutral or cool. It is a measurement of the color of light radiated by a black body while it is being heated. This measurement is expressed in terms of degrees Kelvin. The whiter the light source, the higher the temperature.
Deuteranopia: Green blindness due to an absence of M cones.
Dichromatism: Any form of color blindness in which only two of the three cones are present.
Digital Palette: A color palette created on the computer.
Dye: A soluble colorant that requires a mordant to improve the fastness on the fiber. Dyes can produce brighter colors than pigments, but also are less stable and tend to fade over time.
Dyestuff: A colorant that is fully dissolved in a vehicle may be organic or synthetic.
Egg tempera: A painting medium made from pigment and a water-soluble glutinous binder, often an egg yolk.
Emulsion: The suspension of one liquid in another liquid. In photography it represents a composition that is sensitive to light.
Expressionism: An early twentieth century art movement that was based in Germany. It focused on a subjective rather than a nature based observational approach to color and drawing. It had roots in primitivism utilizing distorted, flattened forms and bright emotive color.
Fauvism: The French term for "wild beast". It was an art movement that was based on a subjective emotive response, rather than the realism of its time. It emphasized strong vibrant color and bold gestural strokes.
Gamut: The full range of colors which can be perceived, produced or represented by a color model. It also refers to the range of color a device can produce.
Gloss: The surface luster of a material. When talking about gloss with respect to color the higher the gloss, the darker a color sample appears. The lower the gloss, the lighter a color sample will appear.
Gouache: Painting using opaque watercolors made from pigments ground in water and a glue like binding agent, usually a gum. This painting style is often used in illustrations and textile design.
Grey scale: The range from white to black and is often used with respect to a black and white design.
Ground: The background on which color and design are placed.
Harmony: A pleasing combination of elements.With respect to color it is a satisfying balance or unity of colors. There are many ways of creating color harmony, including similarity between the colors in hue, value or intensity. There are theoretical harmonic color schemes such as a dyad, triad, tetrad.
HSB Color System: A color model that describes color in terms of hue, saturation, and brightness
Hue: The position of the color on the visible spectrum. It is the attribute of a color that is identified by a color name, such as "red," "green," or "blue." It is the color of an object or a light source.
Impressionism: An art style based on the concept of using paint to capture the experiential moment of time responding to perceived color and light.
Intensity: How clear or muted a color is. A color at its highest intensity is pure pigment. Color decreases in intensity with the addition of a binder or a chromatic or achromatic color.
Kelvin (K) : A unit of measurement for color temperature. The Kelvin scale starts from absolute zero, which is -273 Celsius.
Kodachrome Film: A color film that produces transparencies, which are positive images on a transparent base.
Light: Light can be defined as electromagnetic radiation. Receptors in the human eye are stimulated by wavelengths within the visible light spectrum. Which ranges from 380 to 770nm.
Light Source: An object that emits light or radiant energy, It can be artificial or natural. If it is artificial it comes from one of several types of lamps. Natural light sources come from the sun, moon or stars. Some animals and plants can also emit light, which is termed bioluminescence.
Lightness: The lightness of an object as compared to black or white.
Line: A series of points moving the eye in a direction. At its straightest it defines an edge of a plane. A curvaceous line can enclose an organic shape. It can be thin like a pencil mark, or thick like an Expressionist brushstroke. Lines outline shapes.
Local Color: The ethnic and cultural flavor of a community. It can also be described as a color of an object that has not been modified by light or shadows.
LRV (Light Reflectance Value): The amount of visible light a surface reflects. It refers strictly to the lightness or darkness of a color. The values range from 0% to 100%.
Luminance: A quantitative measurement that describes the intensity or brightness of a surface that is radiating or reflecting light.
Mass: The amount of substance or matter within an object often measured by weight.
Matte Finish: A smooth but dull unpolished surface.
Medium: Used to enhance or change the quality of the paint, whether it's making it dry faster or slower or thickening it, in the case of impasto.
Metameric Match: A color match between physically different stimuli, i.e. a match between stimuli with different reflectances or spectral power distributions.
Metamerism: The phenomenon where two color samples appear to match under one light source, and differ under another. Two such samples are called a metameric pair.
Mid Century Modern: An art movement that reflected design and style developments of the mid twentieth century, with it's main tenants being based on ample windowing and open floor plans. It was influenced by the Bauhaus and Scandinavian Design. The look features organic, quirky geometric and curvilinear shapes made from a mix of natural and manmade materials.
Monochromatic Harmony: A color palette that includes only one hue, a single wavelength of color, but differs in value.
Mood Board: A tool used by color designers to portray a color feeling or story. It is often comprised of collected images/collages of items such as photographs, sketches, clippings, fabric swatches and color samples. A mood board can be physical or virtual.
Mordant: Because dyes have difficulty binding with a substrate, a mordant is required. A mordant is a substance that combines with a dye or stain for the purpose of fixing it to the material. Mordants include tannic acid, alum, urine, chrome alum, sodium chloride, and certain salts of aluminium, chromium, copper, iron, iodine, potassium, sodium, and tin. Mordants can be applied to the substrate, the dye-bath or the dyed material.
Munsell Color System: A three-dimensional color space developed by Albert Munsell in the early part of the 20th century. It is based on the attributes of hue, value and chroma. Munsell defined five principal hues (red, yellow, green, blue and purple) and five intermediate hues (yellow-red, green-yellow, blue-green, purple-blue and red-purple). The hues are equally spaced around a circle, divided into 100 equal visual steps, with the zero point located at the beginning of the red sector. Colors defined around the hue circle are known as chromatic colors.

Nanometer: A unit of length equal to one billionth of a meter Visible light wavelengths are measured in nanometers.
Natural Color System: A system based on how human beings experience color. To establish the system people were asked to visually compare colors to basic elemental colors yellow, red, blue, green, white and black.
Naturalism: The realistic portrayal of objects in a natural environment It was influenced by the principles and methods of natural science.
Neutral Colors: Colors that, due to intensity, value and color mixture, do not have a predominant color. Rather, they have a hint of a color family.

Pop Art: An art movement in the 1950s and 1960s that was influenced by pop imagery and mass production, they used strong flatly applied colors.
Protanopia: Red blindness due to an absence of L cones

Oil paint: Oil based paint made with linseed oil and pigment.
Opacity: The quality of a material that does allow light to pass through a substance
Optical mix: A phenomena that occurs when the mixing of paint viewed on a surface is mixed in the eye rather than on the canvas. This occurs when small amounts of different colors are laid side by side.

Pastels: Colors of subdued shade that have high values, neutral hues, and low to medium saturation. Also an art medium for drawing made from ground pigments and a binder.
Pantone Reference System: Internationally recognized color matching system introduced in the 1960s. Each Pantone color is identified by a specific number. This numeration provides for color specification accuracy across industries.
Perception: The process of receiving and identifying a light source, or other sensory information, and interpreting it in the visual cortex, or other parts of the brain that are subject to sensory input.
Period Color: Color that is readily identifiable as characteristic of a certain period style
Pigment: A colorant that consists of particulate matter It is insoluble and is therefore suspended in a liquid rather than dissolved. Pigments generally have better fade-resistance and permanence than dyes. Pigments are responsible for the color of the object, which means that they selectively reflect and absorb light wavelengths dependent on hue.
Pigments, Natural: Pigments that come from the earth, minerals and plants or animals, precious pigments sometimes were used as tender in history.
Pigments, Synthetic: Pigments that are manufactured from naturally occurring materials, the use of synthetic pigments expanded availability and decreased cost of colored items.
Placement: Where an artist or designer places elements, including color.
Photograms: A photographic image made without a camera.
Photon: A particle that is a carrier for electromagnetic radiation

Phosphor: A chemical compound that emits light when struck by electrons The amount of light that is emitted is dependent on the intensity of the beam. Phosphors are used in RGB monitors.

Photoreceptor: A photo sensitive cell in the eye that reacts to light. There are two type of photoreceptors in the eye called rods and the cones. They emit electrical signals that go to the brain that allow for color perception.

Pixel: Tiny dots which contain red, green and blue information in order to produce color on a monitor or scanner. Monitor resolution is the number of pixels for inch.

Plane: A surface that has length and width, but no depth, it is defined by lines

Plein Air Painting: A type of painting that occurs outdoors.

Point: A position at the beginning or end of a line

Pointillism: A style of painting that uses groups of dots to create color in an image rather than flat color areas. The colors are mixed in the eye rather than on the picture plane. The style imitates the additive mixing process. A prominent artist who used this style was Seurat.

Political color: Color that defines a movement, an event, or a region

Polychromatic: More than one color

Post-impressionism: Rather than focusing on the naturalism of impressionism, post-impressionism revolved around emotional expression. Post-impressionists were also interested in the symbolic underpinnings of what they did. The movement was characterized by simplified color and form.

Primary Color: A color that cannot be made by any combination of other colors, all colors derive from primary colors. Primary colors of light (additive) are red, green and blue (RGB). Primary colors of pigments or dyes (subtractive) are cyan, magenta and yellow (CMY). Painters often refer to primary colors as red yellow and blue. The eye has three primary receptors, red, green and blue, which allows humans to see millions of colors.

Profile: A file of a device that describes how the device is going to act when color is used. It also can be the system of color that a document is created in.

Proportion: A design principle that refers to the relative size of one element of an object in relation to another element or to the artwork as a whole, proportion greatly effects harmony. Often, proportion is viewed in comparison to the human body.

Rainbow: An optical illusion that is created by reflection, dispersion and refraction of light in rain water.

Realism: An artistic style that depicts an image accurately

Refraction: The occurrence when light waves hit material, changing the velocity of the wavelength, and causing the wave to bend.

Reflectance: The percentage of light that bounces off a surface Variables include the quantity of light and its distribution.

Regionalism: An art movement of the 1930s that focused on scenes of rural life

Response: A reaction to something and it may occur on many levels including physiological, psychological and cultural.

RGB: A color model based on the light primaries red, green, and blue.

RYB: A color system based on subtractive painters primaries red, yellow and blue.

Saturation: A quantitative measurement of the amount of color per unit of measurement At its most saturated point, or highest intensity, a hue can be identified as Chroma. Saturation decreases with the addition of other chromatic color, achromatic color, or binders. Achromatic color has zero saturation.

Scale: The size of a shape or an object It is a measurable quantity that can be judged by comparing two objects. Those that are further away tend to be smaller in scale.

Scattering: The method by which electromagnetic particles are dispersed These moving particles are forced by materials to disperse in different directions rather than continue on a straight line. Highly scattering surfaces are described as being dull or having a matte finish, while low scattering surfaces have a glossy appearance, as with polished metal or stone.

Shade: A color with black added to it, making it darker in value.

Shape: The linear form of an object. A shape can be either geometric or organic. Geometric shapes, which include circles, squares, rectangles, triangles, etc., use straight lines and hard edges. Organic shapes, which are are free-form and stem from nature, use curved lines.

Spectral Color: A color that is seen as a result of a single wavelength

Spectral Data: A way of defining color with respect to the specific amount of each wavelength it contains. Typically, spectral data records the amount of reflected light in 10-nanometer or 20-nanometer bands.

Spectral Power Distribution: The amount of light that a light source produces at each wavelength

Spectrophotometer: A photometric measure of the amount of light a color reflects, emits or transmits at each wavelength.

Subtractive Color Mixing: A method of mixing colored materials including, dyes, inks, paints and pigments. It occurs under one light source when various light wavelengths are reflected from a material object. It is called subtractive because it absorbs all colored light except for the color of the object. When all the colors of the visible spectrum are absorbed you get a deep neutral gray.

Subtractive Primaries: Cyan, magenta, and yellow are the subtractive primaries used in printing. Cyan absorbs (subtracts) all red light, reflecting blue and green. Magenta absorbs all green light, reflecting blue and red. Yellow absorbs all blue light, reflecting red and green.

Simultaneous Contrast: A perceptual phenomena that makes the eye see the complement of a color when the color is observed. If more than one color is seen at the same time each of those colors will shift as if mixed with the complementary color. If a red and a blue are viewed next to each other, the red will appear more orange and the blue will appear to be greener.

Successive contrast: The same perceptual phenomena as simultaneous contrast except that when the viewer looks at two colors and then looks across the room at other colors the color shift will be carried over to the newly viewed set of colors.

Stroop Test: A neuropsychological test that demonstrates human brain flexibility by using color terms written in different colored inks. Test takers are asked to name the color of the ink not the word.

Structural Coloration: A scientific term that is used to describe a property of an animal's fur or skin that creates an iridescence due to physical interaction between light and biological nano-structures.

Surrealism: A literary and art movement that focused on the concept of creating with the subconscious mind.

Synaesthesia A neurological phenomena that occurs when a sensation stimulated in the brain cause multiple sensory organs to function simultaneously.

Tertiary Colors: Colors that are a mixture of a primary and a secondary color

Tetradic Color Harmony : A four color scheme inscribed in a circle, square or a rectangle on the color wheel.

Texture: The surface quality of a shape. It can be created visually, by imitating actual textures that appeal to the sense of touch. Pattern is an ornamental texture that provides visual excitement to the viewer. Texture can also refer to actual physical texture, or feeling, of the paint or material.

Tint: A color is tinted by adding white to a hue, making it lighter in value.

Transmission: The light waves that pass through an object. The amount of light that is transmitted is directly related to the degree of transparency of the material quality.

Transparency: When a material allows light to pass through so that the objects or images behind it can be clearly seen.

Transparent: A material that transmits light without diffusion or scattering

Translucent: A material that allows diffuse light to be transmitted.

Triadic Color Harmony
When three colors are chosen for a scheme that are equidistant on the color wheel. The most well known triad is red, blue and yellow, painters primaries. When mixed together they create a neutral grey because they encompass all the colors of the visible spectrum.

Trichromatic/theory: A theory based on the concept that color vision is the result of light being received from three types of cones that have three different color receptors RGB.

Tritanopia: Blue blindness due to an absence of S cones.

Trend: A general direction or tendency that something is following and developing.

Value: The light-to-dark relationship within a color, it is also described as luminance, which refers to the amount of light emitted from a specific area of an object.

Vertex: The spot at which all planes come to a point and can often be a corner.

Visible Spectrum: The range of colors that humans can see, the range of wavelengths in the spectrum lies between 380 and 720 nanometers. The wavelengths in this range stimulate the cones (color receptors) in our retina. We see the shorter wavelengths as blue and violet. The longer wavelengths are seen as red and orange.

Visual weight: Depending on the combination of scale, texture, color, and shape, an object can appear to be "heavy" or "light." Some colors are proportionately heavier than others.

Volume: The amount of space that is occupied by a three-dimensional object mass (length x width x height). Volume is illusory in a two-dimensional artwork.

Warm Colors: Colors starting with yellow and continuing to red-violet on the color wheel, which convey warmth to a viewer. These colors are perceived to come forward on a two dimensional surface.

Watercolor: A transparent paint made with pigments, a water-soluble binder, and water as the medium. Traditionally, the white of the paper painted upon and light shining through it determined the values of the colors.

Wavelength: The curved wave patterns that electromagnetic radiation, sound, light, and infrared make as they travel through space. We distinguish between them by measuring the distance between the peeks.

Way Finding System:
A system that guides individuals around and through a space

REFERENCES

Adamson, J. (2012). *Indigenous Literatures, Multinaturalism, and Avatar: The Emergence of Indigenous Cosmopolitics.* American Literary History.

Akagawa, R. (2013). *Excerpts of Hayao Miyazaki's news conference announcing his retirement. The Asahi Shimbun*. [Online] Available from: http://ajw.asahi.com/article/behind_news/people/AJ201309060087.

Albers, J. (1963). *Interaction of Color*. New Haven: Yale Univeristy Press.

Almond, J. (1998). *Dictionary of Word Origins: A History of the Words, Expressions, and Cliches We Use*. Secaucus: Carol Publishing Group.

Agırel, S. (2009). *Colour Symbolism in Turkish and Azeri Folk Literature*. Folklore.

Ammer, C. (1997). *The American Heritage Dictionary of Idioms*. Boston: Houghton Mifflin Harcourt.

Ammer, C. (1993). *Seeing Red or Tickled Pink: Color Terms in Everyday Language*. New York: Plume.

Annie's Anime Blog. (2012). *Anime Hair Colors: What Do They Mean? (An All-in-One Personality Guide)*. [Online] Available from: http://annesanimeblog.wordpress.com/2012/11/15/anime-hair-colors-what-do-they-mean-an-all-in-one-personality-guide/.

Arango, J. (2010). *Outside In: The Color of Introversion*. Psychology Today.

Austin, B. and Moore, A. (2014). *The Post-Post-Apocalyptic Detroit. The New York Times Magazine*. 13th July, pp.MM22.

Ayto, J. (2005). *Word Origins: The Hidden Histories of English Words From A to Z*. [Online] London: A & C Black.

Baal-Teshuva, J. (2003). *Mark Rothko, 1903–1970: Pictures as Drama*. London: Taschen.

Bailey, J. (2010). *The Cinematographer Today: Evolution or Devolution?—Part One. American Society of Cinematographers*. [Online] Available from: www.theasc.com/blog/2010/08/30/the-cinematographer-today-evolution-or-devolution---part-one/.

Batchelor, D. (2008). *Colour: Documents of Contemporary Art*. London: Whitechapel Gallery and M.I.T. Press.

Batchelor, B. (2009). *American Pop: Popular Culture Decade by Decade*.

Bate, D. (2009). *Photography: The Key Concepts*. [Online] Oxford; New York: Berg. Available from: http://www.ebscohost.com.

Becks-Malorny, U. (2007). *Wassily Kandinsky 1866–1944: The Journey to Abstraction*. London: Taschen.

Bergdorf Goodman. (2011). *Color Exploration: Presenting our New York Fashion Week Windows. 5th at 58th*. [Online] Available from: http://blog.bergdorfgoodman.com/windows/fashion-week.

Berlin, B. and Kay, P. (1969). *Basic Color Terms: Their Universality and Evolution*. Berkeley; Los Angeles: University of California Press.

Bernhard, J. (2011). *Three Cheers for Red, White and Blue*. Phi Kappa Phi Forum.

Berns, R. and Merrill, R. (2002). *Color Science and Painting*. American Artist.

Betts, K. (2004). *Aqua Blue Crush: A first glimpse at the new black. And who decides this stuff anyway?. Time Magazine*.

Birren, F. (1963). *Color: A Survey in Words and Pictures, From Ancient Mysticism to Modern Science*. Secaucus: Citadel Press.

Birren, F. (1978). *Color and Human Response: Aspects of Light and Color Bearing on the Reactions of Living Things and the Welfare of Human Beings*. New York: Van Nostrand Reinhold.

Birren, F. (1982). *Light, Color and Environment*. New York: Van Nostrand Reinhold.

Birren, F. (1986). *Color Perception in Art*. West Chester: Schiffer Publishing.

Birren, F. (1987). *Principles of Color*. West Chester: Schiffer Publishing.

Bleckner, R. (1992). *Artist in Conversation: Adam Fuss. Bomb Magazine*. [Online] 39. Available from: http://bombmagazine.org/article/1524/adam-fuss.

Boulbès, C. (2000). *Lucas Samaras: Galerie Xippas. Art Press*. [Online] EBSCOhost 259, pp.81–82. Available from: http://www.ebscohost.com.

Bower, B. (1992). *Brother Stroop's Enduring Effect. Science News*.

Boynton, R. (1979). *Human Color Vision*. New York: Holt, Reinhart and Winston.

Brewer, E. and Room, A. (ed.) (1999). *Brewer's Dictionary of Phrase and Fable: Millennium Edition*. London: Cassell Reference.

Brownlee, P. (2009). *Color Theory and the Perception of Art. American Art*. 23(2), pp.21–24.

Bruce Mau Design. (2015). *Work: Regent Park School of Music*. [Online] Available from: http://www.brucemaudesign.com/work?project_id=12.

Brusatin, M. (1991). *A History of Colors*. London: Shambhala.

Bruzzi, S. and Church Gibson, P. (Eds.) (2000). *Fashion Cultures: Theories, Explorations and Analysis*. New York: Routeledge.

Bryant, J. and Zillmann, D. (eds) (1991). *Responding To the Screen: Reception and Reaction Processes*. Hillsdale: Lawrence Erlbaum Associates.

Bucholz, E. et al. (2007). *Art: A World of History*. New York: Abrams.

Burgoyne, P. (2005). *Cover Stories. Creative Review*.

Burley, N. and Coopersmith, C. (1987). *Bill Color Preferences of Zebra Finches*. Ethology. 76(2), pp.133–151.

Byrne, A and Hilbert, D. (1997). *A Glossary of Color Science*. [Online] Available from: http://tigger.uic.edu/~hilbert/Glossary.html.

Calouro, E. (2013). *An Interview with Photographer Zhang Jingna*. PetaPixel. [Online] Available from: http://petapixel.com/2013/08/14/an-interview-with-photographer-zhang-jingna/.

Cavallaro, D. (2013). *Japanese Aesthetics and Anime: The Influence of Tradition*. Jefferson: McFarland & Company, Inc.

Chan, T. (2012). *Travel to Tahiti. Wendy Chan Design and Illustrations*. [Online] Available from: http://wendychandesign.com/Travel-to-Tahiti.

Chipp, H. (1968). *Theories of Modern Art: A Sourcebook by Artists and Critics*. Berkeley: University of California Press.

Cieply, M. (2010). *Resistance Forms Against Hollywood's 3-D Push. The New York Times*. [Online] Available from: http://www.nytimes.com/2010/08/03/business/media/03-3d.html?_r=2&.

Clancy, C. (2003). *Health Services Research: From Galvanizing Attention to Creating Action*. Health Services Research.

Clarke, T. & Costall, A. (2008). *The emotional connotations of color: A qualitative investigation. Color Research and Application*. [Online] Wiley 33(5), pp.406–410. Averrable from: http://onlinelibrary.wiley.com.

Cohen, P. (2010). *Color gender by the numbers*.

Conjecture Corporation. (2014). *What are the Origins of the Phrase "the Pot Calling the Kettle Black"? wiseGEEK*. [Online] Available from: http://www.wisegeek.com/what-are-the-origins-of-the-phrase-the-pot-calling-the-kettle-black.htm

Connerlly, M. (2015). *Photographs Described for Blind and Partially Sighted Visitors: Invocation by Adam Fuss*.

Cook, D. (1990). *A History of Narrative Film*. 2nd Ed. New York: W. W. Norton & Company.

Corliss, R. (2014). *The Wind Rises: An Animation Master's Last Flight? Time*. [Online] Available from: http://entertainment.time.com/2014/02/20/the-wind-rises-review-hayao-miyazaki/.

Cotton, C. (2014). *The Photograph as Contemporary Art*. London: Thames & Hudson.

Craven, W. (2002). *American Art: History and Culture*. Boston: McGraw-Hill

Crook, M. (2010). *Being James Cameron. Wall Street Journal*. [Online] Available from: http://online.wsj.com/news/articles/SB10001424052748 70462500457508997280886474.

Crump, J. (1997). *Visceral Photography: The Work of Adam Fuss. Afterimage*. [Online] EBSCOhost 25(1), pp.11-12. Available from: http://www.ebscohost.com. [Accessed: 25th December, 2014].

Cullen, K. (2012). *Design Elements Typography Fundamentals: A Graphic Style Manual For Understanding How Typography Affects Design*. [Online] Beverly: Rockport. Available from: http://www.ebscohost.com.

Daniel, M. (2010). *Edward J. Steichen (1879–1973): The Photo-Secession Years*. The Metropolitan Museum of Art.

De Grandis, L. (1986). *Theory and Use of Color*. New York: Abrams

Delamre, F. and Guineau, B. (2000). *Colors: The Stories of Dyes and Pigments*. New York: Abrams.

DeLong, M. and Martinson, B. (2012). *Color and Design*. London: Berg.

De Proverbio. (2006). *Electric Journal of International Proverb Studies*. [Online] Available from: deproverbio.com.

Design Army (des). (2014). *Neenah Paper Company: Environment Papers*. [Online] Available from: http://www.neenahpaper.com.

Desowitz, B. (2013). *Immersed in Movies: First Look: Designing the Winter Wonderland of 'Frozen'. Animation Scoop*. [Online] Indiewire. Available from: http://blogs.indiewire.com/animationscoop/frozen-preview-designing-arrendelle.

Devika, S. (2010). *Beyond Gutai 1955–2009: Tsuruko Yamazaki*. ArtAsiaPacific.

Di Gregorio, B. (2004). *The Color of Mars*. Discover.

Disney. (2015). *Disney History*. [Online] Available from: http://thewaltdisneycompany.com/about-disney/disney-history.

Disney. (2015). *Walt Disney Studios Animation*. [Online] Available from: http://www.justdisney.com/animation/animation.html.

Downing, S. (2012). *Maverick Mauveine*. Selvedge.

Dresp-Langley, B. and Langley, K. (2010). *The Importance Of Colour Perception To Animals And Man*.

Duchting, H. (2012). *Paul Klee: Painting Music*. Munich: Prestel.

Earth Guild. (2015). *Mordanting for Natural Dyeing*. [Online] Available from: http://www.earthguild.com/products/riff/rmordant.htm.

The Earth Pigments Company. (2014a). *Artist's Watercolor and Gouache*.

Eiseman, L. (1998). *Colors For Your Every Mood: Discover Your True Decorating Colors*. Sterling: Capital Books Inc.

Eiseman, L. (2003). *The Color Answer Book from the World's Leading Color Expert: 100+ Frequently Asked Questions for Home, Health and Happiness*. Sterling: Capital Books Inc.

Eiseman, L. and Recker, K. (2011). *Pantone: The 20th Century in Color*. San Francisco: Chronicle Books.

Elliot, A. et al. (2011). *A subtle threat cue, heart rate variability, and cognitive performance*. Psychophysiology.

Elliot, A. and Maier, M. (2007). *Color and Psychological Functioning. Current Directions in Psychological Science*. 16(5), pp.250–254. Available from: http://www.ebscohost.com.

Failes, I. (2013). *The tech of Disney's Frozen and Get a Horse!*. fxguide. [Online] Available from: http://www.fxguide.com/featured/the-tech-of-disneys-frozen-and-get-a-horse/.

Fairchild, M. (2014). *The Value Proposition: A Metric for the Aesthetic*. Lighting Design & Application.

Fernandez, S. (1998). *History of the Pink Ribbon, Pretty in Pink*. Breast Cancer Action.

Finlay, V. (2002). *Color: A Natural History of the Palette*. New York: Ballantine Books.

Fisher, T. (2013). *A World of Colour and Bright Shining Surfaces: Experiences of Plastics after the Second World War. Journal Of Design History*. 26(3), pp.285–303.

Franklin, A. et al. (2010). *Biological Components of Colour Preference in Infancy*. Developmental Science. 13(2), pp.346–352.

Fraser, B. (1996). *Color. Adobe Magazine*.

Fraser, T. and Banks, A. (2004). *Designer's Color Manual: The Complete Guide to Color Theory and Application*. San Francisco: Chronicle Books.

Freeman, J. (1990). *The Fauve Landscape*. Los Angeles: Los Angeles County Museum of Art.

Funk & Wagnalls. (2014). *Flag of the United States*. Funk & Wagnalls New World Encyclopedia.

Futurebrand. (2013). *Reinvigorating an American Icon: American Airlines*. [Online] Available from: http://www.futurebrand.com.

Gage, J. (1999). *Color and Culture: Practice and Meaning from Antiquity to Abstraction*. Berkeley and Los Angeles: University of California Press.

Gage, J. (1999). *Color and Meaning: Art Science and Symbolism*. Berkeley: University of California Press.

Garau, A. (1984). *Color Harmonies*. Chigago: Univeristy of Chicago Press.

Gatti, T. (2014). *Animating Principle. New Statesman*. [Online] EBSCOhost 143(5209), pp.52–53.

Giesel, M. and Gegenfurtner, K. (2010). *Color appearance of real objects varying in material, hue, and shape. Journal of Vision*.

Goethe, J. (1970). *Theory of colours*. Cambridge: M.I.T. Press.

Goldwater, R. and Treves, M. (eds.). (1972). *Artists on Art: from the XIV to the XX Century*. New York: Pantheon books.

Gombrich, E. (1995). *The Story of Art*. London: Phaidon Press.

Gray, S. (2002). *A Fellowship in Peril. American Cinematographer*. 83(12), pp.36–53.

Greenberg, B. and Patterson, D. (2008). *Art in Chemistry; Chemistry in Art*. Westport: Teacher Ideas Press.

Greenspun, P. (2007). *History of Photography Timeline*. NameMedia, Inc. [Online] Available from: http://photo.net/history/timeline.

Hawking, T. (2012). *The Invisible Beauty of the Microscopic World*. The Atlantic.

Guggenheim, S. (1980). *Expressionism: A German Institution 1905–1920*. San Francisco: Solomon R. Guggenheim Museum.

Hall, M. (2012). *Window Watch: Kate Spade New York Wants You To Go To Bora Bora. The Emerging Designer*. [Online] Available from: http://theemergingdesigner.com/kate-spade-bora-bora/.

Harris, J. (ed.) (2009). *Art and Images in Psychiatry: The Yellow Cow*. Archives of General Psychiatry.

Harry Ransom Center. (2015). *Permanent Exhibitions*. [Online] Available from: http://www.hrc.utexas.edu/exhibitions/permanent/.

Harvey, M. (2013). *Wildlife Photography*. [Online] Available from: http://www.wildimagesonline.com/wildlife-photography/history-of-wild-life-photography.html.

Heard, J. (2006). *Paint like Monet (Masterclass)*. London: Cassell Illustrated.

Herbert, R. et al. (1991). *Georges Seurat (1859–1891)*. New York: The Metropolitan Museum of Art.

Hiskey, D. (2013). *Where Did the Phrase "Caught Red Handed" Come From? Mental Floss*. [Online] Available from: http://mentalfloss.com/article/33503/where-did-phrase-caught-red-handed-come

Holland, J. (2014). *Don't Feed the Bears: Ethics in Wildlife Photography and Filmmaking*. National Geographic.

Holtzsachue, L. (2006). *Understanding Color: An Introduction for Designers*. Hoboken: Wiley.

Homer, W. (1984). *Seurat and the Science of Painting*. Austin, Hacker Art Books.

Hook, E. (2011). *The Importance of 'Enough' Depth of Field in Wildlife Photography*. Digital Photography School. [Online] Available from: http://digital-photography-school.com/the-importance-of-enough-depth-of-field-in-wildlife-photography/.

Hope, M. and Walch, A. (1990). *The Color Compendium*. New York: Van Nostrand Reinhold.

Hope-Jones, M. (2011). *Darkest Arts. American Cinematographer*. [Online] 92(8), pp.40–47. Available from: http://www.theasc.com/site/.

Hornung, D. (2005). *Color: A Workshop Approach*. New York: McGraw Hill.

Huchendorf, L. (2007). *The Effects of Color on Memory*. UW-L Journal of Undergraduate Research X.

Hume, M. (2008). *The Fabric Of Our Lives*. Time.

Itten, J. (1975). *Design and Form: The Basic Course at the Bauhaus and Later*. Rev ed. New York: John Wiley & Sons.

Itten, J. (1961). *The Art of Color: The Subjective Experience and Objective Rationale of Color*. New York: Van Nostrand Reinhold.

Itten, J. and Birren, F. (ed.). (1970). *The Elements of Color: A Treatise on the Color System of Johannes Itten Based on His Book the Art of Color*. New York: Van Nostrand Reinhold.

Jacobs, G. and Nathans, J. (2009). *Color Vision: How Our Eyes Reflect Primate Evolution*. Scientific American.

Jameson, K. (2005). *Introductory Remarks on Cognition, Culture, and Color Experience*. Cross-Cultural Research. 39 (1), pp.5–9.

Janson, H. (1991). *The History of Art*. New York: Harry Abrams Inc.

Johnson Banks. (2015). *Exhibitions & 3D: Ravensbourne Signage*. [Online] Available from: http://johnsonbanks.co.uk/exhibitions-and-3d/ravensbourne-signage/.

Juan, W., Leung, P. and Jiazhi, L. (2007). *A Study of the Composition of Chinese Blue and White Porcelain*. Studies in Conservation. 52(3), pp.188–198.

Jung, W. et al. (2004). Comparison of the Affective Impressions in Chromatic and Achromatic Images. Perception.

Kaiser, P. (1984). *Physiological response to color: A critical review*. Color Research & Application.

Kalderon, M. (2008). *Metamerism, Constancy, and Knowing Which. Mind*. 117(468), pp.935–971.

Kallenberger, R. and Cvjetnicanin, G. (1994). *Film into Video: A Guide to Merging the Technologies*. Boston: Focal Press.

Kaplan Gehring McCarroll. (2015). *KGM Architectural Lighting*. [Online] Available from: http://kgmlighting.com.

Kapoor, A. (1998). *Wounds and Absent Objects*. [Online Video] Available from: http://anishkapoor.com/602/Wounds-and-Absent-Objects.html.

Karlen, M., Benya, J. and Spangler, C. (2012). *Lighting Design Basics*. Hoboken: John Wiley Inc.

Kawin, B. (2012). *Horror and the Horror Film*. London: Anthem Press.

Kay, P. et al. (2009). *The World Color Survey*. Stanford: CSLI.
Keller, M., Taute, M. & Capsule (Firm). (2012). *Design Matters: An Essential Primer*. [Online] Beverly: Rockport.

Kellogg, A. (2002). *In An Influential Fashion : An Encyclopedia Of Nineteenth And Twentieth-Century Fashion Designers And Retailers Who Transformed Dress*.

Kelly, K. and Judd, D. (1955). *The ISCC-NBS method of designating colors and a dictionary of color names*. Washington: U.S. Dept. of Commerce, National Bureau of Standards.

Kelly, K. (1958). *Central Notations for the Revised ISCC-NBS Color-Name Blocks*. Journal of Research of the National Bureau of Standards.

Kent, S. (2001). *The Ultimate History of Video Games: from Pong to Pokemon and beyond...the story behind the craze that touched our lives and changed the world*. New York: Three Rivers Press.

Kessler, A. (2012). *Song Blue And White Porcelain On The Silk Road*.

Keyes, E. (1993). *Typography, Color, and Information Structure*. Technical Communication: Journal Of The Society For Technical Communication. [Online] EBSCOhost 40(4), pp.638–654. Available from: http://www.ebscohost.com.

Kim, S. (2004). *Beyond Black and White: Race and Postmodernism in The Lord of the Rings Films*. Modern Fiction Studies. [Online] EBSCOhost 50(4), p.875. Available from: http://www.ebscohost.com.

Kimura, A. et al. (2013) *Memory Color Effect Induced by Familiarity of Brand Logos*. PLoS ONE. .

Kingslake, R. (1989). *A History of the Photographic Lens*. Boston: Academic Press Inc.

Klein, E. (1971). *A Comprehensive Etymological Dictionary Of The English Language: Dealing With The Origin Of Words And Their Sense Development Thus Illustrating The History Of Civilization And Culture*. [Online] Amsterdam: Elsevier Pub. Co.

Koenig, B. (2003). *Color Workbook*. Upper Saddle River: Pearson Prentice Hall.

Konigsberg, I. (1987). *The Complete Film Directory*. New York: Meridian Book.

Kremer Pigments Inc. (2009). *Making Oil Colors*.

Kuehni, R. (2008). *Philipp Otto Runge's Color Sphere: A translation, with related materials and an essay*.

Kucharski, J. (2014). *Costume Design in Animation—Disney's Frozen. Tyranny Of Style*. [Online] Available from: http://tyrannyofstyle.com/costume-design-animation-disney-frozen.

Kwallek, N., Soon, K. and Lewis, C. (2007). *Work week productivity, visual complexity, and individual environmental sensitivity in three offices of different color interiors*. Color Research & Application. [Online] Wiley 32(2), pp.130–143. Available from: http://onlinelibrary.wiley.com.

Kwallek, N. et al. (1997). *Impact of three interior color schemes on worker mood and performance relative to individual environmental sensitivity*. Color Research & Application. [Online] Wiley 22(2), pp.121–132. Available from: http://onlinelibrary.wiley.com.

Kwallek, N. et al. (1996). *Effects of nine monochromatic office interior colors on clerical tasks and worker mood*. Color Research & Application. [Online] Wiley 21(6), pp.448–458. Available from: http://onlinelibrary.wiley.com.

Landa, E. and Fairchild, M. (2005). *Charting Color from the Eye of the Beholder*. American Scientist.

Lange, R. and Rentfrow, J. (2007). *Color and Personality: Strong's Interest Inventory and Cattell's 16PF*. North American Journal Of Psychology.

Labrecque, L. and Milne, G. (2012). *Exciting red and competent blue: the importance of color in marketing. Journal of the Academy of Marketing Science*.

Larson, E. (2005). *The Cinema of Dreams—A Short History of Fantasy Cinema*. [Online] Available from: http://www.cinemaofdreams.com/fantasy100/fant-04a.html.

Lauer, D. (1990). *Design Basics*. New York: Harcourt Brace.

Lechner, A. and Harrington, L. (2007). *Color effectiveness in environments: Critical review of the current knowledge base*. LH Color White Papers. availabel@lhcolor.com.

Lee, D. (2007). *Nature's Palette: The Science Of Plant Color*. Chicago: University of Chicago Press.

Lenclos, J. (1999). *Colors of the World: A Geography of Color*. New York: Norton and Company Inc.

Lin, L. (2009). *Global Warming*. Graphic Advocacy Posters.

Livingstone, M. (2002). *Vision and Art: The Biology of Seeing*. New York: Harry Abrams Inc.

LoBue, V. and DeLoache, J. (2011). *Pretty in pink: The early development of gender-stereotyped colour preferences. British Journal of Developmental Psychology*.

Lock, J. and Ball, D. (2013). *Why Is the Sky Blue?* Spectroscopy.

Loftus, E. (1977). *Shifting human color memory. Memory & Cognition*. 5(6), pp.696–699.

Long, J. and Luke, J. (2001). *The New Munsell Student Color Set*. New York: Fairchild Publications.

Lorensen, J. (2006). *Between Image and Word, Color and Time: Jacob Lawrence's "The Migration Series". African American Review*.

Lovell-Pank, M. (2012). *David Hockney: The films, photo-collages and iPad works*. Cv/Visual Arts Research. [Online] EBSCOhost 104, pp.24–31.

Lubow, A. (2006). *Edvard Munch: Beyond The Scream*. Smithsonian. [Online] EBSCOhost 36(12), pp.58–67.

Lüscher, M. (2014). *Lüscher Color Diagnostic*.

Lytal, C. (2009). *Michiyo Yasuda makes the story colorful. Los Angeles Times*. [Online] Available from: http://articles.latimes.com/2009/aug/16/entertainment/ca-workinghollywood16.

Madden, T., Hewett, K. & Roth, M. (2000). *Managing Images in Different Cultures: A Cross-National Study of Color Meanings and Preferences. Journal of International Marketing*. [Online] 8(4), pp.90–107. Available from: https://www.ama.org/.

Maddrey, J. (2004). *Nightmares in Red, White and Blue: The Evolution of the American Horror Film*. Jefferson: McFarland & Company, Inc.

Madore, D. (2014). *Colors and Colorimetry*. [Online] Available from: http://www.madore.org/~david/misc/color/.

Magistrale, T. (2005). *Abject Terrors: Surveying the Modern and Postmodern Horror Film*. New York: Peter Lang Publishing Inc.

Mahnke, F. (1996). *Color, Environment, & Human Response*. New York: Wiley.

Mahnke, F. and Mahnke, R. (1993). *Color and Light in Man-made Environments*. New York: Van Nostrand Reinhold.

Marshall, N. (2000). *Communication and camouflage with the same "bright" colours in reef fishes*. Philosophical Transactions of the Royal Society B: Biological Sciences. 355(1401), pp.1243–1248.

Martin, R. (1997). *The St. James Fashion Encyclopedia: A survey of Style from 1945 to the present*. Detroit: Visible Ink Press.

Maxmen, A. (2013). *How Do Tropical Frogs Get Their Stunning Colors*. Smithsonian.

Maxwell, J. (1857). *Experiments on Colour, as Perceived by the Eye with Remarks on Colour-Blindness*. Transactions of the Royal Society of Edinburgh.

Mayer, R. (1957). *The Artists Handbook of Materials and Techniques*. New York: Viking Press.

McCartney, S. (2009). *Chantal Joffe. Interview*. [Online] EBSCOhost 39(5), pp.36. Available from: http://www.ebscohost.com.

McFadden, J. (2010). *Heat Waves in a Swamp: The Paintings of Charles Burchfield*. X-Tra: Contemporary Art Quarterly. [Online] EBSCOhost 12(3), pp.43–47. Available from: http://www.ebscohost.com.

Mehring, C. (2012). *Richter's Willkür. Art Journal*. 71(4), pp.20–35.

Mehta, R and Zhu, R. (2009). *Blue or Red? Exploring the Effect of Color on Cognitive Task Performances. Science*. 323(5918), pp.1226–1229.

Menegaldo, G. (2005). *The color system of Sleepy Hollow by Tim Burton: tribute and author signing. French Review of American Studies*. [Online] 105, pp.53–64. Available from: http://www.cairn.info/article.php?ID_ARTICLE=RFEA_105_64.

Merriam-Webster, Inc. (2014). *Greenhorn. Merriam Webster Dictionary*. [Online] Available from: http://www.merriam-webster.com/dictionary/greenhorn.

Merzbau Design Collective. (2014). *Casa Corbino*. [Online] Available from: http://www.merzbau.com/casa-corbino/64nzj0lxivr6hdjmiazzokp-31y808a.

Millis, J. *Once in a Blue Moon: The Origins and Meaning Behind the Phrase*. About.com. [Online] Available from: http://space.about.com/od/moon/a/Once-In-A-Blue-Moon.htm

Monick, D., Danz, M. and Flake, S. (2013). *Blu Dot 15 Catalog*. Blu Dot Design & Manufacturing, Inc.

Morell, V. (2003). *Animal Attraction. National Geographic*. [Online] 204(1), pp.28. Available from: http://science.nationalgeographic.com/science/health-and-human-body/human-body/animal-attraction/.

Morris, W. (1997). *Morris Dictionary of Word and Phrase Origins*. New York: Harper & Row.

NCS Colour AB (2014). *Natural Color System*. [Online] Available from: http://www.ncscolour.com/en/ncs/how-ncs-works/logic-behind-the-system/.

Nikon Inc. (2014). *Nikon Instruments—Microscopes and Imaging Systems*. [Online] Available from: http://www.nikoninstruments.com. Northern Lights Center. Northern Lights.

Nochlin, L. (1971). *Realism: Style and Civilization*. New York: Penguin Books.

O'Connor, Z. (2011). *Logo colour and differentiation: A new application of environmental colour mapping*. Color Research & Application. [Online] Wiley 36(1), pp.55–60. Available from: http://onlinelibrary.wiley.com.

Olkkonen, M., Hansen, T. and Gegenfurtner, R. (2009). *Categorical color constancy for simulated surfaces. Journal of Vision*.

Palmer, S, et. al. (2013). *Music–color associations are mediated by emotion*. Proceedings Of The National Academy Of Sciences Of The United States Of America. 110(22), pp.8836–8841.

Palmer, S. and Schloss, K. (2010). *An ecological valence theory of human color preference*. Proceedings of the National Academy of Sciences.

Palmer, S. and Schloss, K (2010). *Human preference for individual colors*. Proc. SPIE 7527, Human Vision and Electronic Imaging.

Pantone LLC. (2014). *Pantone—Color, products and guides for accurate color communication*. [Online] Available from: pantone.com.

Parker, C. (2006). Hayao Miyazaki (Studio Ghibli). *Lines and Colors Blog*. [Online] Available from: http://linesandcolors.com/2006/01/07/hayao-miyazaki/.

Parker, W., Smith, H. and Wolf, C. (1985). *Scene Design and Stage Lighting*. New York: Holt, Reinhart and Winston.

Parravano, M. (2014). *Of purple suits and such: The Art of The Wind Rises. The Horn Book*. [Online]. Available from: http://www.hbook.com/2014/05/blogs/out-of-the-box/airplanes-beautiful-dreams-art-wind-rises/#_.

Parsons, G. (1991). *How the Yellow Ribbon Became a National Folk Symbol*. Folklife Center News. 13(3), pp.9–11.

Partridge, E. (1963). *A Dictionary of Cliches*. New York:Dutton and Co., reprinted by Macmillan.

Patten, F. (1996). *A Capsule History of Anime*. Animation World Network Expert Blogs. [Online] Avail-able from: http://www.awn.com/mag/issue1.5/articles/patten1.5.html.

Patterson, I. (2003). *A Dictionary of Colour*. London: Thorogood.

Paul, C. (2003). *Digital Art (World of Art)*. London: Thames & Hudson.

Paul, P. (2002). *Color by numbers*. American Demographics. [Online] EBSCOhost 24(2), pp.30. Pegler, M. (1995). *Visual Merchandising and Display*. 3rd edition. New York: Fairchild Publications.

Pell, B. (2010). *Foreign Office Architects: Ravensbourne College. Architecture Today*. [Online] Available from: http://www.architecturetoday.co.uk/?p=9650.

Peri, D. (2011). *Working With Disney: Interviews With Animators, Producers, And Artists*. [Online] Jackson: University Press of Mississippi.

Peterson, A. and Kellogg, A. (2008). *The Greenwood Encyclopedia of Clothing Through American History 1900 to the Present*. Westport: Greenwood Press.

Phaidon Press. (ed.) (1994). *The Art Book*. London: Phaidon Press.

Pile, J. (1997). *Color in Interior Design*. New York: McGraw-Hill.

Plümacher, M. and Holz, P. (eds.) (2007). *Speaking of Colors and Odors*. Amsterdam: John Benjamins Publishing Company.

Poole, R. (2007). *In Living Color*. Smithsonian.

Poore, J. (1994). *Interior Color By Design: a design tool for architects, interior designers, and homeowners*. Rockport: Rockport Publishers.

Poulin, R. (2012). *The Language Of Graphic Design: An Illustrated Handbook For Understanding Fundamental Design Principles*. (Online) Gloucester: Rockport.

Prideaux, S, and Munch, E. (2005). *Edvard Munch: Behind The Scream*. [Online] New Haven: Yale University Press.

Przyborski, P. (2015). *Mission: Biomes*. NASA: The Earth Observatory. [Online] Available from: http://earthobservatory.nasa.gov/Experiments/Biome/.

Pultz, J. (1981). *Cubism and American Photography, 1910–1930*. Williamstown: Sterling and Francine Clark Institute.

Quinion, M. (2014). *World Wide Words*. http://www.worldwidewords.org/index.htm.

Quinion, M. (1999). *World Wide Words: Blue Blood*. http://www.worldwidewords.org/qa/qa-blu1.htm.

Quinion, M. (1996). *World Wide Words: The Colour of Words*. [Online] Available from: http://www.worldwidewords.org/articles/colour.htm.

Racich, D. (2003). *Creating Interest with the Effects of Egg Tempera*. American Artist. [Online] EBSCOhost 67(737), pp.64–69. Available from: http://www.ebscohost.com.

Rappolt, M. (2012). *Lucas Samaras. Art Review*.

Raven, P et al. (2007). *Biology*. 7th Ed. NYC: McGraw Hill.

Rawsthorn, A. (1996). *Yves Saint Laurent: A Biography*. New York: Nan A. Talese/Doubleday.

Recio, B. (1996). *The Essence of Red*. Salt Lake: Gibbs Smith.

Rensselaer Polytechnic Institute. (2014). The Lighting Research Center.

Reuther, K. (1997). *Heimtextile Home Furnishing Trends for 1998*. Color Marketing Group: Color Chips. 2, pp.14–15.

Rewald, J. (1973). *The History of Impressionism*. New York: Museum of Modern Art.

Riegler, S. (2012). *Master Class: Carleton Varney. House Beautiful*.

Richter, G. (2015). *Gerhard Richter: Biography*. [Online] Available from: https://www.gerhard-richter.com/en/biography.

Robertson, B. (2013). *Winter Wonderland*. Computer Graphics World. [Online] EBSCOhost 36(7), pp.8–15.

Rodriguez, L. and Niemeyer, H. (2001). *Cochineal Production: A Reviving Precolumbian Industry*. Athena Review.

Rogers, J. (1985). *The Dictionary of Cliches: Over 2000 Popular and Amusing Cliches—Their Meanings and Origins*. New York: Wings Books.

Rowe, A., Miller, L. and Meisch, L. (2007). *Weaving and Dyeing in Highland Ecuador*. Austin: ABC-CLIO.

Roy, A. (2007). *Monet's Palette in the Twentieth Century: Water-Lilies and Irises*. National Gallery Technical Bulletin. 28, pp.56–68.

Russell, J. (2013). *Don't It Make My Black Face Blue: Race, Avatars, Albescence, and the Transnational Imaginary. Journal Of Popular Culture*. [Online] EBSCOhost 46(1), pp.192–217. Available from: http://www.ebscohost.com.

Salle, D. (2013). *Alex Katz with David Salle. The Brooklyn Rail*. [Online] Available from: http://www.brooklynrail.org/2013/03/art/alex-katz-with-david-salle. Republished from Interview Magazine Germany.

Saltz, R. (2012). *An Artist at Work, Looking and Judging: 'Gerhard Richter Painting,' a Documentary. The New York Times*.

Sawyer, M. (2007). *Wearing your Politics on your Sleeve: The Role of Political Colors in Social Movements*. Social Movement Studies.

Scoates, C. (2013). *Brian Eno: Visual Music*. San Francisco: Chronicle Books.

Selleck, L. (2010). *Pretty in Pink: The Susan G. Komen Network and the Branding of the Breast Cancer Cause. Nordic Journal Of English* Studies.

Shen, L. (2012). *Dragon and Phoenix. Ceramics Technical*. [Online] EBSCOhost 35, pp.70–73.

Siegel, L. (2014). *Frozen on Ice: rendering frost and ice on Frozen*. SIGGRAPH Talks 2014. [Online] Deepdyve 8. Available from: https://www.deepdyve.com.

Sinervoa, B. et al. (2000). *Testosterone, Endurance, and Darwinian Fitness: Natural and Sexual Selection on the Physiological Bases of Alternative Male Behaviors in Side-Blotched Lizards*. Hormones and Behavior. 38(4), pp.222–233.

Sinopia Pigments. (2014). Recipes. [Online] Available from: http://www.sinopia.com/-Casein-Milk-Paint-Recipe_c_41.html.

Sloane, P. (1991). *Primary Sources: Selected Writings on Color from Aristotle to Albers*. New York: Design Press.

Sobieszek, R. (1985). *Masterpieces of Photography: From the George Eastman House Collection*. New York: Abbeville Press.

Smith, K. (2015). *Color Term Glossary*. [Online] Available from: http://www.sensationalcolor.com/understanding-color/theory/color-term-glossary-1847#.VLQN08ZfEeQ.

Smith, W. (2014). *Flag of the United States of America. Encyclopædia Britannica*.

Sobieszek, R. (1985). *Masterpieces of Photography: From the George Eastman House Collection*. New York: Abbeville Press.

Society for the Confluence of Festivals in India. (2014). *Holi: Let the colours shower joy*. [Online] Available from: http://www.holifestival.org.

Sonzogni, M. (2011) *Re-Covered Rose: A Case Study In Book Cover Design As Intersemiotic Translation*. [Online] Amsterdam: J. Benjamins Pub.

Spence, I. et al. (2006). *How Color Enhances Visual Memory for Natural Scenes. Psychological Science*. 17(1), pp.1–6.

Stein Carter, J. (2014). *Pollination and Plant Families*. UC-Claremont Biology Department.

Stein Carter, J. (2005). *Coevolution and Pollination*. UC-Claremont Biology Department.

Stella, F. (1999). *The Artist of the Century*. American Heritage.

Stock, K. (2009). *Fantasy, Imagination, and Film. British Journal of Aesthetics*. [Online] 49(4), pp.357–369. Available from: http://bjaesthetics.oxfordjournals.org.

Stone, N. (2003). *Environmental view and color for a simulated telemarketing task. Journal of Environmental Psychology*. 23(1), pp.63-78.

Stroop, J. (1935). *Studies of interference in serial verbal reactions. Journal of Experimental Psychology*.

Suddath, C. (2009). *Kodachrome. Time*. [Online] Available from: http://content.time.com/time/printout/0,8816,1906503,00.html

Suqi, R. (2012). *Attention, Class: Show-and-Tell Time With Carleton Varney. The New York Times*.

Swirnoff, L. (1992). *Dimensional Color*. New York: Van Nostrand Reinhold.

Temkin, A. et al. (2008). *Color Chart: Reinventing Color 1950–Today*. New York: Museum of Modern Art.

Terwogt, M. and Hoeksma, J. (1995). *Colors and emotions: Preferences and combinations. Journal of General Psychology*.

The Museum of Modern Art. (1985). *The Museum of Modern Art, New York: The History and the Collection*. New York: Abrams.

Thompson, G. (2007). *American Culture In The 1980s*. [Online] Edinburgh: Edinburgh University Press.

THR Staff. (2013). *The Making of Disney's Animated Oscar Contender 'Frozen'. The Hollywood Reporter*. [Online] Available from: http://www.hollywoodreporter.com/gallery/disneys-frozen-making-oscar-contender-659515.

Tissandier, G and Thomson, J. (Ed.) (1876). *A History and Handbook of Photography*. London: S. Low, Marston, Low, & Searle.

Triedman, K. (2006). *Color graphics: The Power of Color in Graphic Design*. Gloucester: Rockport Publishers.

Triedman, K. (2013a). *Hadestown*. Cincinnati: CW Books.

Triedman, K. (2013b). *Plum(b)*. Charlotte: Main Street Rag Publishing Company.

Triedman, K. (2013c). *The Other Room*. Boulder: Owl Canyon Press.

Troyen, C et al. (2007). *Edward Hopper*. Boston: MFA Publications.

Tufts.edu. (2002). *Adam Fuss*. [Online] Available from: http://www.tufts.edu/programs/mma/fah189/2002/nmadahar/adamfuss.html.

Uhrhane, J. (2005). *Timeline of Color Photography: related to the Leopold Godowsky Jr. Color Photography Awards*. Photographic Resource Center at Boston University. [Online] Available from: http://www.bu.edu/prc/GODOWSKY/timeline.htm.

Varichon, A. (2007). *Colors: What They Mean and How to Make Them*. New York: Abrams.

Variety Staff. (2000). *Cinematographer's Journal: Emmanuel Lubezki on 'Sleepy Hollow'. Variety*. [Online] Available from: http://variety.com/2000/film/news/cinematographer-s-journal-1117761011/.

Vasarely, M. Official Website of Victor Vasarely. [Online] Available from: http://www.vasarely.com.

Villa, A. et al. (2013). *Understanding the gum dichromate process in pictorialist photographs: A literature review and technical study*. Studies in Conservation.

Wagner, C. (1988). *The Wagner Color Response Report*. Chicago: Wagner Institute.

Walch, M. and Hope, A. (1995). *Living Colors: The Definitive Guide to Color Palettes Through the Ages*. San Francisco: Chronicle Books.

Wallin, M. (2002) *Nature's Palette: How animals, including humans, produce colours*. Bioscience Explained.

Walt Disney Treasures: Behind the Scenes at the Walt Disney Studio. (2002). Short Film. Walt Disney. [DVD Set] USA: Walt Disney Studio.

Ward, G. (ed.) (2008). *Grove Encyclopedia of Materials and Techniques in Art*. New York: Oxford University Press.

Watson, A. and Eggington, D. (2002). *Mod to Memphis: Design in Colour, 1960s–80s*. Sydney: Powerhouse Publications.

Washi's Blog. (2011). *Anime Production—Detailed Guide To How Anime Is Made And The Talent Be-hind It*. [Online] Available from: http://washiblog.wordpress.com/2011/01/18/anime-production-detailed-guide-to-how-anime-is-made-and-the-talent-behind-it/.

Wee, D. (2013). *Gutai Artist Tsuruko Yamazaki's New Works at Take Nigawa*. [Online] Available from: http://www.alminerech.com/dbfiles/mfile/120400/120436/Blouin_Artinfo_Tsuruko_Yamazaki.pdf.

Wei, S. et al. (2014). *Package Design: Colour Harmony and Consumer Expectations. International Journal Of Design*.

Whitley, D. (2012). *The Idea Of Nature In Disney Animation: From Snow White To WALL-E*. [Online] Farnham: Ashgate Publishing Ltd.

Wen, R. et al. (2007). *The Chemical Composition of Blue Pigment on Chinese Blue-and-White Porcelain of the Yuan and Ming Dynasties (AD 1271–1644)*. Archaeometry. [Online] Wiley 49(1), pp.101–115. Available from: http://onlinelibrary.wiley.com.

Westland, S. et al. (2007). *Colour Harmony. Colour: Design & Creativity*. 1(1), pp.1–15.

Weta Workshop. (2003). Short Film. Direct by Michael Pellerin. [DVD] USA: New Line Home Video.

Winsor & Newton. (2013). *Choosing Pigments: Old Masters & Contemporary Painters*. [Online] Available from: http://www.winsornewton.com/na/discover/articles-and-inspiration/choosing-pigments-old-masters-contemporary-painters.

Winsor & Newton. (2011). *History of Pigments*. [Online] Available from: http://www.winsornewton.com/na/discover/articles-and-inspiration/history-of-pigments.

Wong, W. (1987). *Principles of Color Design*. New York: Van Nostrand Reinhold.

Wong, W. (1993). *Principles of Form and Design*. New York: Van Nostrand Reinhold.

Wong, W. (1972). *Principles of Two-Dimensional Design*. New York: Van Nostrand Reinhold.

Woo, M. (2013). *Forget little green men, aliens might well be purple. New Scientist*. 220(2943), pp.18.

Woodward, S. (2009). *Introduction To Biomes*. Westport: Greenwood Press.

Woolfson, M. (2012). *The Fundamentals Of Imaging: From Particles To Galaxies*. London: Imperial College Press.

Wyszecki, G. (1969). *The Degree of Color Metamerism and Its Specification*. Textile Chemist & Colorist. 1(1), pp.46–49.

Wyszecki, G. (1977). *Advances in Color Metamerism*. Textile Chemist & Colorist. 9(4), pp.21–23.

Xue, S. et al. (2013). *Learning and Applying Color Styles From Feature Films*. Computer Graphics Forum. [Online] Wiley. 32(7), pp.255–264.

Yates, Y. (2014). *The tech behind Disney's 'Frozen'*. Tech Page One. [Online] Available from: http://techpageone.dell.com/tech-culture/tech-behind-disneys-frozen/.

Yoto, A. et al. (2007). *Effects of object color stimuli on human brain activities in perception and attention referred to EEG alpha band response. Journal of Physiological Anthropology*. 26(3), pp.373–379.

Young, W. and Young, N. (2004). *The 1950s*. [Online] Westport: Greenwood Press. Available from: http://www.ebscohost.com.

Zagzoug, M. (2001). *The History of Anime & Manga. Black Horizon Anime and C.T. Evans*. [Online] Available from: http://novaonline.nvcc.edu/eli/evans/his135/events/anime62/anime62.html.

FOOTNOTES

PART 1 CHAPTER 1

1. (Woodward, 2009) Woodward, S. (2009). *Introduction To Biomes*. Westport: Greenwood Press; (Raven et al, 2007) Raven, P et al. (2007). *Biology*. 7th Ed. NYC: McGraw Hill.
2. (Lee, 2007, pp.192) Lee, D. (2007). *Nature's Palette: The Science Of Plant Color*. Chicago: University of Chicago Press; (Raven et al., 2007) Raven, P et al. (2007). *Biology*. 7th Ed. NYC: McGraw Hill.
3. (Burley and Coopersmith, 1987) Burley, N. and Coopersmith, C. (1987). *Bill Color Preferences of Zebra Finches*. Ethology. 76(2), pp.133–151.
4. (Sinervoa et al., 2000, p.222) Sinervoa, B. et al. (2000). *Testosterone, Endurance, and Darwinian Fitness: Natural and Sexual Selection on the Physiological Bases of Alternative Male Behaviors in Side-Blotched Lizards*. Hormones and Behavior. 38(4), pp.222–233.
5. (Marshall, 2000, p.1247) Marshall, N. (2000). *Communication and camouflage with the same "bright" colours in reef fishes*. Philosophical Transactions of the Royal Society B: Biological Sciences. 355(1401), pp.1243–1248.
6. (Lock and Ball, 2013) Lock, J. and Ball, D. (2013). *Why Is the Sky Blue? Spectroscopy*. [Online] EBSCOhost 28(4), pp.12-17. Available from: http://www.ebscohost.com.
7. (Beish, no date, p.11) Beish, J. *Observing the Planets with Color Filters*. [Online] Available from: http://alpo-astronomy.org/mars/articles/FILTERS1.HTM.

CHAPTER 2

1. (Karlen et al., 2012) Karlen, M., Benya, J. and Spangler, C. (2012). *Lighting Design Basics*. Hoboken: John Wiley Inc.
2. (Karlen et al., 2012) Karlen, M., Benya, J. and Spangler, C. (2012). *Lighting Design Basics*. Hoboken: John Wiley Inc.; (Mahnke and Mahnke, 1993) Mahnke, F. and Mahnke, R. (1993). *Color and Light in Man-made Environments*. New York: Van Nostrand Reinhold; (Boynton, 1979) Boynton, R. (1979). *Human Color Vision*. New York: Holt, Reinhart and Winston; (Livingston, 2002) Livingstone, M. (2002). *Vision and Art: The Biology of Seeing*. New York: Harry Abrams Inc.
3. (Boynton, 1979) Boynton, R. (1979). *Human Color Vision*. New York: Holt, Reinhart and Winston; (Livingston, 2002) Livingstone, M. (2002). *Vision and Art: The Biology of Seeing*. New York: Harry Abrams Inc.
4. (Gage, 1999b) Gage, J. (1999b). *Color and Meaning: Art Science and Symbolism*. Berkeley: University of California Press; (Hope and Walch, 1990) Hope, M. and Walch, A. (1990). *The Color Compendium*. New York: Van Nostrand Reinhold; (Boynton,1979) Boynton, R. (1979). *Human Color Vision*. New York: Holt, Reinhart and Winston.
5. (Livingstone, 2002, p.33) Livingstone, M. (2002). *Vision and Art: The Biology of Seeing*. New York: Harry Abrams Inc.
6. (Livingstone, 2002) Livingstone, M. (2002). *Vision and Art: The Biology of Seeing*. New York: Harry Abrams Inc; (Goethe, 1970) Goethe, J. (1970). *Theory of colours*. Cambridge: M.I.T. Press; (Dresp-Langley and Langley, 2010) Dresp-Langley, B. and Langley, K. (2010). *The Importance Of Colour Perception To Animals And Man*. [Online] New York: Nova Science Publishers. Available from: http://www.ebscohost.com; (Birren, 1978) Birren, F. (1978). *Color and Human Response: Aspects of Light and Color Bearing on the Reactions of Living Things and the Welfare of Human Beings*. New York: Van Nostrand Reinhold.
7. (Fraser, 1996) Fraser, B. (1996). *Color. Adobe Magazine*. [Online] Available from: http://www.arts.rpi.edu/~ruiz/Lessons/lesson8color/color.pdf; (Wyszecki, 1969) Wyszecki, G. (1969). *The Degree of Color Metamerism and Its Specification. Textile Chemist & Colorist*. 1(1), pp.46–49; (Wyszecki, 1977, p.21) Wyszecki, G. (1977). *Advances in Color Metamerism. Textile Chemist & Colorist*. 9(4), pp.21–23; (Berns and Merrill, 2002) Berns, R. and Merrill, R. (2002). *Color Science and Painting. American Artist*. [Online] EBSCOhost 66(714), pp.68. Available from: http://www.ebscohost.com; (De Grandis, 1986) De Grandis, L. (1986). *Theory and Use of Color*. New York: Abrams

CHAPTER 3

1. (De Grandis, 1986) De Grandis, L. (1986). *Theory and Use of Color*. New York: Abrams; (Holtzschue, 2006) Holtzsachue, L. (2006). *Understanding Color: An Introduction for Designers*. Hoboken: Wiley; (Koenig, 2003) Koenig, B. (2003). *Color Workbook*. Upper Saddle River: Pearson Prentice Hall.
2. (Gombrich, 1995) Gombrich, E. (1995). *The Story of Art*. London: Phaidon Press.
3. (Holtzschue, 2006) Holtzsachue, L. (2006). *Understanding Color: An Introduction for Designers*. Hoboken: Wiley; (Itten, 1961) Itten, J. (1961). *The Art of Color: The Subjective Experience and Objective Rationale of Color*. New York: Van Nostrand Reinhold.
4. (Albers, 1963) Albers, J. (1963). *Interaction of Color*. New Haven: Yale Univeristy Press.
5. (Swirnoff, 1992) Swirnoff, L. (1992). *Dimensional Color*. New York: Van Nostrand Reinhold.
6. (Birren, 1963, p.123) Birren, F. (1963). *Color: A Survey in Words and Pictures, From Ancient Mysticism to Modern Science*. Secaucus: Citadel Press.
7. (Becks-Malorny, 2007) Becks-Malorny, U. (2007). *Wassily Kandinsky 1866–1944 : The Journey to Abstraction*. London: Taschen; (Birren, 1963) Birren, F. (1963). *Color: A Survey in Words and Pictures, From Ancient Mysticism to Modern Science*. Secaucus: Citadel Press.
8. (Itten and Birren, 1970) Itten, J. and Birren, F. (ed.). (1970). *The Elements of Color: A Treatise on the Color System of Johannas Itten Based on His Book the Art of Color*. New York: Van Nostrand Reinhold.
9. (Itten and Birren, 1970) Itten, J. and Birren, F. (ed.). (1970). *The Elements of Color: A Treatise on the Color System of Johannas Itten Based on His Book the Art of Color*. New York: Van Nostrand Reinhold; (Goethe, 1970) Goethe, J. (1970). *Theory of colours*. Cambridge: M.I.T. Press.
10. (Mahnke, 1996, pp.68–69) Mahnke, F. (1996). *Color, Environment, & Human Response*. New York: John Wiley Inc.
11. (Bucholz et al., 2007) Bucholz, E. et al. (2007). *Art: A World of History*. New York: Abrams; (Jansen, 1991) Janson, H. (1991). The History of Art. New York: Harry Abrams Inc.

CHAPTER 4

1. (Goethe, 1970) Goethe, J. (1970). *Theory of colours*. Cambridge: M.I.T. Press.
2. (Goethe, 1970) Goethe, J. (1970). *Theory of colours*. Cambridge: M.I.T. Press.
3. (Birren, 1978) Birren, F. (1978). *Color and Human Response: Aspects of Light and Color Bearing on the Reactions of Living Things and the Welfare of Human Beings*. New York: Van Nostrand Reinhold.
4. (Boynton, 1979) Boynton, R. (1979). *Human Color Vision*. New York: Holt, Reinhart and Winston.
5. (Hope and Walch, 1990) Hope, M. and Walch, A. (1990). *The Color Compendium*. New York: Van Nostrand Reinhold.
6. (Boynton, 1979) Boynton, R. (1979). *Human Color Vision*. New York: Holt, Reinhart and Winston; (Koenig, 2003) Koenig, B. (2003). *Color Workbook*. Upper Saddle River: Pearson Prentice Hall; (Westland et al., 2007) Westland, S. et al. (2007). *Colour Harmony. Colour: Design & Creativity*. 1(1), pp.1–15.
7. (Long and Luke, 2001) Long, J. and Luke, J. (2001). *The New Munsell Student Color Set*. New York: Fairchild Publications.
8. (Kelly and Judd, 1955) Kelly, K. and Judd, D. (1955). *The ISCC-NBS method of designating colors and a dictionary of color names*. Washington: U.S. Dept. of Commerce, National Bureau of Standards; (Kelly, 1958) Kelly, K. (1958). *Central Notations for the Revised ISCC-NBS Color-Name Blocks*. Journal of Research of the National Bureau of Standards. [Online] 61(5), pp.427–431. Available from: http://nvlpubs.nist.gov/nistpubs/jres/61/jresv61n5p427_A1b.pdf.
9. (CIE, 2015) CIE. (2015). *International Commission on Illumination*. [Online] Available from: http://www.cie.co.at/; (Hope and Walch, 1990) Hope, M. and Walch, A. (1990). *The Color Compendium*. New York: Van Nostrand Reinhold.
10. (Pantone LLC, 2014) Pantone LLC. (2014). *Pantone—Color, products and guides for accurate color communication*. [Online] Available from: pantone.com.

CHAPTER 5

1. (Delamare and Guineau, 2000) Delamare, F. and Guineau, B. (2000). *Colors: The Stories of Dyes and Pigments*. New York: Abrams.
2. (Mayer, 1957) Mayer, R. (1957). *The Artists Handbook of Materials and Techniques*. New York: Viking Press; (Finlay, 2002, pp.34–36) Finlay, V. (2002). *Color: A Natural History of the Palette*. New York: Ballantine Books.
3. (Downing, 2012) Downing, S. (2012). *Maverick Mauveine*. Selvedge. [Online] EBSCOhost 45 pp.38–43. Available from: http://www.ebscohost.com; (Finlay, 2002) Finlay, V. (2002). *Color: A Natural History of the Palette*. New York: Ballantine Books.
4. (Varichon, 2007) Varichon, A. (2007). *Colors: What They Mean and How to Make Them*. New York: Abrams.
5. (Mayer, 1957) Mayer, R. (1957). *The Artists Handbook of Materials and Techniques*. New York: Viking Press; (Delamare and Guineau, 2000) Delamare, F. and Guineau, B. (2000). *Colors: The Stories of Dyes and Pigments*. New York: Abrams.
6. (Mayer, 1957, p.234) Mayer, R. (1957). *The Artists Handbook of Materials and Techniques*. New York: Viking Press.
7. (Sinopia Pigments, 2014) *Sinopia Pigments*. (2014). *Recipes*. [Online] Available from: http://www.sinopia.com/-Casein-Milk-Paint- Recipe_c_41.html.
8. (Racich, 2003, pp. 64–65) Racich, D. (2003). *Creating Interest with the Effects of Egg Tempera. American Artist*. [Online] EBSCOhost 67(737), pp.64–69. Available from: http://www.ebscohost.com.
9. (The Earth Pigments Company, 2014a) *The Earth Pigments Company*. (2014a). *Artist's Watercolor and Gouache*. [Online] Available from: http://www.earthpigments.com/artists-watercolor-and-gouache/.
10. (The Earth Pigments Company, 2014b) *The Earth Pigments Company*. (2014b). *Artist's Pastels*. [Online] Available from: http://www.earthpigments.com/artists-pastels/.

PART 2 CHAPTER 1

1. (Merriam-Webster Inc, 2014) Merriam-Webster Inc. (2014a). *Cognitive*. [Online] Available from: http://www.merriam-webster.com/dictionary/cognitive.
2. (Loftus, 1977) Loftus, E. (1977). *Shifting human color memory. Memory & Cognition*. 5(6), pp.696–699. Available from: http://link.springer.com/article/10.3758/BF03197418#page-1.
3. (Kimura et al., 2013, p.7) Kimura, A. et. al. (2013) *Memory Color Effect Induced by Familiarity of Brand Logos*. PLoS ONE. [Online] 8(7). Available from: http://www.plosone.org/article/info%3Adoi%2F10.1371%2Fjournal.pone.0068474.
4. (Spence et al., 2006) Spence, I. et al. (2006). *How Color Enhances Visual Memory for Natural Scenes. Psychological Science*. 17(1), pp.1–6.
5. (Stroop, 1935) Stroop, J. (1935). *Studies of interference in serial verbal reactions. Journal of Experimental Psychology*. [Online] PsycNET 18(6), pp.643–662. Available from: http://psycnet.apa.org/?&fa=main.doiLanding&-doi=10.1037/0096-3445.121.1.15.
6. (Mehta and Zhu, 2009, pp.1226–1229) Mehta, R and Zhu, R. (2009). *Blue or Red? Exploring the Effect of Color on Cognitive Task Performances. Science*. 323(5918), pp.1226–1229. Available from: http://www.sciencemag.org/content/323/5918/1226.
7. (Franklin et al., 2010, p.346) Franklin, A. et al. (2010). *Biological Components of Colour Preference in Infancy. Developmental Science*. 13(2), pp.346–352.
8. (Mahnke, 1996, p.13) Mahnke, F. (1996). *Color, Environment, & Human Response*. New York: Wiley.
9. Cohen, Philip N. (2013) *"Children's Gender and Parents' Color Preferences."* Archives of Sexual Behavior.
10. (LoBue and DeLoache, 2011, p.656) LoBue, V. and DeLoache, J. (2011). *Pretty in pink: The early development of gender-stereotyped colour preferences. British Journal of Developmental Psychology*. [Online] Wiley 29(3), pp.656–667. Available from: www.wileyonlinelibrary.com.
11. (Palmer and Schloss, 2010a) Palmer, S. and Schloss, K. (2010a). *An ecological valence theory of human color preference*. Proceedings of the National Academy of Sciences. [Online] DeepDyve 107(19), pp.8877–8882. Available from: https://www.deepdyve.com.
12. (Palmer and Schloss, 2010a) Palmer, S. and Schloss, K. (2010a). *An ecological valence theory of human color preference*. Proceedings of the National Academy of Sciences. [Online] DeepDyve 107(19), pp.8877–8882. Available from: https://www.deepdyve.com.
13. (Wagner, 1988) Wagner, C. (1988). *The Wagner Color Response Report*. Chicago: Wagner Institute.
14. (Palmer et al., 2013, p.8836) Palmer, S, et. al. (2013). *Music–color associations are mediated by emotion*. Proceedings Of The National Academy Of Sciences Of The United States Of America. 110(22), pp.8836–8841. Available from: http://www.pnas.org/content/110/22/8836.full.pdf+html
15. (Eiseman, 1998, p.18) Eiseman, L. (1998). *Colors For Your Every Mood: Discover Your True Decorating Colors*. Sterling: Capital Books Inc.

CHAPTER 2

1. (Bernhard, 2011) Bernhard, J. (2011). *Three Cheers for Red, White and Blue*. Phi Kappa Phi Forum. [Online] EBSCOhost 91(2), pp.16–18. Available from: http://www.ebscohost.com; (Smith, 2014) Smith, W. (2014). *Flag of the United States of America. Encyclopædia Britannica*. [Online] Available from: http://www.britannica.com/EBchecked/topic/563712/flag-of-the-United-States-of-America.
2. (Bernhard, 2011, p.16) Bernhard, J. (2011). *Three Cheers for Red, White and Blue*. Phi Kappa Phi Forum. [Online] EBSCOhost 91(2), pp.16–18. Available from: http://www.ebscohost.com; (Funk & Wagnalls, 2014) Funk & Wagnalls. (2014). *Flag of the United States. Funk & Wagnalls New World Encyclopedia*. [Online] EBSCOhost pp.1. Available from: http://www.ebscohost.com.
3. (Lenclos, 1999) Lenclos, J. (1999). *Colors of the World: A Geography of Color*. New York: Norton and Company Inc.
4. (Paul, 2002). Paul, P. (2002). *Color by numbers. American Demographics*. [Online] EBSCOhost 24(2), pp.30. Available from: http://www.ebscohost.com.
5. (Sawyer, 2007). Sawyer, M. (2007). *Wearing your Politics on your Sleeve: The Role of Political Colors in Social Movements*. Social Movement Studies. [Online] EBSCOhost 6(1), pp.39–56. Available from: http://www.ebscohost.com.
6. (Elliot et al., 2011) Elliot, A. et al. (2011). *A subtle threat cue, heart rate variability, and cognitive performance*. Psychophysiology. [Online] Wiley 48(10), pp.1340–1345. Available from: http://onlinelibrary.wiley.com; (Kaiser, 1984) Kaiser, P. (1984). *Physiological response to color: A critical review*. Color Research & Application. [Online] DeepDyve 9(1), pp.29–36. Available from: https://www.deepdyve.com.
7. (Recio, 1996, pp.7–8) Recio, B. (1996). *The Essence of Red*. Salt Lake: Gibbs Smith.
8. Black, (Graphic Advocacy, 2012) *Graphic Advocacy*. (2012). *International Posters for the Digital Age*. [Online] Available from: http://graphicadvocacyposters.org/posters/.
9. Lin, (Graphic Advocacy, 2012) *Graphic Advocacy*. (2012). *International Posters for the Digital Age*. [Online] Available from: http://graphicadvocacyposters.org/posters/.
10. (Parsons, 2014b) Parsons, G. (2014b). *Yellow Ribbons: Ties with Tradition*. The American Folklife Center. [Online] Available from: http://www.loc.gov/folklife/ribbons/ribbons_81.html.
11. (Romesburg,1998, p.20) Romesburg, D. (1998). *1978: She's a gay old flag*. Advocate. [Online] EBSCOhost 763, p.20. Available from: http://www.ebscohost.com.

CHAPTER 3

1. (Finlay, 2002) Finlay, V. (2002). *Color: A Natural History of the Palette*. New York: Ballantine Books.
2. (Rowe et al., 2007) Rowe, A., Miller, L. and Meisch, L. (2007). *Weaving and Dyeing in Highland Ecuador*. Austin: ABC-CLIO; (Rodriguez and Niemeyer, 2001) Rodriguez, L. and Niemeyer, H. (2001). *Cochineal Production: A Reviving Precolumbian Industry. Athena Review*. [Online] 2(4), pp.76–78. Available from: http://abulafia.ciencias.uchile.cl/publicaciones/pdf/169-AthenaRev-2-76-2001.pdf.
3. (Juan et al., 2007) Juan, W., Leung, P. and Jiazhi, L. (2007). *A Study of the Composition of Chinese Blue and White Porcelain*. Studies in Conservation. 52(3), pp.188–198; (Wen et al., 2007) Wen, R. et al. (2007). *The Chemical Composition of Blue Pigment on Chinese Blue-and-White Porcelain of the Yuan and Ming Dynasties (AD 1271–1644). Archaeometry*. [Online] Wiley 49(1), pp.101–115. Available from: http://onlinelibrary.wiley.com.
4. (Roy, 2005) Roy, C. (2005). *Traditional Festivals: A Multicultural Encyclopedia*. [Online] Santa Barbara: ABC-CLIO. Available from: http://www.ebscohost.com; (Society for the Confluence of Festivals in India, 2014) Society for the Confluence of Festivals in India. (2014). *Holi: Let the colours shower joy*. [Online] Available from: http://www.holifestival.org.

CHAPTER 4

1. (Peterson and Kellogg, 2008, p.173) Peterson, A. and Kellogg, A. (2008). *The Greenwood Encyclopedia of Clothing Through American History 1900 to the Present*. Westport: Greenwood Press.
2. (Eiseman and Recker, 2011) Eiseman, L. and Recker, K. (2011). *Pantone: The 20th Century in Color*. San Francisco: Chronicle Books; (Walch and Hope, 1995) Walch, M. and Hope, A. (1995). *Living Colors: The Definitive Guide to Color Palettes Through the Ages*. San Francisco: Chronicle Books.
3. (Peterson and Kellogg, 2008, p.238) Peterson, A. and Kellogg, A. (2008). *The Greenwood Encyclopedia of Clothing Through American History 1900 to the Present*. Westport: Greenwood Press.

4. (Walch and Hope, 1995, p.108) Walch, M. and Hope, A. (1995). *Living Colors: The Definitive Guide to Color Palettes Through the Ages*. San Francisco: Chronicle Books.
5. (Riegler, 2012) Riegler, S. (2012). *Master Class: Carleton Varney. House Beautiful.* [Online] EBSCOhost 154(4), pp.36. Available from: http://www.ebscohost.com; Tyrnauer, 2010) Tyrnauer, M. (2010). *Modern Classic. Vanity Fair.* [Online] EBSCOhost 601, pp.172. Available from: http://www.ebscohost.com.
6. (Batchelor, 2009) Batchelor, B. (2009). *American Pop: Popular Culture Decade by Decade*. [Online] Westport: Greenwood Press. Available from: http://www.ebscohost.com.
7. (Eiseman and Recker, 2011) Eisemen, L. and Recker, K. (2011). *Pantone: The 20th Century in Color*. San Francisco: Chronicle Books.
8. (Peterson and Kellogg, 2008) Peterson, A. and Kellogg, A. (2008). *The Greenwood Encyclopedia of Clothing Through American History 1900 to the Present*. Westport: Greenwood Press.
9. (Reuther, 1997) Reuther, K. (1997). Heimtextile Home Furnishing Trends for 1998. Color Marketing Group: Color Chips. 2, pp.14–15.

PART 3 CHAPTER 1

1. (Hurt, 2013) Hurt, P. (2013). *Never Underestimate the Power of a Paint Tube. Smithsonian Magazine*. [Online] pp.20. Available from: http://www.smithsonianmag.com/arts-culture/never-underestimate-the-power-of-a-paint-tube-36637764/ .
2. (2006, p.21) Heard, J. (2006). *Paint like Monet (Masterclass)*. London: Cassell Illustrated.
3. (Homer, 1984) Homer, W. (1984). *Seurat and the Science of Painting*. Austin, Hacker Art Books.
4. (Prideaux and Munch, 2005, p.251) Prideaux, S, and Munch, E. (2005). *Edvard Munch: Behind The Scream*. [Online] New Haven: Yale University Press. Available from: http://www.ebscohost.com.
5. (Gage, 1999a, p.207) Gage, J. (1999a). *Color and Culture: Practice and Meaning from Antiquity to Abstraction*. Los Angeles: University of California Press.
6. (Gombrich, 1995, p.604) Gombrich, E. (1995). *The Story of Art*. London: Phaidon Press.
7. (Rothko Chapel, 2014) *Rothko Chapel*. (2014). [Online] Available from: www.rothkochapel.org/; (Baal-Teshuva, 2003, p.74) Baal-Teshuva, J. (2003). *Mark Rothko, 1903–1970: Pictures as Drama*. London: Taschen.
8. (Karabenick and Stanczak, 2012) Karabenick, J. and Stanczak, J. (2012). *An Interview with Artist Julian Stanczak*. Geofrom. [Online] Available from: http://geoform.net/interviews/an-interview-with-artist-julian-stanczak/.
9. (Sloane, 1991, p.160) Sloane, P. (1991). *Primary Sources: Selected Writings on Color from Aristotle to Albers*. New York: Design Press.
10. (Lorensen, 2006) Lorensen, J. (2006). *Between Image and Word, Color and Time: Jacob Lawrence's "The Migration Series". African American Review*. [Online] EBSCOhost 40(3), pp.571–586. Available from: http://www.ebscohost.com.
11. (The Museum of Modern Art, 1985) The Museum of Modern Art. (1985). *The Museum of Modern Art, New York: The History and the Collection*. New York: Abrams.
12. [Online] www.gerhard-richter.com.

CHAPTER 2

1. (Dougal et al., 2005, p.215) Dougal, R,. Greated, C. and Marson, A. (2005). *Then and now: James Clerk Maxwell and colour. Optics and Laser Technology*. [Online] DeepDyve 38(2006), pp.210–218. Available from: https://www.deepdyve.com.
2. (Uhrhane, 2005) Uhrhane, J. (2005). *Timeline of Color Photography: related to the Leopold Godowsky Jr. Color Photography Awards*. Photographic Resource Center at Boston University. [Online] Available from: http://www.bu.edu/prc/GODOWSKY/timeline.htm.
3. (Pultz, 1981) Pultz, J. (1981). *Cubism and American Photography, 1910–1930*. Williamstown: Sterling and Francine Clark Institute.
4. (Bleckner, 1992) Bleckner, R. (1992). *Artist in Conversation: Adam Fuss. Bomb Magazine*. [Online] 39. Available from: http://bombmagazine.org/article/1524/adam-fuss.
5. Rappolt, M. (2012). *Lucas Samaras. Art Review*. [Online] EBSCOhost (62), pp.84–87. Available from: http://www.ebscohost.com.
6. (M+B, 2014) M+B. (2014). Mariah Robertson. [Online] Available from:http://www.mbart.com/artists/141-Mariah-Robertson/press/.

CHAPTER 3

1. Triedman, K. (2013b). *Plum(b)*. Charlotte: Main Street Rag Publishing Company.
2. Triedman, K. (2013b). *Plum(b)*. Charlotte: Main Street Rag Publishing Company.
3. Triedman, K. (2013b). *Plum(b)*. Charlotte: Main Street Rag Publishing Company.
4. Triedman, K. (2013b). *Plum(b)*. Charlotte: Main Street Rag Publishing Company.
5. (Melissa, 2012) Melissa. (2012). *The Origin of the English Names of Colors*. Today I Found Out. [Online] Available from: http://www.todayifoundout.com/index.php/2014/01/origin-english-names-colors/.
6. (Brenner, 1982, pp.4–7) Brenner, A. (1982). *Colour Terms In The Old Testament*. [Online] Sheffield: JSOT Press. Available from: http://www.ebscohost.com.
7. (Berlin and Kay, 1969) Berlin, B. and Kay, P. (1969). Basic Color Terms: Their Universality and Evolution. Berkeley; Los Angeles: University of California Press.
8. (Kay and Berlin, 2002) Kay, P. and Berlin, B. (2002). *The World Color Survey*. [Online] Available from: http://www1.icsi.berkeley.edu/wcs/.
9. (2001, p.389) Zentner, M. (2001). *Preferences for colours and colour-emotion combinations in early childhood*. Developmental Science. [Online] Wiley 4(4), pp.389–398. Available from: http://onlinelibrary.wiley.com.
10. (Zentner, 2001) Zentner, M. (2001). *Preferences for colours and colour-emotion combinations in early childhood*. Developmental Science. [Online] Wiley 4(4), pp.389–398. Available from: http://onlinelibrary.wiley.com.
11. (Almond, 1998, p.41) Almond, J. (1998). *Dictionary of Word Origins: A History of the Words, Expressions, and Cliches We Use*. Secaucus: Carol Publishing Group.
12. (Rogers, 1985, p.216) Rogers, J. (1985). *The Dictionary of Cliches: Over 2000 Popular and Amusing Cliches—Their Meanings and Origins*. New York: Wings Books.
13. (Rogers, 1985, p.27) Rogers, J. (1985). *The Dictionary of Cliches: Over 2000 Popular and Amusing Cliches—Their Meanings and Origins*. New York: Wings Books.
14. (Makkai, 1984, p.216) Makkai, A. (1984). *Handbook of Commonly Used American Idioms*. Woodbury: Barrons Educational Series.
15. (Rogers, 1985, p.27) Rogers, J. (1985). *The Dictionary of Cliches: Over 2000 Popular and Amusing Cliches—Their Meanings and Origins*. New York: Wings Books.
16. (New World Encyclopedia, 2008) *New World Encyclopedia*. (2008). *Censorship: Etymology*. [Online] Available from: http://www.newworldencyclopedia.org/entry/censorship.
17. (Rogers, 1985, p.289) Rogers, J. (1985). *The Dictionary of Cliches: Over 2000 Popular and Amusing Cliches—Their Meanings and Origins*. New York: Wings Books.
18. (Patterson, 2003, p.317) Patterson, I. (2003). *A Dictionary of Colour*. London: Thorogood.
19. (Martin, 2014) Martin, G. (2014). The Phrase Finder. [Online] Available from: http://www.phrases.org.uk.
20. (Almond, 1998) Almond, J. (1998). *Dictionary of Word Origins: A History of the Words, Expressions, and Cliches We Use*. Secaucus: Carol Publishing Group.
21. (Almond, 1998) Almond, J. (1998). *Dictionary of Word Origins: A History of the Words, Expressions, and Cliches We Use*. Secaucus: Carol Publishing Group.
22. (Almond, 1998) Almond, J. (1998). *Dictionary of Word Origins: A History of the Words, Expressions, and Cliches We Use*. Secaucus: Carol Publishing Group.
23. (Almond, 1998) Almond, J. (1998). *Dictionary of Word Origins: A History of the Words, Expressions, and Cliches We Use*. Secaucus: Carol Publishing Group.
24. (Almond, 1998) Almond, J. (1998). *Dictionary of Word Origins: A History of the Words, Expressions, and Cliches We Use*. Secaucus: Carol Publishing Group.
25. (Almond, 1998) Almond, J. (1998). *Dictionary of Word Origins: A History of the Words, Expressions, and Cliches We Use*. Secaucus: Carol Publishing Group.
26. (Martin, 2014) Martin, G. (2014). The Phrase Finder. [Online] Available from: http://www.phrases.org.uk.
27. (Almond, 1998) Almond, J. (1998). *Dictionary of Word Origins: A History of the Words, Expressions, and Cliches We Use*. Secaucus: Carol Publishing Group.
28. (U.S. Department of State, 2014) U.S. Department of State. (2014). Office of the Historian. [Online] Available from: history.state.gov.
29. (Almond, 1998, p.206) Almond, J. (1998). *Dictionary of Word Origins: A History of the Words, Expressions, and Cliches We Use*. Secaucus: Carol Publishing Group.
30. (Hendrickson, 1997, pp.135–138) Hendrickson, R. (1997). *The Facts on File Encyclopedia of Word and Phrase Origins*. New York: Facts on File.
31. (Almond, 1998) Almond, J. (1998). *Dictionary of Word Origins: A History of the Words, Expressions, and Cliches We Use*. Secaucus: Carol Publishing Group.

PART 4 CHAPTER 2

1. (Keyes, 1993) Keyes, E. (1993). *Typography, Color, and Information Structure. Technical Communication: Journal Of The Society For Technical Communication*. [Online] EBSCOhost 40(4), pp.638–654. Available from: http://www.ebscohost.com.
2. (Pearce, 2009) Pearce, H. (2009). *Conundrums: Typographic Conundrums*. New York: It Books.
3. (Dwell Media LLC, 2015) Dwell Media LLC. (2015). *Dwell Magazine*. New York: Dwell.
4. (Johnson, 2013) Johnson, *Boston Magazine*, April 2013.
5. (Davenport, 2015) Davenport, 2015, vocal quote: www.jaddavenport.com
6. (Davenport, 2015) Davenport, 2015, vocal quote: www.jaddavenport.com
7. (Domaradzki, 2015) Domaradzki, 2015, vocal quote.
8. (Martinson and Waldron, 2002, p.211) Martinson, B. and Waldron, C. (2002). *Color in graphic design: an analysis of meaning and trends*. Proceedings of SPIE. [Online] 4421, 9th Congress of the International Colour Association, 221. Available from: http://dx.doi.org/10.1117/12.464555.
9. (Kapoor, 1998) Kapoor, A. (1998). *Wounds and Absent Objects*. [Online Video] Available from: http://anishkapoor.com/602/Wounds-and-Absent-Objects.html.
10. (Design Army, 2014) Design Army (des). (2014). Neenah Paper Company: Environment Papers. [Online] Available from: http://www.neenahpaper.com.

CHAPTER 3

1. (2012) Labrecque, L. and Milne, G. (2012). *Exciting red and competent blue: the importance of color in marketing. Journal of the Academy of Marketing Science*. [Online] EBSCOhost 40(5), pp.711–727. Available from: http://www.ebscohost.com.
2. (O'Conner, 2011, p.56) O'Connor, Z. (2011). *Logo colour and differentiation: A new application of environmental colour mapping*. Color Research & Application. [Online] Wiley 36(1), pp.55–60. Available from: http://onlinelibrary.wiley.com.
3. (Chermayeff et al., 2015a) Chermayeff & Geismar & Haviv. (2015a). Grey Advertising. [Online] Available from: http://www.cgstudionyc.com/identities/grey.
4. (Chermayeff et al., 2015b) Chermayeff & Geismar & Haviv. (2015b). Tennessee Aquarium. [Online] Available from: http://www.cgstudionyc.com/art-architecture/tennessee-aquarium.
5. (Osborne, 2014) Osborne, M. (2014). San Francisco Museum of Modern Art. [Online] Available from: http://www.modsf.com/sfmoma.
6. (Snøhetta Design, 2014) Snøhetta Design. (2014). Olympic Games Oslo 2022. [Online] Available from: http://snohetta.com/project/117-olym-pic-games-oslo-2022.
7. (Futurebrand, 2013) Futurebrand. (2013). Reinvigorating an American Icon: American Airlines. [Online] Available from: http://www.futurebrand.com.
8. (Wei et al., 2013) Wei, S. et al. (2014). *Package Design: Colour Harmony and Consumer Expectations. International Journal Of Design*. [Online] EBSCOhost 8(1), pp.109–126. Available from: http://www.ebscohost.com.
9. L'Occitane. (2015). L'Occitane en Provence. [Online] Available from: www.loccitane.com.
10. (FITCH, 2015a) FITCH. (2015a). Nestlé: Greater Visibility for Nestlé at Festival Time. [Online] Available from: http://fitch.opolis.co.uk/case-study/nestle-gifting/.

PART 5 CHAPTER 2

1. Kate Spade. (2012). Travel to Tahiti Window. NYC.
2. (Bergdoff Goodman, 2011) Bergdorf Goodman. (2011). Color Exploration: Presenting our New York Fashion Week Windows. 5th at 58th. [Online] Available from: http://blog.bergdorfgoodman.com/windows/fashion-week.
3. Zoological Society of London. (2015). Project Ocean. [Online] Available from: http://www.zsl.org/conservation/habitats/marine-and-freshwater/project-ocean.
4. (Bruce Mau Design, 2015) Bruce Mau Design. (2015). Work: Regent Park School of Music. [Online] Available from: http://www.brucemaudesign.com/work?project_id=12.
5. (Ravensbourne, 2013) Ravensbourne. (2013). Ravensbourne College. [Online] Available from: http://www.ravensbourne.ac.uk/.
6. (Jason Banks, 2015) Johnson Banks. (2015). Exhibitions & 3D: Ravensbourne Signage. [Online] Available from: http://johnsonbanks.co.uk/exhibitions-and-3d/ravensbourne-signage/.
7. (Pegler, 1995) Pegler, M. (1995). *Visual Merchandising and Display*. 3rd edition New York: Fairchild Publications.
8. (Kaplan Gehring McCarroll, 2015) Kaplan Gehring McCarroll. (2015). KGM Architectural Lighting. [Online] Available from: http://kgmlighting.com.
9. (Philips Solid-State Lighting Solutions, Inc., 2015c) Philips Solid-State Lighting Solutions, Inc. (2015c). Selfridges. [Online] Available from: http://www.colorkinetics.com/showcase/installs/Selfridges/.

CHAPTER 3

1. (Mughannam, 2013) Mughannam, E. (2013). EM Design Interiors: Her Elegant Escape. [Online] Available from: http://emdesigninteriors.com/napa-valley-showcase-house#/id/i6513847.
2. (Merzbau Design Collective, 2014) Merzbau Design Collective. (2014). Casa Corbino. [Online] Available from: http://www.merzbau.com/casa-corbino/64nzj0lxivr6hdjmiazzokp31y808a.
3. (1996) Mahnke, F. (1996). *Color, Environment, & Human Response*. New York: Wiley.
4. (1997) Pile, J. (1997). *Color in Interior Design*. New York: McGraw-Hill.
5. (Kwallek et al., 2007, p.142) Kwallek, N., Soon, K. and Lewis, C. (2007). *Work week productivity, visual complexity, and individual environmental sensitivity in three offices of different color interiors*. Color Research & Application. [Online] Wiley 32(2), pp.130–143. Available from: http://onlinelibrary.wiley.com.
6. (Lechner and Harrington, 2007) Lechner, A. and Harrington, L. (2007). *Color effectiveness in environments: Critical review of the current knowledge base*. LH Color White Papers. availabel@lhcolor.com.

PART 6 CHAPTER 1

1. (Weta Workshop, 2003) Weta Workshop. (2003). Short Film. Directed by Michael Pellerin. [DVD] USA: New Line Home Video.
2. (Gray, p.37, 2002) Gray, S. (2002). *A Fellowship in Peril. American Cinematographer*. 83(12), pp.36–53.
3. (Gray, p.37, 2002) Gray, S. (2002). *A Fellowship in Peril. American Cinematographer*. 83(12), pp.36–53.
4. (Crook, 2010) Crook, M. (2010). *Being James Cameron. Wall Street Journal*. [Online] Available from: http://online.wsj.com/news/articles/SB10001424052748704625004575089972808864774.
5. (Lytal, 2009) Lytal, C. (2009). Michiyo Yasuda makes the story colorful. Los Angeles Times. [Online] Available from: http://articles.latimes.com/2009/aug/16/entertainment/ca-workinghollywood16.
6. (Akagawa, 2013) Akagawa, R. (2013). Excerpts of Hayao Miyazaki's news conference announcing his retirement. The Asahi Shimbun. [Online] Available from: http://ajw.asahi.com/article/behind_news/people/AJ201309060087.
7. (Corliss, 2014) Corliss, R. (2014). *The Wind Rises: An Animation Master's Last Flight? Time*. [Online] Available from: http://entertainment.time.com/2014/02/20/the-wind-rises-review-hayao-miyazaki/.
8. (Siegel, 2014) Siegel, L. (2014). *Frozen on Ice: rendering frost and ice on Frozen*. SIGGRAPH Talks 2014. [Online] Deepdyve 8. Available from: https://www.deepdyve.com.
9. (Desowitz, 2013) Desowitz, B. (2013). *Immersed in Movies: First Look: Designing the Winter Wonderland of 'Frozen'*. Animation Scoop. [Online] Indiewire. Available from: http://blogs.indiewire.com/animationscoop/frozen-preview-designing-arrendelle.
10. (Robertson, 2013) Robertson, B. (2013). *Winter Wonderland. Computer Graphics World*. [Online] EBSCOhost 36(7), pp.8-15. Available from: http://www.ebscohost.com; (Desowitz, 2013) Desowitz, B. (2013). *Immersed in Movies: First Look: Designing the Winter Wonderland of 'Frozen'*. Animation Scoop.
11. (Kucharski, 2014) Kucharski, J. (2014). *Costume Design in Animation—Disney's Frozen*. Tyranny Of Style. [Online] Available from: http://tyrannyofstyle.com/costume-design-animation-disney-frozen.

INDEX

07.01 appendix / bibliography

ACKNOWLEDGMENTS

There are so many people involved in a project of this nature. I would like to extend my thanks to all those involved in all aspects and roles. I want first and foremost to thank my family—my husband Ron and my three daughters Sidra, Allegra, and Stephanie, and her husband CJ for their tolerance, flexibility, and support in this endeavor. I owe a great deal of gratitude to my assistant, Emma Hammel for her steady, detail-oriented approach, resolve and research skills. I would like to thank Florence Markoff for enticing me to explore the relationship between language and color.

I would like to acknowledge the professionalism shown by the staff at Ilex, Octopus Publishing Group. I would like to thank Commissioning Editor, Zara Larcombe, who helped me develop the initial premises and directions for this book, and Ilex Publisher, Roly Allen. I would like to give a special thanks to Senior Project Editor, Natalia Price-Cabrera. It is her expertise, professionalism, and flexibility that has guided me through the process bringing this to completion. I would also like to thank Assistant Editor, Rachel Silverlight and Art Director, Julie Weir for all their hard work getting this book over the final hurdle and to Katie Greenwood, picture researcher, and the image researchers at Octopus Publishing Group, for tracking down all the fantastic images that grace the pages of this book.

I would also like to thank the experts that took time to speak with me in detail about some of the intricacies of their life's work and its relationship to and perspective of color. I would therefore like to thank the following people for their expertise and consideration:

Dr Julia Hartling, Dr Joseph Markoff, Dr Margaret S. Livingstone, Mark Fairchild, Dr Florica Zaharia, Karen Schloss, Leatrice Eiseman, Clark Schoettle, Leslie Harrington, Nancy Friese, John Rohrbach, Kim Triedman, Adrian Burke, Michael Osborne, David Kunitz, Frank Mahnke, Jonathan Weiner, Harry Adler, and Betsy Connors.

Karen Triedman

PICTURE CREDITS